A small man holding chopsticks sat in the graying dimness of the jungle. He was not more than five feet away. He appeared to be eating out of a small bag. Ten feet to his right were two more men, also sitting on the ground, eating and talking. The horror of it hit me. I realized what I was looking at. Enemy soldiers! For a brief moment, time froze.

Lucky for me, the enemy soldiers seemed to be doing what every GI did at that time of day—eating. The last thing they expected was an uninvited GI showing up for breakfast.

I stood perfectly still, not sure what to do. My instincts told me to run, my training told me to shoot, but my good sense told me to do neither, not yet. I held my fire, and without taking my eyes off the man closest to me, I slowly backed away.

As my eyes adjusted to the shadows, I could see more NVA sitting among the trees. They looked like ghosts. It was hard to see, even harder to think.

Two of them looked in my direction. I stopped in mid-step. A strange, cold sensation of dread and terror coursed through my veins. I felt paralyzed, unable to move.

How I spent Christmas at Camp Eagle: This is my not so typical team preparing to leave on a different type of LRP mission. Our job was to keep the Bob Hope USO show safe from sneak attack. Author smiling, standing next to teammate and best friend John Meszaros, holding M-60 machine gun. John didn't sleep all night worrying that we might mistakenly kill Santa or worse, his reindeer in our ambush.

RECONDO

LRRPs in the 101st

Larry Chambers

PRESIDIO
PRESS

BALLANTINE BOOKS • NEW YORK

A Presidio Press Book
Published by The Random House Publishing Group
Copyright © 1992, 2003 by Larry Chambers

Published in the United States by Presidio Press, an imprint of The Random House Publishing Group, a division of Random House, Inc., New York, and simultaneously in Canada by Random House of Canada Limited, Toronto. Originally published in slightly different form by Ivy Books, an imprint of The Random House Publishing Group, a division of Random House, Inc., in 1992.

ISBN 0-89141-840-7

Manufactured in the United States of America

First Ivy Books Mass Market Edition: August 1992
First Presidio Press Mass Market Edition: January 2004

Cover photo of Larry Chambers, Gary Linderer, and Jim Schwartz of Co. L RANGER 75th Inf., attached to 101st Airborne division, Republic of Vietnam 1969–1970, courtesy of Larry Chambers.

Page iii photo of Larry Chambers and LRP team courtesy of Larry Chambers.

OPM   9   8   7   6   5   4   3

Acknowledgments

We had some of the best LRP team leaders in the U.S. Army, but there was only one I would have followed into North Vietnam—Sgt. John Burford.

The men of 5th Special Forces who served as cadre at Recondo School, and the men who served in the LRPs and Rangers.

Gary Linderer, who gave me constant support and inspiration.

I wrote *Recondo* because I'm proud of being a U.S. Army Ranger. It seemed to me that every Vietnam movie portrayed American Marines and soldiers as bloodthirsty, mindless drug addicts, burning villages and killing innocent people. I wrote *Recondo* to show a different point of view, not a glorification of war but a piece of Americana. I experienced a bunch of heroic young Americans fighting a very tough and seasoned foe—the North Vietnamese Army. Our GIs and Marines, especially our "helicopter crews," were the bravest, boldest, most audacious bunch of guys I've ever had the pleasure to be with. I wrote this book to tell my story but also to tell theirs.

Dedication

Gary Lotze flew home on a Christmas leave from Vietnam, December 1967. We kept him awake all night telling us one story after another of his SF unit in Vietnam—some heroic, some painful, some foolish—but always with an unrivaled sense of duty, pride, and loyalty. He left the next morning to spend Christmas visiting friends in Alaska, but his plane never arrived. After weeks of searching, the place was declared lost. Gary never got to return to Vietnam or Special Forces Recondo school where he had been an instructor.

Gary's disappearance remained a mystery for fourteen years, until the plane and passengers were discovered in a glacier near Anchorage.

Gary loved what he did and wore his green beret proudly. This reissue is dedicated to his memory. May he rest in peace.

Introduction

What most distinguished the Special Forces Recondo school from any other in the history of the American military was its final exam—a reconnaissance mission under the worst of conditions—within enemy territory, miles from friendly ground troops, and with absolutely no support. To graduate from Recondo school, you had to prove you could blend into the surroundings and gather information about the enemy units—right under the enemy's nose. It was a trial by fire, where students were sometimes wounded or even killed. That's how Recondo school got its reputation as the "deadliest school on earth."

The conflict in Vietnam called for drastic measures, and among these drastic measures was the establishment of a unique school by the 5th U.S. Special Forces Group in Vietnam. The guerrilla warfare tactics of the Vietcong and constant infiltration to the South by the North Vietnamese Army created a need for reliable reconnaissance. To gather this crucial intelligence, small groups of soldiers had to travel deep within enemy territory without detection and without support. The men being rotated into recon units had only minimal stateside training with methods based on conventional tactics. The harsh jungles of Vietnam demanded further training specific to that environment. A school that taught guerrilla warfare was required where the classrooms were the jungles of Vietnam and the instructors were members of Special Forces. Given the nature of reconnaissance teams—

small 5–6 man groups—a weak link on the team could not only jeopardize himself, but his teammates and the mission. Over a few short weeks, students had to be drilled 24/7 to react automatically when there's no time to think with a *what-to-do-when-everything-goes-wrong* process.

"Welcome to Recondo school— all volunteer, all on-the-job-training, and all brutally real."

Almost a year before the Marines hit the beach at Da Nang, Special Forces members were already in Southern Vietnam. Activated on May 15, 1964, project Leaping Lena was created with the purpose of conducting classified long range recon missions throughout Vietnam.

Special Forces A detachments were put in charge of training members of the Civilian Irregular Defense Group (or CIDG) and Vietnamese Special Forces in long range patrolling and recon techniques. These initial recon missions for Special Forces would begin to change the face of the war, as the enemy was beginning to lose his advantage of invisibility.

To further standardize the demand for recon teams, Project Delta was created from Leaping Lena in October 1964. Project Delta, headed by Maj. Charlie A. Beckwith, grew quickly from a single twelve-man detachment to a battalion-size command containing nearly one hundred Special Forces personnel and more than twelve hundred indigenous soldiers.

Special Forces Detachment B-52 was organized into twelve recon teams, twelve CIDG "Roadrunner" reams, a Chinese Nung camp security company, and a South Vietnamese Airborne Ranger battalion. By June of the following year, B-52 was given the task of creating a control headquarters to train recon students. An exclusive program, Project Delta was created both as a series of reconnaissance missions and as a training program to keep the Delta teams staffed. Their primary mission was to infiltrate hostile areas inaccessible to conventional units.

Delta trained Special Forces members and indigenous fighters in long range reconnaissance, artillery spotting, intelligence gathering, forward air control, and bomb damage assessment. But more importantly, it taught them how to stay alive.

Delta was a success. By 1966, awareness of the program had spread and conventional commanders were constantly asking to send members of their best infantry units in for training. Soon classes swelled to fifty students per class, which now also included members of the Australian SAS and Korean Army. The Delta school was now overwhelmed, and problems began to occur. Staffed by members of the actual Delta recon teams who taught the incoming classes, a conflict of interest surfaced. The Delta missions were imperative, and keeping the team members as teachers kept them out of the field. Yet there was a constant demand to continue to train new recon teams.

General William Westmoreland decided to solve the problem by establishing a formal reconnaissance training program that he dubbed *Recondo*, a name derived from three common terms of soldiering—*recon*, for reconnaissance; *commando*, an elite member of a small force; and *doughboy*, a nickname for the determined soldiers of World War One. Westmoreland was no stranger to the Recondo idea. During his command of the 101st Airborne Division in Fort Campbell, Kentucky between 1958 and 1960, Westmoreland had already started a Recondo type school.

Since Westmoreland fully backed the Recondo concept, and MACV was already funding project Delta, the pair was combined to create the MACV-Recondo school. He directed Col. Francis J. Kelly, commander of the 5th Special Forces Group, to establish Recondo School. Kelly, in turn, looked to the Project Delta veterans to get the school started. On September 15, 1966, Recondo school was officially opened.

The MACV-Recondo school was based at the coastal city of Nha Trang, 140 north of Saigon and neighboring the headquarters for the 5th Special Forces group. Using the Delta model of success, Delta officer in charge Maj. A. J. Baker hand-selected the cadre. Maj. Edward Rybat became the first assistant commandant of the school, as the main commandant position was honorarily reserved for the 5th Special Forces Group commander . . . Colonel Kelly.

The Recondo school staff was initially limited to five officers and forty-one sergeants, with eight positions being added through the course of the war. The instructors combined qualities of being excellent teachers, recon team advisors and veterans of the field, at least on their 3rd or 4th tour of duty.

All of the teachers were members of the 5th Special Forces Group, and many were veterans of Delta. The staff took their job seriously and were relentless in discovering the type of man who could operate efficiently under the pressure of a reconnaissance mission.

The staff was ready to challenge the students as they had never been challenged before. In fact, the school was so challenging that many company commanders who were sending their men in for training attempted to create makeshift pre-Recondo schools to better prepare their men for the challenges ahead.

To gain entry into the school each applicant had to be in peak physical fitness, have served at least one month in Vietnam, and still have at least six months of their tour left. And as is common practice with participation in extremely hazardous military operations, Recondo school was for volunteers only.

Students included troops from the U.S. Marine Corps, the Royal Thai Army, the Australian SAS, the Korean Army, and the South Vietnamese Army. But chief among the participants in Recondo school were the U.S. Army LRPs—an acronym for Long Range Reconnaissance Patrols.

Some LRPs were Ranger qualified, while others were volunteers who simply learned from the experience of the veteran LRPs while in the field. For the LRPs, they considered Recondo school their finishing school, and given their need to be on the field and the long waitlist of students to enter the school, the LRPs often waited months just to get an opportunity to get a shot at it.

The LRPs already had the built-in advantage of being veterans of recon, but many also brought with them bad field habits. Once in Recondo school, students would begin their crash course in the art of reconnaissance, which consists of traveling deep within enemy territory and, in essence, becoming the eyes and ears for the rest of the military.

- The program lasted 3 weeks with 18-hour work days beginning at 4:30 A.M.
- The failure rate was immense—upward of 50 percent.
- The school's capacity was 130 students, with classes of 65 being trained every two weeks.

The first week consisted of academics—combat intelligence, terrain analysis, map reading, basic photography, the handling of POWs, and basic first aid. Students were also expected to learn the ins, outs, and sounds of every weapon the Communists used. Students were taught to anticipate and think like the enemy. Physically, the challenges were immense and sometimes overwhelming.

The day would begin with typical PT (physical training) consisting of sit-ups, pull-ups, and push-ups. Students were tested on their rappelling techniques, which for most was a review of skills they already possessed, but skills they would still need during helicopter operations. However, unless they were Navy SEALs, most students were not prepared for the swim test—a grueling 100 meter swim against an ocean current.

The worst of the physical tests was the notorious Recondo sandbag run, in which the students were expected to run with their fully loaded rucksacks on their backs. The typical rucksack contained everything they would need in the field—claymore mines, grenades, sixteen magazines of ammunition, six quarts of water, rations, and communication equipment. It was also common practice for the men to carry military-issued pills to keep them alert, and also to carry a serum to expand their blood in case a team member was wounded and needed to run like hell. All in all, it was forty to fifty pounds of equipment.

Most important to bring was their rifle, commonly the CAR-15, as even just outside of the Recondo school compound, the enemy was capable of attacking. However, even with all of this equipment, in an almost diabolical idea, instructors forced the students to carry a forty-pound sandbag in their rucksacks, pushing the total weight to now almost one-hundred pounds on their backs. And they were expected to run.

The sand bag runs occurred every day for the first week and became progressively more difficult. By the seventh day, students were expected to run nine miles in ninety minutes with the one-hundred-pound rucksack. Students who did not complete the sandbag runs or failed any of the academic tests were automatically dropped from the school.

As recon soldiers these men learned the benefits of "invisibility," since, for small teams, stealth is one of the only advantages in enemy territory. Many of the rules of invisibility seem like common sense when you hear them, but not knowing them in the field can lead to the compromising of the entire team.

Rules to keep you alive: Never remove your equipment even when you sleep. Tape up every part of your equipment to prevent jingling and rattling. The lightest rattle, especially from metallic objects, can travel hundreds of feet. Always have tape for the mouths of prisoners; it only takes a yell to alert the enemy to your position. Do not use insect repellent because it makes the team traceable. It's a huge sacrifice: you may be eaten alive by the jungle insects, but the Vietcong doesn't use insect repellent, and neither should the recon teams.

For the same reason, soap cannot be used. Captured VC claimed that anticipating French ambushes during the first Indochina Wars was easy because they smelled the soap before they saw the army.

Cigarette smoking, a bad habit even for the LRPs, was prohibited. Cigarette smoke can be detected up to one quarter mile away if wind conditions are right. Heighten your sense of smell: learn every aroma of the enemy, from body odor to cooking habits. Heighten your sense of hearing: hear the safety snap of an AK-47, learn when birds or jungle animals make startling noises. Detect the enemy before he detects you and stay alert.

After basic training, the fun really began. Those who survived the first week were able to participate in helicopter and field training exercises conducted on the remote Hon Tre Island, located five miles off the coast of Nha Trang. Here, students would put into practice the techniques learned during the first week of classroom instruction and see how they are immediately applicable.

During this section of the training in Recondo school, it was a time to improvise, making sure that recon skills were always updated and that equipment and techniques refined.

One such example of Recondo school ingenuity was the invention of the "Stabo" rig as a means of extracting a soldier. Unlike the Maguire rig, the Stabo rig could be worn as a field harness–belt combination around the body, enabling a soldier to hook up to the extraction ropes while also keeping their hands free. This allowed soldiers to operate radios, use their weapons, or just protect themselves from being dragged through trees. The Stabo rig proved to be one of the most useful inventions for recon teams during the entire Vietnam War.

However, as far as training, what distinguished Recondo school from any other school in the history of the American military was the third week, called "you bet your life" by the students.

Third Week

If the men weren't so highly trained to survive, you could almost call it a death wish. It was at this time that students were broken up into teams of six and deployed on 4–5 day recon patrols in hostile areas west of Nha Trang. Students were expected to be able to put the previous two weeks into practice in a real situation in which contact with the NVA was expected to be made. Along with the team would be a Special Forces observer, who would come along to grade each member as they operated in every team position, from team leader to point man.

The mission was operated like a typical LRP mission, which included gathering intelligence and locating enemy reserves, combat patrols, and command posts. The helicopter was the primary means for insertion and exfiltration. Once on the ground the recon team normally tried to avoid contact with the enemy. If enemy troops were spotted the team would try to remain hidden, relying on helicopter gunships or jets to deliver air strikes.

Teams were too small to engage the enemy in a pitched battle, but if it did come down to a firefight then the team would try to hit hard and fast, and then try to exit the area as quickly as possible.

The third week of Recondo school was a brutal but necessary initiation to the reality of a combat situation in which the enemy could be anywhere and had the advantage of numbers.

The End of Recondo School

The Tet Offensive in 1968 was the first and only temporary closing of Recondo school, though its instructors and some students still operated, this time to defend the area of Nha Trang from North Vietnamese infiltration. For some students, the Tet Offensive was their graduation exam.

By 1970, Recondo school had run its course. Before it shut its doors forever on December 31, 1970, the MACV-Recondo school had graduated 3,000 troops.

The school was not a substitute for Ranger school, but it served an essential role in improving recon and ranger operations in Vietnam.

In retrospect, it was perhaps the most difficult training school in the world. Graduates proudly wore the distinctive Recondo patch. The downward-pointing arrowhead symbolizes the air-to-ground method of infiltration into enemy territory and the American Indian skills of field craft and survival. The dark pattern with a light background indicates the capability for both day and night operations. The V stood for both valor and Vietnam. But more important, the "school from hell" gave its student the skills to outwit a deadly enemy in its own environment—skills that saved lives in the jungle and laid the groundwork for the future military surveillance operations.

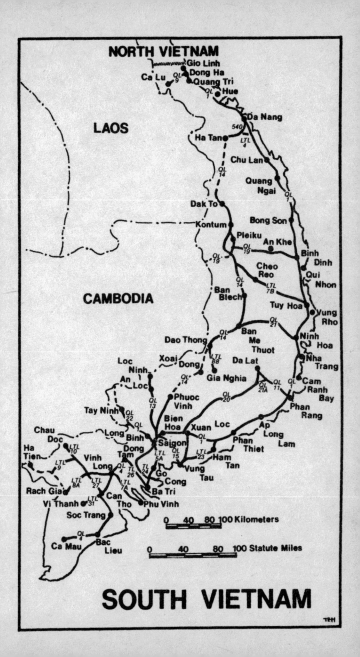

Prologue

MACV RECONDO SCHOOL, Nha Trang, South Vietnam

March 17, 1969

The morning sun broke through the clouds high above the Special Forces training compound in Nha Trang, South Vietnam. A U.S. Army helicopter came beating in, head-on, and with its approach, the roar of its turbines and the clatter of its rotors filled the camp. A yellow smoke grenade popped on the ground below. The pilot locked his ship into a hover. Inside the chopper sat six volunteers, each nervously awaiting his turn to rappel to the ground some ninety feet below. The bellyman signaled me to stand in the door.

I stood up, faced him and adjusted my Swiss seat. I grabbed hold of the nylon rappelling rope, and with both my legs shaking, backed toward the open helicopter door. The instructor clipped the steel D ring from my Swiss seat to the rope. Then it hit me . . . the realization of what I had gotten myself into and what I was about to do . . . jump out of a helicopter holding nothing more than a damn rope tied to my ass! My arms felt heavy; the sweat collecting under my shirt began to drip and made my skin crawl. I couldn't have released my grip on the rope if I'd wanted to. I tried to remember what I practiced on the ground, but my mind was a blank. I looked over to the guys sitting in line and felt a surge of adrenaline as my body prepared itself for what was about to happen. I took a deep breath and thought, *There is no turning back now . . . no stopping . . . I gotta piss.*

As I stepped back, the downdraft from the main rotor blades hit me. It was like walking into a hurricane. Its force was almost unbearable. I was blown down and to the side, momentarily standing on one foot—trying to regain my balance. I was a paratrooper. I'd jumped out of aircraft in flight. I'd rappelled too—under conditions that should have been scarier than this. And here I was—terrified.

"Look at me, troop!" the Special Forces instructor bellowed. "Look here!" Even over the deafening sound of the swirling blades, less than five feet from my head, I could still hear the gravelly-voiced Green Beret. He was holding on to my web gear and shouting, "Hey, where do you think you're going! I ain't through talking to you!"

I'm falling, you asshole! I thought to myself, still fighting against the downdraft.

I checked my slide and tried to listen to what the instructor was saying. Suddenly, his grip on the rope broke, and I went toppling into the void.

The overweight rucksack forced me back and upside down under the hovering helicopter. My feet slammed into the bottom of the chopper with a thud. I was now hanging, head down, ninety feet above the ground.

The instructor, a Special Forces sergeant, roared at the top of his lungs, "C'mon, troop, shape up! I'm not coming down to get your sorry ass!"

I could see the training grounds below. Two Green Beret NCOs pulled on the dangling rope. My fear was suddenly replaced by panic—and embarrassment.

Oh my God! I'm going to die! All I could think of was holding on.

I knew I had to do something. I pushed away from the helicopter. *Pop!* The rope straightened out, and the knot snapped loose. I started a fast slide to earth, this time in an upright position, and landed on my feet.

As I untangled myself at the bottom, another instructor

barked an order, "Get down, troop, and give me thirty push ups! And one for Airborne, and one more for Recondo!"

Welcome to MACV Recondo School. From the day I arrived, it was up at four in the morning, hard runs that progressively lengthened to eight miles. On the runs each morning, we had to carry forty-pound sandbags on our backs, our weapons, and everything else we'd need in case we were attacked by the VC before we got back to the compound. Even the streets of Nha Trang weren't safe.

Eighteen-hour days were filled with tough physical training and endless hours of map reading, medical training, prisoner handling, memorizing North Vietnamese military tactics, and firing every weapon the Communists used.

Volunteers came from a variety of reconnaissance units throughout South Vietnam, including those of Thailand, Australia, and Korea. We were trained to become the eyes and ears of our units. That is, if you weren't one of the 39 percent that washed out.

Even the basic things were drummed in—never remove your equipment, even while sleeping. Our rifles were taped to prevent the slightest rattle. Extra tape was carried on the stock to cover the mouths of any Vietcong prisoners we might capture.

Medical supplies included pills to keep us awake and a serum that would expand our blood in case we were wounded and had to keep running. No insect repellent was carried on missions because of its scent.

The second week consisted of field training on a remote island just off the coast of Nha Trang. Graduation week entailed a reconnaissance mission—deep into enemy territory.

The cadre was relentless. They didn't want half-trained men who could jeopardize a mission on LRP teams. No other school in the history of the military was like it or will be like it again. They may make tougher schools, with more physical demands, but they will never be able to duplicate the 5th Special

Forces Recondo School in South Vietnam and the training that provided its graduates with something that we needed in Vietnam—pride, self-confidence, and formal training.

1 Preserve, Protect and Defend

February 1968

The highway to Fort Lewis from the Sea-Tac Airport was covered with a thin film of water that reflected the lights from the oncoming cars. I leaned my head against the cold window. The air smelled clean, like fresh-cut wood. The bus ride was long, and I sat in silence.

Once we arrived at the base, we were greeted in the parking lot with friendly words from a well-starched drill instructor.

"Now get your sorry butts off my bus. Get down and give me push-ups until I get tired!"

George Ellis, my high-school buddy, muttered something obscene my way.

The fort was quiet except for the echo of the fifty of us counting out push-ups in the rain.

The next morning we shed our civilian clothes for olive-drab fatigues. The pants were too big, and the shirts were too stiff—and then to the barbershop, where *zip zip*, off came the hair.

The next few weeks of basic training were pretty rough. After the first week, our DI finally started to lighten up, even joked around a bit, although he never smiled. We had a theory that the drill instructors never slept. They had a nasty habit of pulling surprise inspections in the middle of the night.

We were all sitting in the corner of the large open bay of the 1st Platoon, A Company, 1st Battalion, 2d Brigade, building.

Dave Smith had just punched Dumpy Drivold in the arm as our drill instructor, Sergeant Koffman, began his instructions on night watch.

Koffman said, "One of these nights you're going to be walking on fire watch, you'll walk into the latrine, and you might find someone masturbating."

Everyone started laughing.

"Don't turn the poor guy in. It will embarrass him, it will embarrass you, and it will embarrass the sergeant you turn him into."

Everyone was really laughing by now.

I raised my hand—then grabbed Ellis and shouted, "Sergeant Koffman, what if you already caught someone?"

Ellis and I had played sports together all through high school and college; we were always playing jokes on each other.

"What? Not me!"

Ellis struggled to get free of my grasp. The more Ellis tried to explain, the harder everyone laughed.

After basic training, Ellis got a thirty-day leave and truck-driving school in Fort Ord, California. I couldn't believe it! My orders were to leave immediately for AIT.

"I thought you volunteered for infantry school, like we agreed, right? Remember our pact?" I asked Ellis.

He shrugged. "I couldn't help it, they asked me what I wanted to do, so I put down drive a truck."

George was the worst driver in our high school class. The only truck he had ever driven was his brother's old pickup, and he couldn't park *that* without hitting something. George left for truck-driving school.

George stayed in the States and never left California. I headed across the base to report to Company E, 2d Battalion, 3d Advanced Individual Training Brigade. Our company commander was Capt. Boudewijn Van Pamelen, an ex-Special Forces A Team leader. His example encouraged me to volunteer for Airborne.

AIT went by quickly, and soon I was on my way to Fort Benning for Airborne training.

I walked up to the airline ticket counter and was told I would be flying military standby. The attendant handed back my ticket and told me to go wait in line with the others. I looked in the direction she indicated and saw what must have been two hundred GIs, who looked like they'd been camping in the airport for weeks. I turned back to the ticket salesgirl and asked, "Is there a bar in this place?"

We finally boarded the Boeing 707 jet, and I celebrated my twenty-first birthday on the long flight to Georgia.

I arrived late in the evening, the day before training. I picked up my bag, tossed it over my shoulder and walked down the hot, dusty road, which led to the only building left with an empty bunk.

No sooner had I closed my eyes than I was awakened by a short, squatty staff sergeant who told me to follow him down to the mess hall. I thought I could orient myself to the school, but instead I was greeted with a work detail. This was one detail I would soon learn to avoid at all cost—KP!

Once inside, he introduced me to a hundred-pound bag of potatoes and a potato peeler. I learned to never arrive early in the army again.

We began orientation by standing in formation on the open grounds in front of a large, white sign with huge letters that read JUMP COMMITTEE, painted above a set of jump wings. Our instructor was a white-haired, wiry gentleman who introduced himself as Colonel Welch and then spent the next twenty minutes officially welcoming us to jump school. He told us that our training would last three weeks and while we were there we would observe a few rules. Attendance at all formations was mandatory, and we were to run everywhere we went. Because the training was during the hottest part of Georgia's long summer, we were required every hour to roll through the specially arranged outdoor showers set up at every training station and to take a couple of salt tablets. We soon learned to love those showers and hate the salt tablets.

One morning during our second week, we heard that one of the holdovers killed himself. As we ran past the Animal Farm, the holdover barracks, we could see the outline of his body hanging just inside the doorway. Seeing someone dead made the training take on a more serious tone. Death had suddenly become a reality.

Later that night, as we ran back past the Animal Farm, his body was still hanging there. What possibly could have pushed this guy this far? Was it because he didn't make it through jump school? I wondered how his parents would react and what they'd think when they got word that their son had killed himself.

By the third week we were in great shape. We ran everywhere, even to and from the mess hall. We were now ready for the real training to begin.

Down on the airfield, we boarded an old, silver C-119. She shook like hell as we taxied down the runway. It took forever for the plane to begin the climb. I became more afraid of the flight than the upcoming jump.

They called the C-119's flying boxcars. They would take up a planeload of fifty paratroopers, fly us into Alabama, and dump us out over the drop zone.

Up in the sky, we sat nervously along both sides of the cargo compartment, waiting to stand and hook our static lines to one of the two cables which ran the length of the plane. It was very hard to be brave inside that bouncing plane, but I was trying. I had my eye on the two lights near the exit door.

One was red, warning us to get ready. The green one meant go.

The jumpmaster yelled, "Get ready!" He lifted his arms over his head, causing all of us to tighten up.

"Stand up! Hook up!"

It was just as we had trained. The jumpmaster, with his

hands held high, crooked his index finger, the sign to hook up. We fastened our static-line snap links to the parallel cables running down both sides of the airplane. We checked our reserve chutes, then turned and checked the main chute of the guy behind us.

"Stand in the door!" the jumpmaster screamed. I shuffled to the open door. I was one of the first ones to jump. I tightly grasped the doorway and waited for the tap of the jumpmaster. I leaned back a little to see the red light on the side. A sick feeling washed over me. It was the same one I had when I watched the shower scene from the movie *Psycho*. I stood, almost paralyzed with fear. But this time I couldn't go out to the lobby for a Coke.

The ground below didn't look real. The green light came on. I tucked in my head, grabbed my reserve, and jumped! A blast of wind blew me back against the side of the plane. I started rolling as I fell.

Wham!

My main chute opened—partially. I looked up and saw the shroud lines wrapped around each other. The chute was tangled, and I was spinning uncontrollably.

I reached up. I couldn't free the tangled mess. Then I remembered the training. Run in place! There wasn't much time before I would have to make a major decision. Cut loose the main or pull the reserve. I had maybe fifteen seconds before I would hit the ground. I ran like hell! With a loud *pop!* my main chute fully deployed.

As the wind whistled past me, I looked down. The earth was still coming up too fast! The instructors had explained ground rush to us during training.

"If you fix your eyes on the ground, you start reaching for it. You involuntarily straighten your legs out, and if you hit that way, it's broken-leg city."

I quickly pulled my head up, looked straight out at the horizon, then pulled down on the front risers.

Crunch! I hit with a jarring blow and rolled to the right. I lay on my back, looking up at the sky. I had done it.

The three C-119's, off in the distance, flew back to Georgia.

"Welcome to Alabama, Private."

One of the jump school's cadre watching me hit laughed because I was just lying there talking to the sky.

"Yes, you're alive, but you'd better give me five, troop," he said as he bent over and held out his hand. When I reached out, he grabbed me by the wrist and pulled me to my feet.

"Better yet, make it ten."

Then, still chuckling to himself, he walked away.

I uncoupled my harness, pulled in my chute and started doing push-ups.

"One Airborne, two Airborne . . ."

Later in the week, after our fifth and last qualifying jump, we all met back at the parade ground, and Platoon Sergeant Williams, our head instructor, awarded us our jump wings.

With a hard blow from his fist, the big NCO hammered the bare metal pins into our chests. My pride quelled the pain.

After the formation, a group of us went down to the small soda shop nearby to show off our new "blood wings."

I told the guys about my high-school buddy, Dave Kranig, and how he'd volunteered for the paratroopers back in 1965. He ended up in the 101st and got shot up bad in Nam.

"Shot thirteen times, he spent fifteen months in an army hospital. He almost bought it. He tried to take out a VC bunker by himself, and a group of Vietcong ambushed him."

Everyone listened intently. The whole place got quiet.

"His left arm was shot almost completely off. He rolled over on it to slow the bleeding with the weight of his body. The VC ran back and shot him three more times, but even that didn't finish him off. He survived it all."

Kranig had come back and visited me at college. I told the guys that shortly after being released from the hospital for bone-graft surgery, Kranig got into a fist fight.

"No way, man!" one of the guys said.

"It wasn't much of a fight," I said. "A peacenik gave him some lip, so he hit him with his cast."

One of the guys said, "Man, that Kranig's cool!" as we walked back to the training grounds.

We all got our orders the next day and left Fort Benning for a month of "good-byes" before we left for Nam.

The leave was over before it started. The next thing I realized, I was stepping off a Boeing 707 at Bien Hoa Air Base, Republic of Vietnam. It was nine in the morning when they opened the airplane doors. A blast of searing heat hit me. Before we walked halfway across the tarmac, my fatigue shirt was soaked with sweat. Nothing had prepared me for this.

"Move out!" one of the black-hatted NCOs shouted.

"Get on those buses. Move it now, troop!"

I climbed aboard and grabbed a front seat. I stared out the window at the Vietnamese countryside. Rows of palm trees broke up the flat, stark landscape. An occasional rice paddy or a Vietnamese farmer drew everyone's attention. We passed an endless series of small villages with children playing in the streets. The driver seemed barely aware of them as they darted back and forth in front of our bus. The locals casually went about their business, as if unaware that a war was going on. ARVN soldiers lounged at every outside cafe we passed.

As we drove into the 90th Replacement Center in Long Binh, I noticed an above-ground swimming pool. One of the guys behind me yelled, "Hey, this doesn't look too bad!"

The four buses stopped in front of an open parade ground, and we quickly filed off. A stocky specialist fourth class gave us a Welcome-to-Vietnam speech. He then told us to line up outside the administration building to process in and be assigned to our units.

This was my first introduction to REMFs—the guys in the rear. There was no glory in being support personnel. In many ways, their jobs were the worst. They probably found the boredom and constant stress excuse enough to bully the replacements.

In less than four hours, I felt more like I was starting a one-year prison sentence than fighting a war. We were told that everything but the building we were standing in was officially off-limits.

Those of us who were Airborne qualified were told that the 101st had just lost one thousand men up North, and would be needing "fresh meat."

Fresh meat? I thought, *I'm fresh meat?*

Finally, almost begrudgingly, we were led to the mess hall to wait in an endless line for what we were told was food. It didn't taste like any food I'd eaten back home. I was more thirsty than hungry and grabbed a second cup of lime Kool-Aid. I was told that this was a new record. I would come to hate green Kool-Aid. After sampling some interesting pound cake, we had a few minutes outside to grab a smoke. Instead, I found a meal-on-wheels conveniently outside the mess hall and grabbed a Coke. I gulped it down. Everything seemed so strange and different here, but Coke still tasted the same.

Later, in my bunk, I tried to rest but couldn't. I guess it was a combination of jet lag and being treated like an animal. The hooch was hot, muggy, and noisy. The sounds of people moving in and out all night kept me awake. I couldn't tell if they were on our side or the enemy's. I tried to keep my eyes shut, but it was no use.

The next night, a hard-looking sergeant walked into our hooch.

"Hey, you three! Draw weapons and come with me. You're on bunker four."

"What do we do?" I asked. That question really pissed him off. *Did he think we could read his mind?*

He drove us to a sandbag-covered bunker, dropped us off, gave us some quick instructions, then stormed on up the berm to the next bunker.

For the next three hours, we stood around inside the hot,

humid bunker, looking out through the narrow slot in the sandbags. I never took my eyes off the two claymore mines just in front of the coiled concertina wire, less than twenty feet from our position. We had been told the Vietcong would sneak up in the night and turn the claymores around, face them back at us. Then they would sit back and make a bunch of noise to get us to blow ourselves up. I was determined that this was not going to happen to me, at least not on the first night.

After a while, it appeared that no one was going to tell us anything more. We split into shifts and took turns pulling watch on top of the fortification.

None of us could sleep. Every time a flare went up, it made a loud *pop!*, and we'd all run back inside the bunker to wait for the enemy to attack.

The next day I had to pull bunker guard again. This time I was a little more confident, and lucky for the Vietcong they didn't attack. I knew their claymore trick.

Flares went off all that night, like an endless celebration of the Fourth of July. They burned slowly, under small parachutes, as they drifted back to earth, casting long shadows across the open fields.

I began thinking that maybe I'd made a mistake coming here. I was really feeling homesick.

One of the guys on the guard was Lennie White. He was from Kansas City. One of his friends had told him the boonies was like living in hell for a whole year.

"Man, look at the faces in the mess hall tonight. Watch for the blank stare. When you see a guy with that stare, you know he's been in the boonies."

I was starting to hate this place, and I'd only been here two days.

It was all very confusing. It was as if I'd stumbled into some kind of weird movie. Those were the hardest five days I had ever spent. And they called it "adjustment."

SERTS

Soon I received orders for the 101st Airborne Division, which had its rear area nearby.

We packed up our gear, jumped into the back of an army deuce-and-a-half, then drove to Bien Hoa. As we pulled into the flat, dusty, army base, we passed a sign that read, SERTS (Screaming Eagle Replacement Training School) THE 101ST AIRBORNE DIVISION.

After in-processing and completion of a five-day training program, we would be shipped north to join a combat unit as replacements. The school's mission was to get us ready to survive in real combat.

The 101st Airborne Division believed that the treatment a soldier received during this first contact with the division was crucial to his attitude for the remainder of his tour. So the cadre at SERTS was better than the REMFs had been at the 90th Replacement. They worked us much harder, but there seemed to be a purpose behind it.

My initial processing included a records check, getting paid, and the opportunity to visit one of the many "swinging" night spots that Vietnam had to offer. And I never even had to leave camp.

Besides providing time to adjust to the tropical heat, the school offered a refresher course in all the subjects we'd covered back in basic and AIT. We received day-and-night training under the watchful eyes of handpicked, combat-experienced NCOs. There was a realistic enemy village and a jungle trail, complete with mines and booby traps. There were classes in first aid, field sanitation, and sometimes unscheduled, simulated mortar attacks. Sometimes there were rocket attacks too—and they were not simulated. You had to be on your toes.

The second day was hotter than the first, as our group practiced counterambush drills. We had just walked past a jungle trail when our black-capped instructor yelled, "Ambush!"

I jumped to the side. I hit the ground, then looked up. Dust was flying everywhere. I felt something moving under me and felt a burning pain, like my skin was on fire. I raised my bare forearm to look. Hundreds of half-inch-long ants were clinging to the skin on my arm. Fire ants! The shock of feeling and seeing all those nasty-looking insects biting into my flesh sent me jumping back away from the trail.

As I tried to remove the remaining ants, the instructor yelled in my ear.

"You are dead meat, son! I don't care if you got razor blades up your ass, you don't jump up in an ambush, you cherry—drop and give me twenty-five!"

I was now certain that coming here was not a good idea.

That night we were gathered together to listen to a recruiter for an all-volunteer, special-operations unit called the LRPs. I was interested, but I didn't know what a LRP was.

A guy named Lennie White filled me in.

"The LRPs are some bad dudes. I knew one in the 173d. They work in six-man teams behind enemy lines at night. If the NVA caught them, they all got wiped out. The gooks even had a bounty on their heads. They are some bad dudes," he repeated, shaking his head. "Bad dudes."

We moved into the large conference tent. About eighty of us sat down on the benches in front of the SERTS instructor.

"A-ten-hut!" We jumped up.

This recruiter looked different. He wore a black baseball cap with a Recondo patch on it. His jump wings were pinned above the patch. His shirt was starched, and he had jump wings and a Combat Infantry Badge (CIB) above his left pocket. On the right side of his shirt, he wore another Recondo patch. I wondered what it stood for. Even his jungle boots were polished, though there was not much leather left on them.

His look was intense. He didn't have the blank stare of a boonie rat. He looked normal—well, almost normal.

"Good afternoon, men! I'm Sergeant McDougal, F Company 58th LRPs."

Some of the guys nudged each other.

We had already been warned about the LRPs by our SERTS instructor, who told us, "They're the long range patrol. No support, some way-out crazies. So don't go and volunteer unless you got a death wish."

But this guy seemed okay. Like a breath of fresh air in a place that smelled of burned shit.

I listened to his spiel.

"Our unit is better trained. Everyone is a volunteer and a paratrooper. We have the highest body count per man in the division. We work in six-man teams, and we are as far from friendly ground troops as we can get. Our primary mission is reconnaissance, but *occasionally* we'll snatch a prisoner or pull an ambush."

Everyone laughed at his emphasis on the word *occasionally*.

"If you volunteer and qualify, you will get more training and have more privileges than in a line unit. You might even get an extra R & R; plus, you won't have to live in the boonies. We just work there. Usually a mission lasts three to six days, followed by a two- or three-day stand-down in the rear."

Some guy in the back cracked, "If you live that long."

Some of the guys laughed nervously.

"Any questions?"

One hand went up.

"Yeah, Sarge. I have been hearing about different life expectancies, you know, for different duty assignments. Like, the life expectancy for a door gunner in combat is five seconds, and an infantry second lieutenant is twenty seconds. What's the life expectancy of a LRP in combat?"

The salty NCO frowned, then a sly smile came over his face. In a low voice he explained, "LRPs don't have a life expectancy in combat. If you find yourself in combat, either you started it—in which case the gooks die. Or they start it, in which case you die. We don't make mistakes. We don't let them start fights."

The spec-four who asked the question fidgeted nervously in his chair as if he wanted to leave now. Without any more explanation, McDougal asked for any volunteers to stand up.

This was the first guy who had truly impressed me since I had joined the army. He seemed pretty squared away. I thought, *if the other guys are like this, it won't be so bad.*

I felt that if I walked away, I would regret it for the rest of my life, so I stood up.

Everyone looked at me like I was nuts, especially Wallace, our sergeant. Wallace was a line NCO from the O'deuce—the 502d Parachute Infantry. He looked at me and whispered, "You're steppin' on it now, boy! I'm glad it ain't my ass. I've only got twenty-nine days and a wake-up."

The next afternoon, I was notified that I'd been accepted. I would be going to the LRPs as a replacement.

I would be going up north to Camp Eagle, near the ancient imperial capital of Vietnam—the city of Hue.

I was apprehensive about what I'd done. But, what the hell! If there were only six guys working alone, then everyone would be more careful. Maybe these guys were okay. Besides, it sounded like the kind of unit my dad was in during World War II.

In more normal times, these special unit assignments were hard to get. You had to sign up and wait forever to get into them. But this was war, and the lines were a lot shorter.

Not many others shared my drive and enthusiasm, but I had something to look forward to now. All that the other ground pounders had to look forward to was humping the boonies for 360 days with a line company.

Three days later I had my orders to F Company, 58th Infantry, LRP, 101st Airborne Division. *Airborne!* I wondered what it would be like. I knew I didn't want to be just a ground pounder. I heard that LRPs flew in helicopters everywhere they went—even had choppers specifically assigned to them! It was their mission to gather intelligence for the whole damn division.

2 Cherry

September 1968

The traffic was light as Don Lynch, the LRP company's driver, took me from Phu Bai Airport to the LRP compound at Camp Eagle. Lynch, who had driven this road a hundred times, seemed deeply absorbed in something else as he drove past the endless Vietnamese concession stands. But I tried to take in everything. The roadside buildings made from cardboard and old, flattened soda cans fascinated me.

As the scenery rolled by, I tried not to breathe. But the smell of burning fuel oil and human feces was everywhere. I grabbed the underside of my seat with my left hand and held onto my duffle bag with my right. I studied everything as if it would give me a clue as to what was ahead. I kept hearing my dad's voice as we bumped along, *"Keep your noggin down, Son."*

Art Heringhausen, a nineteen-year-old from a line company who had volunteered for the LRPs, sat next to me but didn't speak. He seemed lost in thought.

Lynch smiled, flashing peace signs to every American jeep or truck passing from the opposite direction. We turned left and headed down the dusty road to Camp Eagle, home of the 101st Airborne Division.

On the corner, an MP sat alone beside an old weather-beaten bunker. The bunker was made of layers of frayed and rotten sandbags. He waved us on. We left him choking in a cloud of dust.

Lynch turned and said, "Here we are."

I looked up. A small sign announced CAMP EAGLE—GIA LAI GATE.

We drove past endless strings of barbed wire, looped concertina, and bunkers—lots of bunkers.

I thought, *this is it?* Yet neither our driver nor Heringhausen seemed tense, or even concerned that we were in a war zone.

The jeep slowed. We entered a second gate marked F CO. 58TH INF. LRP, EYES BEHIND THE LINES. It was already difficult to remember what the outside world was like, and I hadn't been here five minutes.

I was told to report to Sgt. Phil Byron, an E-6 from Killeen, Texas. Byron hadn't lost a man on twenty-five patrols. Being assigned to his team was the first good news I had heard since I arrived here.

I found him in his hooch, sitting on the edge of his cot. He was wearing worn-out tiger fatigues and chewing on a cigar. He was stocky, five feet eight, and weighed about 180 pounds. He took out a book of matches, folded back the cover, rolled the match over his thumb and struck it.

"Where you from, Chambers?"

"Corning, California."

"Where?"

"It's a small town in northern California."

He lit the cigar, blew out the match, then began to show me the sort of gear I'd be carrying.

He began a methodical inspection of his equipment, taking out each item and then replacing it so he could find it by feel. He continued to speak.

"You've got to find everything quickly in the pitch-black of a triple-canopy jungle."

Byron had just returned from a six-day mission the day before, and was already preparing to go out on his next assignment. Three days earlier, Byron's team had made contact. Glen Martinez, his point man, had been on a narrow trail next to the Song Bo. He heard movement and stopped the team. It was on one of those trails that ran along the side of a mountain river, a high sidewall of jungle flanked the trail on both sides. The trail funneled into the team's position and left no place to hide, so they didn't try.

In the distance, a lone figure was coming toward them on foot. Everyone froze. He walked closer.

The enemy soldier didn't seem to realize they were Americans. He never tried to take his AK-47 from his shoulder. He just looked at Marty and nodded his head as if to say, "Good morning." Without flinching, Martinez emptied a magazine into the NVA soldier. As he fell through the cover and into the stream, Martinez sprayed him again. The enemy soldier never knew what hit him.

Byron, shifting his weight on his cot, continued cleaning the moisture from his ammunition. He laid his boonie towel out, emptied each magazine onto it, and wiped down each round. Then one by one, he fed them back into the magazine.

He continued, "Always keep eighteen rounds in your magazines, no more. Leave out two rounds. It puts less stress on the spring and gives you more snap, less risk of a jam."

Sergeant Burnell, a burly E-7, walked into Byron's hooch. He started to tell Byron that he had a new replacement for his team when he noticed me standing next to him.

Without looking up, Byron answered, "I know."

Burnell turned, then walked out of the hooch without saying another word.

Byron was short. He was down to twenty-nine days and a wake-up. This would probably be his last mission. He stood up, and all of the loose M-16 rounds rolled toward the center of the cot. He grabbed his black baseball cap and headed out the door.

Motioning for me to follow, he said, "C'mon, I'll show you where you can bunk. Find the mess hall yet?"

"Nope, where do I go?"

"Look behind you."

I turned and looked past the row of green mosquito nets to the rear of the hooch.

"Just go out the back of the hooch, turn left and follow the wall down past the next three hooches and the TOC. Look up and you'll see the 17th Cav mess tent. You have to go through the barbed-wire fence."

He continued walking to where I'd bunk.

"You're going to pull bunker guard tomorrow night. I'll try to put you on a watch detail without any of the heads."

I gave him a puzzled look.

"Heads?" I'd never heard that term before.

"Heads are the pot smokers."

He stopped abruptly and looked me in the eye. "You don't smoke dope?"

"No way, Sarge! I never tried that stuff, don't even smoke cigarettes."

"You don't *yet*. We got more heads in the company than Vietnam's got mosquitoes. But you hang out with Schwartz, he'll square you away."

He paused, then continued.

"We'll be going out in a few days, I think I'll have you carry a radio. Don't worry, you'll do okay. Just keep your mouth shut, your eyes open, and your head down. Watch what the old guys do."

Byron took the time to explain, in great detail, what was going to happen from the time we walked down to the chopper pad until we returned from our mission six days later.

I was to be the artillery radioman. We would be headed for a spooky valley next to a range of jungle-covered hills, dominated by an obscenely rugged peak, known as Nui Khe. Rugged terrain, steep triple-canopy jungle, and an NVA sapper battalion—that's what G-2 suspected would be waiting for us.

I carried a radio during AIT (Advanced Infantry Training),

and it was a piece of cake, yet I was worried that I wouldn't remember my radio procedure. Byron assured me I wouldn't have to talk. He called in all the radio reports himself.

My job was to watch, learn, and not make any noise. I was beginning to feel that I had made the right decision about volunteering.

We were sitting in the 2d Platoon hooch when Jim Schwartz burst in. He also wore camouflage pants, no shirt, and looked as if he hadn't shaved in a week.

He was excited that I was here because now *he* would have someone to call a "cherry" instead of it being him.

Schwartz was thin and wiry and looked a couple of years younger than he really was. He told me he was from Chicago and wanted to know what I thought of the Cubs. He talked nonstop.

"They never win anything, they get close and blow it."

"It's lunch time. Ya wanna hit the chow line?"

I had not eaten since dinner back at SERTS, almost fifteen hours before.

He reached up, grabbed a shirt, and pulled an unopened pack of cigarettes out of its pocket.

"You smoke?"

I shook my head.

"You will. Let's go. Don't drink the green Kool-Aid, it tastes like shit. All the REMFs down south get the good stuff. We're the last stop on the food chain."

On the way to the mess hall, he proceeded to tell his life story and the stories of everyone in the 2d Platoon.

As we stood in line, I was beginning to feel a little more at home. *This ain't so bad.*

"How was SERTS?" Schwartz asked.

"Terrible. I got stung by a bunch of ants."

"That's nothing. Wait until you meet Dave Biedron. When he went thru SERTS, the gooks rocketed his hooch on his first night in country. He watched three guys get blown away."

"Jesus!" I said.

Schwartz went on. "A 122 rocket came through the top of the tin roof. It hit in the middle of their bunks."

I had almost forgotten where I was. Biedron's story immediately brought me back to the war.

He asked me how I managed to get on Byron's team.

"Byron is one of the best team leaders in the company. You lucked out man, you really lucked out. Do you snore?"

"I don't think so."

"Good, I don't want to go out with no cherry that snores."

Just then a few more LRPs arrived from out of nowhere.

"Hey, Schwartz, you got shit-burning detail tomorrow. Take the new guy and break him in. Hah, Hah."

"Who was that?"

"That's Glenn. He can be a real asshole."

We finished lunch, and for the rest of the afternoon, I sat on my bunk and tried to imagine what the jungle would be like. Every time I heard a chopper fly over, I ran out of the hooch and watched it. I had to suppress my excitement while watching the helicopters. I wanted to wave at every one that flew over. There was something very rugged about this place, like being in a logging camp. If I could make it here, I could make it anywhere.

As I tried to write my first letter home, I was aware of the thumping of a helicopter flying directly over my hooch.

Schwartz walked back in. He started telling me what to do if we got rocketed.

"Here's the rule about the 122 mm rockets; if you can hear them, that's good. If you can't, you're dead."

"That's the rule? What do you mean, if I can't hear them?"

"It means it hit you. We only get rocketed about once or twice a month, so, no big deal."

"What do they sound like?" I asked.

"You'll find out. The gooks launch them from a no-fire and no-fly zone, not far from here."

"What do mean no-fire, no-fly?" I asked. "You mean like King's X? If you cross your fingers, no one can bother you?"

"It means we can't even go in after the little bastards, even though we know where they are. Ain't that the shits?"

"Yes! I can't believe it."

"You'll find a lot of things here you won't believe. It don't mean nothin'."

I spent the rest of the afternoon thinking over what I'd heard and running outside the hooch every time a helicopter flew over.

At 1700 hours, Schwartz appeared like clockwork. "Come on, they got hot dogs up at the Cav mess."

Once again we walked the path behind the hooches and headed for the chow tent. *So far so good. This wasn't so bad. Until now, all I had to do was listen to the advice of the kid from Chicago.*

"Let's go eat. There's Harris. Have you met him yet? He's going to be walkin' point on your team."

"No, I haven't . . ."

Schwartz cut me off and proceeded to tell me how he had seen Harris kill two dinks with one shot.

A midwestern voice came from the table behind us.

"Come on, Schwartz," said a big guy with the name "Linderer" on his fatigue shirt. He and some of the other guys had also been listening to Schwartz's stories.

"One shot? Did you tell the new guy how you captured the entire NVA Army on your first mission? Or was it your second?"

"Very funny, Linderer," Schwartz said as he pulled out his second cigarette in as many minutes.

"This is Chambers, he's another Californian."

The big farm boy from Missouri spoke up. "Well that's appropriate. They put you with the 2d Platoon, they're all from California. The only thing to ever come out of California was queers and hot rods. I don't see any tail pipes sticking out of your ass, so I guess you'll fit in. How ya doing?"

He stuck out his big hand and introduced himself.

"Gary Linderer! I'm also in the 2d Platoon, but thank God I'm not in that tent full of California faggots."

Everyone was laughing, including me.

Dave Biedron came over to get in on the fun. He was a big muscular guy from Chicago.

"Hey, man, leave the new cherry alone. Schwartz has him believing he's a team leader."

"Come on you guys," Schwartz complained.

"Hey, Schwartz, who's going to win the pennant? The Cubs don't have a chance, man."

Linderer asked where I went to school. I told him Shasta College in northern California. Just then Sergeant Burnell walked in.

"Hey, Burney, we got another cherry college boy in the second," Biedron said.

Burnell paid no attention and walked past everyone, profiling like John Wayne.

"He's on a fantasy lifer beer run," Linderer said. "It's as close as they come to orgasm."

I tried to see what Burnell looked like. He seemed older than everyone else by about ten years, and his arms looked like they were covered with open sores. I asked Linderer about Burnell's arms.

"Cigarette burns. You'll see soon. He plays some game where he puts a lit cigarette between his arm and yours and the first one to move is a pussy. No one can stand pain like Burnell. Wait till you see him eat a razor blade or a light bulb."

"What?"

Linderer nodded.

"He can take a double-edged razor blade and chew it! That's the truth. Loves light bulbs. Says it gives his turds body."

Schwartz broke into the conversation. "Two weeks ago Burnell was drunker than shit and was messing with the Cav medic. The medic wants to be a Ranger, so he copies Burney.

Bad move. He thinks he can eat razor blades, too. So this idiot puts a double-edged razor blade between his teeth and tries to bend it in half. The blade snapped and flew right through the side of his cheek. He didn't even know what happened."

The group broke into wild laughter.

"Hey, you going out with Byron's team in two days?"

"Ya." It was my first chance to speak. Just as I opened my mouth, a thin, young buck sergeant interrupted.

"Come on, you guys. We got to get ready, we're supposed to be at the TOC at 0630 for our briefing."

As I walked back to the hooch, I realized that these guys were okay. I crawled in my cot and adjusted the mosquito netting. I fell asleep, thinking about the day's events.

The next day, Schwartz handed me three grenades that had been under Penchansky's bunk.

"He's on R & R, so use these. Come on, I'll make sure you get a CAR."

"What's a CAR?"

"Man, you don't know shit! It's a commando version of an M-16."

"But what's wrong with my 16?"

"Nothing, but when you see what this rifle can do, you'll want one. Come on, let's see if there's one left in supply."

We headed for the supply tent.

"Hey, Wiley," said Schwartz, "We need a CAR-15. You got one?"

A big smile crossed the supply clerk's face as he reached under the table at the entrance to the supply tent.

"You mean one of these?"

"Whoa!" I'd never seen such a mean-looking weapon. "I think I'm in love."

"I told you you'd like it."

Schwartz was beaming.

As we walked back to the hooch, I felt like a kid again, playing army back at Fort Berry, when my dad had upgraded my wooden rifle to a BB gun. This was the kind of rifle I had pictured in a commando unit. We went back inside the dimly lit hooch.

"Tomorrow we'll sight it and fire it a few times down at the pit so that you can get the feel of it. We've got a fifty-gallon drum filled with sand just to test-fire our weapons before we go out on a mission. You gotta keep 'em well oiled, man. The humidity is the shits out here. Oh yeah, find yourself a boonie towel and keep it around your neck. It's good to have for everything from wiping down a wet gun, wiping the sweat off your face, and keeping the mosquitoes off your neck. Come here!"

Schwartz handed me three two-quart, plastic canteens.

"Bring lots of water. You'll need it. Put your poncho liner around the radio, like this. Your claymore goes here."

Schwartz explained to me how to pack my equipment, punctuated with stories about his last mission. Finally, it was time for us to head down to the TOC for our briefing.

A handful of LRPs were already sitting in small groups throughout the TOC. At the front of the room was an unfinished wooden table, piled high with captured guns and an NVA radio. Behind it sat a tough-looking E-6 named Vaughan— Johnny Vaughan.

Schwartz and I stood in the back of the room. It reminded me, somewhat, of football practice with the coach going over the other team's plays.

Just then Zoschak walked in. He was a tough, sandy-haired, average-size guy, with a Massachusetts accent and a soft, slow, way of talking that people listened to with respect.

"Where'd you go in Bangkok, Zo?"

Everyone whistled except me. I felt like someone told a joke, and I didn't get it.

Then Harris and Jody Gravett walked in, taking seats up front like a couple of starting halfbacks. Gravett turned and spoke.

"Hey, Byron, can you believe some 17th Cav asshole

colonel wouldn't let me and the Shadow on his friggin' chopper with our weapons loaded?"

Byron didn't respond.

"Man, where do they get these dumb-shit lifers? He even asked us to put the seat belts on."

Laughing, Gravett continued, grabbing Harris by the neck.

"So Harris looks at this colonel and belches."

Jody made the same belching sound.

"Just like that, *urrrrp!*"

"Atten-hut!"

Lieutenant Williams walked in and moved to the front of the room. Hung directly in front of us was a large, acetate-covered map which took up most of the wall. The map was a composite of several smaller topo maps that made up the entire I Corp area of operation. At the top of the map was the DMZ, to the west was the Laotian border—marked in red. Jungles were in light and dark green, with the lowlands and swamps in white. The map was covered with tightly packed contour lines, showing steep mountains and deep valleys. The right side of the map bordered on the South China Sea. Firebases were red triangles drawn with grease pencils.

Schwartz pointed to a valley called the A Shau. He said it was a bad mother. "The 1st Cav went in there last year and lost twenty-two helicopters in fifteen minutes. The gooks had radar-controlled 12.7 mm antiaircraft guns up in the hills, and you can't see shit because it's always foggy and raining."

He also said he had heard we were going to be pulling missions in there real soon. Just then, a lanky sergeant walked in and sat down in an open chair reserved for the old guys. He was tall and thin, and spoke in a slow, but methodical, southern drawl. He turned back and looked at me.

"You the new cherry?"

John Burford was country to the bone. He was on his sixth year in the army. Airborne all the way.

"Honest John Burford, son! But you can just call me Honest John."

He held out a friendly hand.

"Chambers!" I reached over the chair and shook his hand.

Burnell appeared, and everyone turned to look his way.

Someone next to the door yelled, "Hey, Burney, you leading this show?"

"No. If I were, I'd just dismiss you bunch of peckerwoods, and we'd jump onto the next chopper headed to Hanoi."

Everyone laughed.

"Come on, you guys," said Lieutenant Williams. "Can I get on with this?"

"Yes, sir, please do."

A few of the guys started to shift in their seats. Lieutenant Williams went over the weather forecast.

"The weather for the next few days will be hot, cloudy, and humid. Today's high will be ninety-six degrees. Sunrise tomorrow is 0630 hours, sunset 1900 hours. No rain for the next twenty-four hours. The AO will be foggy in the morning, and in the late afternoon, clouds will again move in. The winds will be light and variable out of the southwest. As you know, we have been experiencing a lot of problems because of the fog."

I listened to every word Lieutenant Williams said, but I noticed a few of the LRPs were nodding off.

I kept my eyes on the briefing officer. Williams wrapped up the weather report about the same time the division G-2 intelligence officer arrived. He was an older man who reminded me of the captain on "Gilligan's Island." He was here to recount recent enemy activity in the operation area and establish the intelligence basis for the operation.

"Good evening, men. Over the past several months since the Tet offensive, we have been trying to cut off Charlie's supply lines from the north. Heavy enemy activity has been reported in the eastern sector of your AO."

He pointed to a location on the wall map.

"Your mission will be to monitor traffic on a network of high-speed trails running through your AO. We have reason to believe there is an enemy base camp there. Be at the chopper pad with your gear and ready to go at 1800 hours. You'll go in at last light, tomorrow. Thank you, gentlemen."

Byron got us together after the preop was over.

"I want to rehearse with the new guy. Chambers, meet me after breakfast at 0900 hours. Schwartz, take him with you."

Schwartz spoke up, pointing my way. "Sarge, me and the new guy got shit-burning detail in the morning? That's what Sergeant Burnell says."

Byron walked over to Burnell who was talking with Zo.

"Burney, I got to get my new men ready for the mission, and you got 'em burnin' shit. Don't you have anyone else?"

Burnell looked annoyed. He got up and walked around to where we were sitting.

"No! See you jerk offs at 0900 hours."

"Come on, Chambers, I think we pissed him off," mumbled Schwartz as we headed toward the supply tent.

I had no idea what they were talking about, but nodded in agreement with Schwartz. Schwartz continued.

"Byron told us to draw enough rations for six days for the entire team. Let's go."

As the sun went down I was becoming apprehensive. I thought, *In a few hours, I'll be on my first mission.* I was very anxious. We were going to try to locate an enemy regimental base camp. Whoa! I still couldn't believe it—not yet.

I walked back down to the helicopter pad with Schwartz. We could hear a lone helicopter warming up across the open valley.

We stood at the edge of the tarmac and waited.

Perched on the ridge across from our company area, the deadly looking helicopters sat motionless on their metal skids. Every fifty feet were two rows of sandbags. These bags were piled six high and must have stretched for twenty feet. Between each of these protective walls sat one of the new Cobra gunships. At the end of the ridgeline, directly behind the Cobras, sat a teardrop-shaped helicopter, called an LOH—

light observation helicopter, or Loach. It was our company commander's command-and-control ship. Schwartz called it the C & C ship.

As Schwartz and I watched, the LOH's rotor began to revolve. It lifted and flew the short distance to the company acid pad. It passed over us, then circled back around and landed within twenty feet of where we stood. The sides of the chopper bore the crossed-swords emblem of the cavalry. We watched a barrel-chested officer as he walked up behind us and headed for the LOH. The rotors slowed to idle speed as the big captain climbed aboard. We held on to our caps as the helicopter rose straight up, moved back a few feet, then swung around and headed out toward the distant mountains.

"He sleeps in that bird," Schwartz remarked.

"Who?" I asked.

"Eklund, Captain Eklund, our CO. He lives in that chopper, he never comes in. When there is a team in the field, he stays up until they get extracted," Schwartz explained.

That's reassuring, I thought. My first impression of Nam was that nobody really gave a shit. But I could tell by the way Schwartz talked about this CO that here was an officer who cared for his troops.

By 1600 hours the next day, puddles of water dotted the acid pad. The weather report was wrong. It had rained all day. After painting some last-minute camouflage on my face, hands, and forearms, I was ready.

"Let's go do it," Schwartz said.

Less than a month ago, this was just practice. Now it was real. Somehow, it didn't feel like I thought it would. At least not yet.

"Hey, Schwartz, how do I look?"

"Like John Wayne, man."

It felt like I was carrying half a ton on my back. Inside my rucksack and on my LBE harness, I had a PRC-25 radio, twelve freeze-dried meals, fourteen magazines of extra ammunition, two hand grenades, three smoke grenades, one white phosphorous grenade, one claymore mine, one pair of socks, a jungle sweater, poncho liner, a poncho, ten packs of cocoa powder, survival knife, a pen gun with flares, and six quarts of water. Schwartz had to pull me to my feet.

We walked slowly down to the staging area. I quickly understood why the radio was referred to as an ass-kicker. Sergeant Byron was already there, checking his map. He had a very serious look on his face. There was a flurry of last-minute activity. I tried to imagine what was ahead. I was a little light-headed and was not sure what to do next.

Each radio had to be checked and rechecked. Byron opened my pack and turned down the squelch button until he couldn't hear the static. Everyone was adding last-minute touches to their camouflage, checking packs, and smoking final cigarettes.

I looked over at Schwartz. His back was to me, and I could see that the hair on the back of his neck was standing straight up. He nervously lit a cigarette, turned around, and rechecked my gear.

"You set?"

I was becoming even more aware that this was the real thing. All the bullshitting had stopped, and everyone was now concentrating on the job at hand. I felt ready.

"Here," Byron said. "Stand here, next to me."

I nodded. He turned to Schwartz.

"Come on, Schwartz. You are going out the right side with Harris and Smitty."

The choppers were deafening as they landed. Byron had to yell at us.

"Check again, is your radio on?"

"Yes!"

"Make sure you keep that fucking rifle pointed out the door and keep your safety on until we insert. You okay?"

"Oh I'm fine." I switched my rifle back on safe. I'd jumped the gun, but even after screwing up, I was still very excited.

"Okay, chamber a round and get in next to me," said Byron.

I stepped on the skid, climbed in, then turned and sat down on the cargo-bay floor.

I'd never been near a helicopter before, let alone in one. It was a lot different than that wooden mock-up we practiced on at SERTS. From what I'd heard, some of the other guys had Ranger and Special Forces school behind them, or at least six months in the field in Vietnam, before coming to LRPs. I'd never been in a helicopter, and here I was going out on an LRP mission. They had to be desperate people to be taking me.

I was startled when the chopper rocked back and lifted off the ground. I grabbed a vertical brace that separated the door gunner's compartment from the cabin. I was very uncomfortable. I couldn't get my legs straight. One minute we were on the ground, solid and firm, the next we were airborne.

Once underway, I couldn't get over how smooth the ride was. In the background was the ever-present, high-pitched whine of the turbine engine. The chopper made a deafening *whap* sound when we turned sharply to head west.

I looked down and could see all of Camp Eagle. It was big, and as far as I could see, there was nothing but bunkers, sandbagged hooches, shitters, and tin-roofed buildings.

I had a death grip on the retaining post as I tried to look over Sergeant Byron's shoulder. I looked out toward the mountains and saw the most beautiful sunset I had ever seen. The sun was a vibrant orange as it began to drop behind the horizon. It reminded me of back home along the river. I relaxed my grip on the pipe.

We had been airborne about twenty-five minutes when Byron tapped me on the leg.

"Get ready!" he shouted over the roar of the Huey.

I felt the same feeling I had sitting in the locker room before the kickoff of the big game against Humboldt State.

After the thirty-minute flight, the helicopter made a wide circle over a jungle-covered mountain, and we started to drop. Our pilot headed toward an opening the size of a small basketball court. It was a one-ship LZ, surrounded by single-canopy jungle. I clutched my weapon tightly, took a deep breath, and prepared to jump.

The floppy hat I brought with me from training was too small. I was afraid I would lose it if the wind from the rotor wash caught it. I took it off and jammed it under my web belt.

Burford, the lanky sergeant from Georgia, was the first one out, followed by Byron, then me. On the port side, Harris leaped from the skid and disappeared into the jungle, followed by Looney and Schwartz.

We had to jump about three feet to the jungle floor. I hit the ground and stood there, momentarily confused as to where I should go.

Once on the ground, things started to happen quickly. Byron grabbed me by my web gear and pulled me after him as he ran for the cover of a thicket. *God,* I thought, *I've got to be the dumbest cherry alive! I hope I don't fuck up and get us all killed!*

Sergeant Burford was already there, listening intently for any sounds of the enemy. The rest of us huddled around Byron. After a few seconds, Byron motioned Burford and Harris to move out toward the tree line. The sound of the chopper faded in the distance. The silence was deafening, as we lay waiting for Burford and Harris to return.

The radio crackled over the handset clipped on my web gear. Byron was getting anxious. He wanted to check the place out. Finally, Burford and Harris returned. Burford folded his map over, showed it to Byron, then checked his compass.

Byron pointed in the direction they had scouted out three days earlier on the overflight. He'd spotted a high-speed trail from the air and wanted to monitor it for enemy activity. It was close to our LZ.

Burford told Byron he had heard four shots down in the valley as we inserted. Burford said it had probably been trail watchers firing all-clear shots.

Byron thought for a moment, then changed our route of

march. Instead of going in the direction of the shots, we would parallel the side of the hill. With luck, we could slip past the NVA who fired those shots.

Usually, the chopper bracketed the real insertion point with several false insertions to conceal our location. A trail watcher would fire a series of all-clear shots if he checked and found no one after the chopper left the area. So it was not uncommon to hear shots. It didn't mean we had been discovered. In fact, it probably meant the opposite.

The team spread out at intervals of five meters. I stayed on Byron's tail, so he could get to the radio if he needed it.

Harris was at point and didn't seem to make a sound, as he moved in and out of brush thirty meters ahead of the team. Suddenly, he disappeared behind a bush. All I could see was his hand, signaling Byron to halt the team.

He found the trail they had spotted on the overflight. It ran parallel to a muddy stream.

Harris and Burford, the point man and the assistant team leader, moved out to check the trail. I saw Harris turn and point down the path, then vanish into the jungle. We followed.

As Byron and I approached, we looked down at what appeared to be dozens of sets of tracks. The muddy prints were still wet. I thought, *This is it*.

If these had been deer tracks, I'd have estimated that a small herd passed by less than twenty minutes before. We must have alerted them when we came in.

Burford walked back and said he wanted to recon the trail. "I'll take the new kid as my radio," he said, pointing my way with a smile.

I was beginning to trust Byron but felt uneasy following anyone else on a gook hunt.

Burford whispered, "C'mon, Chambers, you might get a chance to bust your cherry."

The two of us followed Harris up the trail. Burford leaned close and whispered that he wished he'd brought his Ho Chi Minh sandals, and then said, "Stay quiet and behind me.

Watch the right side of the trail. If we get hit, shoot back, and don't run until you know where the running might help."

Don't run. I thought, *Where would I run to?*

As we moved farther up, skirting the trail, the steep valley closed in behind us, cutting off our escape route and leaving us vulnerable to an ambush. At times, the trail ran through the middle of the creek. Crossing it, I felt the cool water fill my boots, then run back out as we stepped up onto the muddy bank.

Burford stopped and bent over, reaching for something in the bushes. He pulled out several pieces of paper, a cigarette pack and a candy wrapper. He licked the wrapper, then turned his head my way and whispered, "Sugar. Wrapper's still covered with sugar; if it had set out overnight, the sugar would be gone. The gooks are close."

My stomach tightened at his words.

We moved on until we came to a log jam across the slow-moving creek. The greenish-looking water was covered with algae and full of small water bugs swimming in circles. Next to the stream's edge, the moss was torn. The gooks must have gotten out of the water here and gone around. Several logs and branches lay on the south side. Harris froze and pointed at the logs. I looked and could see mud still dripping from them. Harris backed up. We couldn't have been more than fifty feet behind them. Harris signaled Burford to turn around and retrace our steps. Not more than twenty meters ahead, Harris spotted the back of a soldier through the brush, moving into the jungle. We'd found the enemy. But this was not the time or the place to take them. We moved quietly back down the stream to link up with Byron and the rest of the team. Moving in the stream made us all nervous, but it was quieter and quicker than skirting it.

Back with the team, Burford whispered to Byron. I couldn't hear, but I knew what he had to be saying. "Let's set up off the trail up there and see what comes by."

Burford got up and disappeared into a wall of vegetation, leaving no sign that he'd ever been there. Byron pointed to an opening in the brush just off the edge of the trail. He told me to hide there and wait. I was ten feet to the left of Looney, the soft-spoken kid from West Virginia, who carried the other radio for Byron. We were close to a bend in the trail where it broke and turned sharply south.

Byron couldn't have seen the bend from the direction he'd come in. If he'd seen it, he would have noticed how close Looney and I were to the edge of the trail. He would have never put us there. But with us in this position, he would be within reach of both radios.

Harris was farther up the trail, next to Burford. He had taken his poncho liner out of his ruck, and pulled it over his head. He took out a pack of Camels, tapped the bottom of the pack, then bent over and pulled one of the cigarettes out with his teeth. He lit it under the poncho. I couldn't see anything, but I could smell the smoke of the burning tobacco. Being a nonsmoker, I didn't like the smell—particularly out here. I hoped the gooks were all smokers, and wouldn't notice it.

Looney took the radio out of his pack, and turned the squelch down to the lowest setting. He had told me earlier that you could still communicate without picking up any "white noise."

Burford and Harris sat together and whispered between themselves. It was getting dark. I had to piss. I held it as long as I could, thinking we might get into a fire fight at any moment. But I couldn't wait any longer.

As I stood up to piss, Byron came to full alert. I motioned and pointed to my fly. He shook his head, "no." I couldn't hold it, so I sat back down, and peed anyway. What the hell. This was a war, and I was trying to be an LRP. I could piss in place if I had to.

I could feel the dampness of the ground come through my pants as I sat staring into the jungle. No one talked or moved. I watched the last light of day disappear. I wanted it to hurry and get dark. If the bad guys heard us, and they came back, they'd see our boot tracks in the mud.

My prayers were answered. It got dark—very suddenly, and very dark. I was a real cherry, and this was my first night in the jungle.

I sat facing the trail, frozen, afraid to move for most of the night. At 2300 hours, Byron passed me the watch.

During my guard shift, I was tempted to pull my camouflage poncho liner over my head so I wouldn't hear the swarm of mosquitoes I was attracting, but I was afraid that if I did that, I wouldn't be able to hear any gooks. My neck itched. I could feel welts swelling up like an uncontrolled rash. The little bastards were eating me alive.

At 2400 hours, I passed the watch to Looney, then fell asleep. Ten minutes later, Byron woke me.

"You're snoring!" he whispered. He told me to sleep on my stomach. I rolled over and lay facedown. I couldn't sleep much. I kept passing in and out of a dreamlike state, but it wasn't really sleep. I thought about the changes in my life. Basic training, AIT, then jump school, and home for thirty days. My leave had ended just three weeks ago. And now, here I was, in the jungle. Just a place on a map in Vietnam. It seemed unreal—and all too real, at the same time.

I was dreaming about pheasant hunting. Kranig, Craig, and I found the biggest flock of pheasants I had seen in years. There must have been a hundred hens and roosters mixed together, feeding on the fresh-cut alfalfa. But just as I was about to shoot . . . I woke with a start. I wasn't sure where I was; the pheasants were gone. I looked at my watch, 0500. It was still dark. It was cold and damp from the morning fog. I pulled my poncho liner even tighter around me. Byron and Burford were sitting a few feet away. I could see that they were whispering into the radio. Byron was getting ready to call in his sitrep. I was only half-awake, not paying much attention. Suddenly, something behind me caught Byron's eyes. I watched as he reached out and put his hand over Burford's mouth, then pointed over my head.

Everything grew quiet. I was still tightly wrapped up in my

poncho liner. I lifted my head to see what had attracted Byron's attention. I heard someone coming. I saw the shadow of a man. I froze. He walked within three feet of me. My eyes focused on his face. I held my breath and prayed that he wouldn't turn his head my way. I felt helpless, like an Egyptian mummy. Wrapped in my poncho liner like a dumb shit, I couldn't even move my arms. Silhouettes of several people followed behind the first man.

Peeking nervously from the corner of my eye, I could see rifles slung over their shoulders. If they'd been any closer, I could have reached out and grabbed them—except that my arms were wrapped in that damn poncho liner. As the first man passed, I tried to let the air out of my lungs and breathe before the next man got even with my position. I eased back toward the ground and lay on my side, facing the trail. I had wrapped the poncho liner so tight, trying to stay warm, that now I had trapped myself in it. I'd never felt so helpless—or so stupid—in my life.

Terrified, I waited and didn't move. One soldier looked right at me as he passed, but he didn't see me and continued down the trail. My stomach was knotting, but I stayed in position. My weapon was next to me, but my hands were still trapped inside my poncho liner.

Now what was I to do?

The fourth enemy soldier passed without a sound. I could hear the sound of banging metal, like two empty canteens knocking together. A fifth and sixth man passed. I didn't know how long I could stay motionless in this position. All I knew was that I couldn't move.

After the full column of seventeen VC passed, I fell back and quickly undid the poncho liner which had held me prisoner. I reached for my rifle and quietly pulled it up to my chest. I looked back at Byron who motioned for me to stay still. The mosquitoes were almost unbearable, but my shame was worse. I brushed the mosquitoes and dead leaves from my face and thought about what I would do if the bad guys returned. I was really screwing up. The army hadn't prepared me for this sort of job. I'd never been to Ranger School, Special Forces Training Group, Jungle Expert School. I was a lifer's kid, son of a World War II Alamo Scout, and I was a paratrooper. But I was a two-year, voluntary draftee on a break from college. I wasn't prepared for this, but I'd asked for it, and I was going to have to smarten up.

In the middle of the night, I had taken off my boots and had put them next to me, at the bottom of my tightly wrapped poncho. No boots, no weapon. How dumb can you get? I swore I would never do that again.

Thirty minutes after the gooks were past, Byron tapped me on the shoulder. He motioned for me to move quietly back to his position. My boots were still untied but at least I had something on my feet. He keyed the mike and whispered.

"One seven Victor Charles headed November Whiskey my position. Do you copy?"

He described what the enemy was wearing and the weapons they carried. I looked at Looney. He was as white as a ghost, but at least he had the good sense to sleep with his rifle on his chest and his boots on. I think it was me that scared him, not the gooks.

We got up, and pulled back. We moved into thicker vegetation and set up in a tight, defensive perimeter.

As we set up, I noticed that Harris had a big smile on his face, and Byron was grinning from ear to ear. I felt pretty cool, too. Maybe I wasn't an incurable screw-up. I hadn't panicked, and the gooks hadn't seen me. I don't think anyone realized how helpless I had been, all wrapped up in that poncho liner. No one, except maybe Looney.

As the sun began to rise, the sounds of jungle birds could be heard all around us. We relaxed a bit. The adrenaline high from our encounter was starting to wear off.

Byron whispered, "Good job, kid. You did all right."

I told him I had counted seventeen gooks. The first ones were carrying AK-47s, and the rest were packing canteens and something that rattled. I was trying to be cool. I was beginning to believe he had no idea how helpless I'd been, and I was determined to never be so helpless again.

Byron radioed the Old Man and asked him what he wanted us to do. The CO radioed back that he wanted us to watch them for the next few days and see what they were up to.

Burford crawled over and whispered to me in his country drawl, saying that I still might get the chance to kill my first gook, but not to rush it or go doing anything rash.

I wasn't about to do anything rash. Volunteering for the draft, going Airborne infantry, and raising my hand for the LRPs had just about expended my store of rashness.

Like clockwork, at 1800 hours that afternoon, the bad guys came walking back down the trail—but this time there were twice as many. They were talking, and they seemed relaxed and unaware that there was an LRP team anywhere nearby.

They walked right by us, but this time, we weren't as close to the trail, so it didn't seem as frightening. And this time, I had my weapon off safe and my finger on the trigger.

As soon as they had passed by us, Byron grabbed the headphone from Looney, and reported the size of the enemy element. From the size of the element, he suspected that they had a big base camp back in the jungle—possibly a regimental headquarters.

Back at the TOC, Captain Eklund decided to send in two heavy teams to pull an ambush and try for a prisoner. Eklund called Byron and told him that he would extract us the next afternoon. We were to lay dog all day and not initiate contact. I overheard Byron talking on the radio. He was going to leave one man behind to guide the other teams in. I had this fantasy that it would be me.

"Harris, you're staying behind to guide the other teams back in."

"Right, Sarge."

Just as we were rising to move out, a dink came running up the trail. He must've spotted us. I looked up just in time to see him leveling his AK-47. I heard a loud *click* as he switched it off safe.

Harris heard it too.

Pow!

Harris fired a single shot, killing the man instantly. The concussion from the round passing my head left my ears ringing. A second gook appeared down the trail. Harris opened up again and dropped him.

I raised my CAR-15 and was about to open up, when Byron grabbed me and pulled me back into the thicket. We ran deeper into the jungle. Byron called in on my radio and told the radio-relay team that we had been compromised and were in contact, and I tried to be as cool as the other men, who all covered their security zones and worked as a team, even though they were running. I would have felt like a real dumb shit, except I was too scared.

Schwartz broke trail through the bush. Harris and Burford dropped back to protect our rear. I didn't hear any more shots. Byron moved us fifty meters away from where Harris had made the initial contact, and we set up a small perimeter and waited for Burford and Harris to join us. When they were back with us, Byron took the handset from my web gear and held it to his ear.

"Six, just broke contact. Moving to PZ, over."

I wondered why he was using this radio now. Was it standard procedure to switch frequency after a contact? And if so, why?

Without waiting for a response, Byron tossed the handset back to me, and we continued through the jungle.

Burford and Harris had detected a lot of movement on the other side of the trail. The gooks apparently thought we'd broke in that direction.

Looney's radio crackled, and Byron grabbed the handset. It was Captain Eklund. Byron reported that we had broken contact and had two enemy KIAs. He turned to Burford and whispered for him to adjust fire from our last position. Burford reached for my handset and switched the frequency to the artillery net. I was glad he knew what he was doing, because I sure didn't.

Burford radioed the artillery unit on Firebase Normandy. Looney looked up from his handset and whispered that we had a reaction force coming in soon.

We moved out again.

"Let's move it!" Byron ordered as I stashed the handset in my web gear.

As Byron ran past me, he grabbed my web gear and pulled me after him. Without taking my eyes off the trail behind us, I followed.

As we reached the edge of an open field, I could hear artillery rounds coming in overhead.

About two hundred meters back down the stream, I could see puffs of smoke. Seconds later, I could hear the explosions—*Shoowhacaboom! Shooowhacaboom! Boom!*

Schwartz, at point, stopped near an open field and passed the word back, "Choppers coming in from the west."

Looney turned back to me and whispered that it was the reaction force, coming to develop the situation.

Schwartz and Looney swept their security zones, and I tried to remember mine. Harris and Burford quickly set out a claymore. Burford took out a thirty-second delay fuse and placed it in the mine but didn't arm it yet.

I looked up to see a helicopter overhead, dropping down toward our position.

Schwartz popped a smoke, then threw the yellow smoke grenade out into the center of the field. Looney turned back to Byron and told him that the pilots identified yellow smoke, then gave the pilots an affirmative.

The first chopper came in fast. It was one of the Kingsmen's ships. I recognized the big ace of spades painted on the nose of the chopper. Schwartz had said they were the best. As it settled in the grass, six infantrymen in steel helmets spilled out through the open doors. They formed a line behind us.

The guy closest to me was carrying an M-60 machine gun and had a peace sign drawn on his helmet.

A second chopper came in, and six more troops jumped out and moved quickly over to our position. A stocky sergeant pulled out a map and asked Byron where we had broken contact. As he turned, I noticed a dried human ear on a dirty shoelace around his neck.

I could hear other helicopters farther to the north. I figured they were trying to trap the enemy between us.

Byron yelled for us to go.

I jumped up and ran for the incoming chopper. Byron was running with my radio handset still clenched tightly in his hand. I was just trying to keep up with him. We hopped into the last chopper and headed back for Camp Eagle. Inside the chopper I couldn't resist letting out a war whoop.

"Ya hoooooo!" We were punching each other in the arms, slapping hands, and trying not to fall out the open chopper.

3

November 1968

Sergeant Burnell's jaw was set, and his eyes bored straight through me. I stood, feeling very much out of place. Burnell reached into the pocket of his fatigue shirt, took out a cigar, and lit it, blowing smoke into the center of the hooch. Burnell grinned.

"Ever fire an M-60, Chambers?"

I nodded. Sure, what did he think I was? A clerk? I wasn't even a cherry anymore—at least in my mind.

"Good, you'll be carrying the 60 this trip out."

The 101st Airborne Division was conducting operations in coordination with the 1st ARVN Division to provide external defense for the ancient imperial city of Hue. The operation was called Nevada Eagle, in honor of the home state of the division commanding general, who was generally despised by all those under him, except the clowns who named the operation for him. Nevada Eagle's primary mission was to locate and destroy NVA and VC forces around the city of Hue.

Normally, six-man LRP teams were used in reconnaissance or small ambushes. But on this mission, we were on a twelve-man heavy team. Our target was to find and destroy a radio transmitter that some radio-research unit had been monitoring for the past few weeks.

Enemy radio activity could only mean one thing—more bad guys moving into our area of operation. Monthly order-of-battle summaries estimated that North Vietnamese troops infiltrating down into South Vietnam were averaging about eight thousand men. But rumors around camp had twice that many coming down.

Five helicopters were to be used on this mission—a lift ship, a chase ship, two Cobras, and a command-and-control chopper. The pilots and crew were from the 160th Aviation Group, the Black Widows and the Kingsmen. They were an integral part of the company. They were highly respected and deeply appreciated by every member of the outfit, and I would soon find out why.

I walked outside the hooch. John Meszaros was sitting on a five-foot pile of PSP steel sections. He and Joe Bielesch were playing with Tiger, the small, brown, striped mutt that hung out at our company area, trying to avoid being eaten by the local Vietnamese. Tiger was smart as a whip, but refused to learn a word of English.

Burnell walked by, studying his clipboard. As he walked past us, he told us that we had op orders. He wanted to go over insertion and immediate-action drills.

Doyle Smith was writing a letter against the side of a sandbag.

"Smitty, come here!" Burnell barked. "Here's how I want the positions."

He pointed at the board.

"Harris can trade off with Schwartz at point. Meszaros, Proctor, and the new kid take turns walking slack. Evans, Burford switch at tail gun. Lieutenant Williams, Looney, and Miller will carry radios. Smitty, I want you to run everyone through the drills. I'm going on the overflight over the Roung Roung Valley. Meet me back at my hooch at 1900 hours."

Smitty nodded. "Right, Sarge."

Later, back at the hooch, I sat under the mosquito net draped over my cot and tried to write a letter to my cousin, Donna. She had written me every week since I had joined the army, and I wanted to answer her last letter before we went out on this mission.

The back door of the hooch flew open. I couldn't see for a second, as my eyes adjusted to the light. It was Meszaros. He was standing in the doorway; the bright sun behind him made him look almost foreboding.

"Come on, man. We've got to get down to the chopper pad, more drills."

I stashed the pen and paper under my cot and followed him out of the hooch.

We walked down to the chopper pad. I heard a Huey coming in fast. We looked up as it passed over us, swung around, then landed. It was the guys returning from the overflight. Burnell, Lieutenant Williams, Venable, and Contreros were sitting on the edge of the open-cabin floor. The chopper rocked back and forth as it set down. The four hopped out, ducking their heads as they walked over to the steps which led back up to the company area.

A second chopper flew over. It was much smaller than the Huey. It was a Loach, a light observation helicopter. The Loach was carrying Captain Eklund. It landed fifty feet on the other side of the larger slick.

Captain Eklund slowly got out of the helicopter and started walking up the steps. He was carrying a CAR-15 and a PRC-25 radio. He joined the other four men. They had been waiting for him at the top of the stairs. As they walked toward the TOC, Eklund pointed to a spot on the map. No one was smiling.

Schwartz and I stood waiting, not saying a word but taking in everything. I was still a little afraid to open my mouth around any of the old guys. Even though the average age of the so-called "old foul dudes" was only twenty, they looked more like they were in their thirties. I felt like an awkward kid.

It was almost 1600 hours. We were scheduled to insert at last light the next evening. We spent almost two hours going over the escape-and-evasion drills. The idea of escaping into the enemy-infested jungle, twenty miles from the nearest friendly forces, didn't thrill me. We continued to practice immediate-action drills. Charging into the direction of an attack was an unnatural human reaction. The natural response to an ambush was to hit the ground or run for cover. The gooks prepared their ambushes, sometimes days before, planting mines and punji stakes along the trail. They counted on our natural tendency to dive for cover off the trail, straight into their traps.

As we walked back up the hill, Schwartz told me that word was the 5th NVA Regiment was in one of the AOs we were going into. Then he asked, "Is this your third mission?"

I nodded. I hoped it wasn't my last.

On the earlier missions, I had learned how to sleep without snoring by lying facedown. But the thought of sleeping next to an entire NVA Regiment would be a new problem. Somehow I didn't feel ready to deal with this one.

The next morning, Sergeant Burnell woke us at 0430. I was still groggy, as I slowly pulled on my green-canvas jungle boots and thought about Schwartz's explanation of why I should thread a dog tag through one of my bootlaces. It was supposed to make for easier identification if the upper half of my body got blown away.

We funneled into a single line as we walked up the hill for breakfast. We could smell the chow long before seeing the mess tent. Inside, the cooks had huge piles of steaming French toast, and there were large bricks of butter on each table. I grabbed a stainless-steel tray and got into line. Our two team leaders, Sergeant Contreros and Sergeant Burnell, joked with each other as they stood in the chow line ahead of us. I filled my tray, then sat down next to the exit, still feeling a little nervous about my surroundings.

The two team leaders were bragging about who was going to get the bigger body count. Higher echelons were full of clerks who measured success by the number of dead enemy soldiers. It was called "the war of attrition." The theory was that we were winning the war if we could kill more enemy troops than they could replace. Whoever invented this theory obviously hadn't taken a census in Vietnam lately. It was pretty stupid if you asked me. Unfortunately no one did.

The sound of rain beating down on the tin roof merged with the sound of Cobra gunships landing as I finished my coffee. I hurried back to my hooch. The day before, Sergeant Burnell had told us that the new Cobras would be making their debut, flying escort for us.

It was time. I was getting tense. I would be on the second ship. The twelve of us were going up against eighteen hundred hard-core NVA regulars. I was wondering how many each one of us would have to kill if we got caught. I leaned over and tapped Schwartz's shoulder.

"Jim, if things get bad out there and we get into a firefight, the way I figure it, we are going to have to kill 150 gooks each. Conservatively, if it only takes three rounds per gook, I figure we are five hundred rounds short. Save my place."

I was assigned to carry the M-60 machine gun for the six-day mission, trading off with Meszaros. I had spent the previous day carrying that heavy gun around while we drilled. I rigged a shoulder strap for the gun so that it would balance under my arm. Meszaros was my loader. He had to carry his own M-16 plus five hundred additional rounds of M-60 ammo.

Each of us had a hundred-round belt of ammo at the top of our rucksacks. That way, whoever was near the guy carrying the machine gun would be able to reach into the pack of the LRP in front of him and pull out a belt to feed into the M-60. Since we intended to trade off carrying it, we both had to practice loading and firing the gun.

The CO had upgraded the mission. It seemed that there were now closer to six thousand NVA regulars reported in the area. Hearing this, Meszaros went back for more ammo.

While our primary mission was to locate and observe enemy movement, our secondary mission was much more interesting. We were to locate and destroy a COSVN radio transmitter that had been sending messages from somewhere near our insertion LZ.

We had finished the preop briefing and were down on the acid pad, sitting around waiting for the order to load up. Burnell came down to the edge of the tarmac and shouted that it was time to go. I slipped into the shoulder straps of my rucksack, and extended my hand up to Burford. He grunted as he pulled me to my feet. I reached down and grabbed the heavy machine gun. My gear weighed a ton and the gun added another twenty-six pounds.

The first ship came in. Sergeant Burnell, the team leader; Lt. O.D. Williams, junior RTO; Sgt. "Snuffy" Smith, rear security; Sp4c. Jim "Boom Boom" Evans, junior scout; Kenn Miller, artillery RTO; and Sp4c. Jim "Stinky" Schwartz, junior scout, boarded in reverse order of how they were going to get off at the LZ.

The rest of us—Sgt. "Honest John" Burford, the ATL; Sp4c. Joe Don Looney, the senior RTO; Sgt. Bruce "Doc" Proctor, medic; John "May-Zeus" Meszaros, assistant gunner; Don "The Shadow" Harris, point man; and yours truly, the cherry—headed over to the second ship. I took my time getting into the chopper with the M-60 machine gun. It was a real handful.

Behind our chopper was Captain Eklund's C & C ship. He was waiting for Burnell's helicopter to take off. The other heavy team had already been inserted and was already on its mission.

The aircraft commanders were going through their preflights. Our pilot, W.T. Grant, looked up and gave Burford the thumbs-up sign. Grant had inserted damn near every LRP team at one time or another and had promised us that any place he put in a team, he would come back and get them out again. Just knowing we had pilots like that made me feel better.

The high-pitched whine of the turbines began as the rotor blades started their lazy rotation. Keith Hammond and Wiley Holland loaded some last-minute rations aboard the C & C ship for our radio-relay team. This time, they were going to be out there as far as we were, with none of our freedom of movement.

Across the hill, at the 2/17th Cavalry's helipad, two brand-spanking-new Cobra gunships were warming up. They would soon join us on our trip to the Roung Roung Valley. It was the same valley where Ray Zoschak's team had killed an estimated hundred and fifty NVA only two months earlier. From a distance, the Cobras looked more like futuristic toy models than army helicopters.

I sat behind Burford on the floor of the chopper, next to the door gunner's open compartment. I gripped the M-60 tightly. There weren't many weapons in the U.S. arsenal you could call a "gun." An M-16 or a CAR-15 was called a rifle, but this bad mother was affectionately dubbed a "gun."

As the rotor blades picked up speed, I pulled my boonie hat off my head and stuck it in my shirt. Sergeant Bowman was flying as the bellyman in our ship. His job was to coordinate functions between the helicopter crew, the C & C ship, and the team. We were packed in tightly, hoping no one would fart or get airsick. Bowman passed the word to Grant over the ship's intercom that we were ready to get the show on the road. Grant pulled back on the cyclic. I felt the chopper shudder, rise gently on its skids, then lunge as it broke away from the ground. The ship turned 180 degrees as it dropped its nose and started to climb. The ground fell away as we gained speed and altitude. We climbed out over the concertina wire that circled Camp Eagle. I leaned forward for a single look at Camp Eagle. I was amazed how it looked more like a papier-mâché model than a real army camp.

I could see the command-and-control ship and the two Cobra gunships as they pulled into formation ahead of us. We flew west toward the jungles of northern I Corps. Camp Eagle faded away behind us.

The sun was beginning to set to the west, and the mountains turned from bright green to a dark, colorless gloom. The hillsides and valleys were pocked with bomb craters, but they were anything but ugly. Emerald green vegetation was already growing in some of them, and the water accumulated in the center of the fresher craters shone dark in the fading sunlight. From up here, Vietnam looked so peaceful and beautiful, it was hard to believe that a war was going on below. The air rushing through the open cabin made conversation almost impossible. I sat back and thought about what was coming.

We were to land on an abandoned firebase, then walk into our AO. I tried to gauge the distance to the ground as we circled above.

This was a critical time for a chopper. Any helicopter in a descending flare is an easy target.

We sat down on the muddy ground and quickly off-loaded.

I asked Burford, "Why the rush?"

"Those Hueys are sittin' ducks up here, son. The grunts have been getting rocketed and mortared night and day. When the choppers come in, they seem to draw incoming like blood attracts sharks."

I ran over to an old bunker and sat down. It felt good to get the heavy ruck off my back.

Burnell growled, "Don't get *too* comfortable, cherry, we're moving down the hill as soon as I square away our radio-relay team."

Burnell had changed the Grape code, and he needed to give the relay team the new SOIs. (The "Grape Code" was a radio code that used a common, predetermined point of reference on a map—called the "grape point"—and allowed us to give our location in coordinates from the grape point while on a mission.) The firebase looked eerie and unreal to me, like an abandoned war-movie set. They had double-rolled concertina wire around the outer perimeter, like they were expecting a lot more gooks than they thought they could handle, but the only "they" manning the place was a terrified Aero Rifle platoon of infantry, usually used as a reaction force, that didn't relish securing our radio relay out here. They were more vulnerable than we, but they looked at us like we were madmen.

I sensed that it would be safer down in the jungle below. At least the enemy wouldn't know our every move. This firebase just didn't seem like a good place to set up housekeeping. I felt sorry for our relay team. There'd be only four of them, and they'd have to reassure and protect these guys and still handle our commo.

There was no artillery on the mountaintop, just this platoon of air rifles pulling security for our radio relay team. There was a rumor going around that there had been some real hairy battles around this mountain firebase, and I was glad I wasn't one of those "air rifles" trying to secure it—or a member of our relay team.

"Move out! Move out!" Burnell roused us.

I hurried into my position, number-three man. I pulled back the charging handle on my M-60, and pushed the safety to on.

We moved out of the perimeter, walking single file through a small gap in the wire. I looked back at the relay team, who had come over to see us off. I got the impression that they would sleep more soundly knowing that there was one more buffer between them and the enemy.

I tried not to think about what might be waiting below. I was good at keeping my mind on something else.

It was getting dark, and we had covered quite a bit of ground, when I slipped and fell. I tried to catch myself, but the heavy machine gun threw me off balance. I hit with a thud, landing in something sticky and slimy. Then the smell hit me. I retched involuntarily.

I had stumbled onto a decomposing enemy soldier.

Oh God! I'm standing on a dead guy! I got up quickly, trying to brush the rotten flesh off my clothing. Gagging, I stepped out of the slop that had once been a man. I was trying not to think about what had just happened.

They weren't going to believe *this* back home.

A few yards away, next to a large tree, we found what was left of his head. Some animal had had a field day with it. Bits of black hair were still plastered to it, but most of the skin was gone. It was hard to believe that this had once been a person. Everyone went on full alert. It was unusual for the Viet Cong not to collect their dead.

The enemy's style was to prepare the battlefield, controlling every aspect of it, whether they really had a chance or not. The VC would prearrange fighting positions and bury extra weapons and ammo in strategic places. They would also carefully determine the best avenues of escape, or dig tunnels to pull the dead and wounded into, and lay out routes to recover their dead. Throughout the war, it was not uncommon for American units to blindly stumble into an ambush that the gooks had set up weeks in advance.

I pulled myself back together and moved out. My assignment was to watch the trail on my right.

It started raining, and I hoped some of the slime would wash off my clothes. The ground became muddier as we moved. We climbed over some bamboo that had fallen across our path. I leaned the M-60 against a tree and grabbed an overhanging limb to pull myself over the bamboo. The rest of the patrol followed close behind. We moved quickly on, anxious to get out of the area.

Everyone seemed to sense the danger. We moved in silence, slowly. The mountain trail disappeared into the fog at its base, then appeared again through the vines.

Two hours later, Burnell drew an arrow on his map, folded it, then shoved it back into his pocket. He readjusted a wad of tobacco he'd been chewing on.

We were on the steep side of the mountain and hoped the gooks would not expect us to come down this side.

The mud and light rain made the trail almost impassable. With each step, the red mud built up on my boots until it felt like I was wearing heavy lead weights. We stopped, and I scraped off as much mud as possible, then we moved on.

It began to grow dark as we reached the bottom of the hill. We moved deeper into the jungle. Harris found a narrow creek bed with thick, green vines hanging from the trees overhead. I watched him disappear into the ground fog ahead. It looked like a scene from a horror movie.

The rainfall had intensified, and soon everything and everybody seemed to just blend together. The jungle was so dense it hid our view of the stream just a few feet away. Harris stepped into the water and startled a bird from the brush on the other side. It flew, squawking, through the jungle canopy. We could hear the percussive sounds of our own artillery off in the distance.

We were miserable, as we made our way along the valley floor. The birds warned each other of our approach. I thought, *Even the birds have trail watchers.*

In many ways this place was very much like the swamps along the rivers back home, except here there were more trees and bigger vines. Even the smells were similar.

Every few feet, I had to arch my back as I readjusted the heavy machine gun. The shoulder strap was digging into my collar bone, and it was beginning to ache. I had broken my collar bone in a high-school basketball game, and it still bothered me.

The wind increased and covered the sounds of our movement. The damp, cold air went right through my tiger fatigues. Finally, Burnell signaled for us to pull off next to the trail. It was getting darker, and he wanted to set up a night defensive perimeter.

We had just moved up to the edge of the trail from the jungle. I set the M-60 down next to a large hardwood tree. The first thing I did was pull out my canteen and take a big swig of water. Suddenly, I heard something above me. It was fifty meters away on the next ridgeline. It sounded like people running. The sound was growing louder. *More than one,* I thought. The wind blew harder through the leaves over my head, momentarily drowning out the noise on the hill above us. I strained to hear the sound, it was too dark to see. When the wind stopped, the noises became even louder. I stood, looking up the steep trail into the darkness.

The clamor had drawn everyone else's attention, too. I looked at Burford, standing motionless next to me with his M-16 at the ready. I rested the M-60 on my gas-mask cover for balance. The sounds moved closer. Something was coming our way!

Burford pushed me down. I dropped to the ground, propped myself up on my right elbow, and waited. The enemy wouldn't be able to see us until they were right on top of us.

Burnell snapped his fingers, softly. I turned back to see what he wanted. He pointed up the hill, then made a fist meaning "hold your fire."

I held my breath. It sounded like the entire North Vietnamese Army was running down the hill toward us.

I was thinking, *Why were they running? How many of them are there? Is that what an attack sounds like?*

I pointed the M-60 in the direction of the trail. They were less than thirty feet away. *God, it sounds like there must be a hundred of them.* I wondered what it would feel like to shoot a man. I felt someone move up next to me. I didn't want to take my eyes off of the trail to see who it was.

"Easy." It was Burford. Even in a whisper, I recognized that unmistakable Georgia drawl, "Take the ones on the right side of the trail. Hold her low, she's gonna rise on ya a bit."

He reached into my ruck, pulled out the one hundred-round belt of M-60 ammo, and snapped it to the free link. Burford tapped me on the back. I nodded without taking my eyes off the trail.

Here they come! I thought. At fifteen feet they broke trail. I could see a silhouette. I started to pull the trigger, when a small deer ran out.

Not more than ten feet behind her came two small monkeys, racing as fast as they could. They got to my position and hit the skids, turned, and scampered back up the hill. I rolled over on my side and let out my breath

"Jesus, they scared the living shit out of me!" I whispered to Burford. He was busting a gut trying not to laugh. He grabbed my wrist and held my arm up in the air for everyone to see, as if I had won the match. I looked back at Schwartz. He grinned and flipped me the victory sign. Meszaros snickered cynically.

Holy shit! I almost blew away two monkeys and a pygmy deer! I could have sworn they were dinks.

Burford uncoupled the extra belt, folded it over and put it back in my pack. As he tightened the straps on the back of my ruck, he leaned over and whispered in my ear, "Good job, dude."

I held my fire and didn't panic. The OJT, on-the-job training, was working.

They could never teach you *this* back in the States. In training all we did was shoot 'em up. No one warned me about monkeys chasing deer.

I was just getting over the experience when Burford knelt down and whispered that Contreros's team had spotted a large force. A chill went down my spine. LRP teams are not set up to deal with large enemy units, especially at night. Most firefights were over in minutes. Our unit was just too small to withstand a pitched battle with a large enemy force. We monitored Contreros's transmissions.

Burnell held up his right hand and, with two fingers pointed upward, gave the double-up sign, then waved in a circular motion, instructing the team to double up and lie out in a ten-meter circle. Each man faced out like spokes on a wheel, but within arm's reach of each other.

Suddenly, gunfire erupted above us. M-60 and M-16 automatic fire tore the night apart. Burford crept up next to me and told me it was only the grunts on the firebase pulling a "mad minute," sixty seconds of automatic fire from the perimeter of the firebase. My entire nervous system was in a spasm.

We were all exhausted and worried about the other team. It was raining lightly as I set my M-60 and rucksack on the ground and went about running out forty feet of detonation cord. Burford followed me, then carefully removed a blasting cap from his shirt pocket and handed it to me. I slid it over the end of the cord and crimped it. I found a spot on the other side of a stand of bamboo and set up my claymore. I aimed the mine so that the direction of its blast would open a hole in the thick jungle and its backblast would knock down the stand of bamboo. This would serve two purposes: First, anyone in its path would be killed instantly, and second, the blast would cut a large hole in the jungle for us to escape through. I finished preparing the mine, then crawled back, slid my web gear off, and put it where I could quickly pull it back on. I took out a couple of frags and placed them on the ground next to the clacker, the firing device for the claymore mine. Now everything was in place, only a few inches from my hands, neatly laid out on my poncho liner.

Burnell signaled Looney, the senior radio operator, to contact the relay team on the firebase. He told him to inform them that we were in our NDP and that the situation report (sitrep) was negative, meaning all was quiet.

Harris was to take the first watch. At the end of his shift, he would pass his watch to the next man, and so on. Each man would stand guard for one hour at a time, then wake up the next man and hand him the watch. This passing of the watch continued around the circle until it arrived back to Harris, six hours later. The watch would be handed to me at 2200 hours, then again at 0400 hours. *That* would be the tough one.

Then, like someone took a sledgehammer and knocked a hole in the night sky, the rain began to pour. It came down so heavy that I felt like I was trying to breathe underwater.

I was soon soaked to the skin, the jungle was soaked, no one could sleep. Meszaros moved up against me, back-to-back, in an attempt to preserve some of our body heat. Everyone else paired up, too. The temperature must have dropped twenty degrees in ten minutes.

We pulled our guard shifts and tried to catch a few minutes of sleep between the downpours. We kept track of the developments on Contreros's team. It wasn't looking good. During the night, enemy soldiers had come down the trail several times, looking for their team.

The next morning, November 20th, the fog came in heavy, like someone had set the jungle valley on fire. I sat in the dense, damp jungle. Anxiety crept over me. Burnell told Burford to take Lieutenant Williams and me out to make an early-morning recon of the southern ridgeline.

I fell in behind Burford, with Lieutenant Williams following close behind. We took our time, stopping after an hour's patrol. The jungle had opened up around us, and the rain began again. Then the vegetation got so thick again that you couldn't see five feet ahead. The gooks could be waiting in ambush anywhere, and we would never know they were there until we walked up on them. We passed an abandoned bunker complex, complete with fighting trenches along one side of the trail. Burford said it looked as if a battalion-size unit had been here only days before.

Burford decided it was not in our best interest to continue up that hill. We backed off and returned to the team. Burford and Burnell had a few words about the likely direction the gooks had taken. I could tell Burnell wanted to find the gooks before Contreros. He wasn't bloodthirsty, just competitive.

It was near 0900. I had just finished eating and was concerned about the reports coming in from Contreros's team. They had spotted a couple of enemy patrols the night before, and they seemed to be looking for the team. I had a feeling that something terrible was about to happen. Then Contreros was on the radio, calling in for a medevac for one of his men, who had broken an ankle on their insertion.

A few hours later, we heard shots far off in the distance,

then the radio crackled to life. It was Contreros's voice, and we could hear gunfire in the background. He was excited; they had sprung an ambush. They had nine NVA down and had captured a lot of documents. The CO radioed that the team would be extracted then reinserted to the south of us. Burnell seemed upset. A muscle jumped on his jaw, and he tried to monitor all three radios at once.

About a half hour later, the CO came back on the air and told Contreros that he could not get the team extracted. All of the division's choppers were committed. Contreros had just radioed back that he was going to move up the ridge to the west when we heard more gunfire coming from the direction of their position. This time it was a heavy volume of fire that didn't let up. Captain Eklund was told by G-2 to keep our team in position. We monitored the action. We would hear gun shots, then the radio would come alive telling the CO what was going on. All we knew was one of Contreros's men had been hit and they were trying to get a medevac in for him, but they were having a rough time. Every time we'd hear the distant sounds of our Cobra's miniguns blasting away, everyone would smile and give the thumbs-up sign. We were like a bunch of guys at a bar rooting for the home team. Then it got quiet—too quiet. Contreros's team had sprung an ambush on ten NVA and only killed nine of them. If the other enemy soldier escaped, he would be back with reinforcements ricky-tick.

Contreros's team stayed near the ambush site, waiting for a reaction force. When they finally decided to move, they were hit from all sides. It was bad, really bad, and there was nothing we could do to help. Their ATL, trying to signal a chopper from outside the perimeter, went down in the initial attack. The team pulled him back inside the perimeter and returned fire. They remained in contact with a reinforced company-size NVA unit for the next four hours. Except for the Cobras and Captain Eklund's presence in the Loach, they received no help. We momentarily lost radio contact with them. Burford told me the Cobras had expended their ammo and had to return to Camp Eagle to rearm and take on fuel. Suddenly, we heard 105 mm rounds impacting. The team was back on the air again, Burford monitored Contreros's fire mission, then turned and whispered, "They're walking artillery rounds within fifty meters of their perimeter. The gooks must be right on top of them."

Another salvo hit, and we had lost radio contact with them a second time.

Suddenly, we heard a tremendous explosion from the direction of the team. It had a different sound than the *crump* of the artillery rounds. Harris hurried back to talk to Burnell, then moved back up to the point position. I tried to hear what was being said. It was obvious that something was dreadfully wrong. I could tell by the way everyone was acting. The explosion we heard sounded like one of those huge Chicom claymores. We were only five klicks away from Contreros's team, but in the dense jungle, we were too far away to reach them by going overland. We may as well have been in China.

Burford sat down next to me.

"We may have lost Contreros's team."

"What?" I felt only shock. The same feeling in my gut when I'd heard President Kennedy had been assassinated. I felt angry and sad at the same time—and totally helpless.

Burford left and went back to where Burnell was listening intently to the radio.

A terrible sadness overwhelmed me. I could feel my chest tighten. I fought to control my emotions. The rain hid my tears. I could only imagine the worst possible scenario.

A few minutes passed, then Burnell stood and said, "Get up, get up, let's go!" He was visibly upset.

"We've been ordered back up to the top of the hill. We're going to get the team out. Let's go, now!"

A surge of energy shot through my body as word circulated that we would be used as the reaction force. But with each passing minute, the odds of rescuing the team dwindled. By now it was getting so late in the day that it would take until dark to get us to the team. They didn't have that long.

Then the radio crackled again. They were sending in a re-action force from our company and the Aero Rifle Platoon from the 2/17th Cav. They were already in the air.

Burford said that he could hear the pilots talking as they reached the team's location. He reported that they could see the dead bodies of enemy soldiers all around the hilltop where the team lay trapped. All we could do was to keep pray-ing for them.

Burnell got on the radio with Captain Eklund and de-manded to be picked up and dropped in to help get Contreros out. The CO told him to stay put. All that could be done was being done.

We were still waiting when the terrible news came over the radio; the team leader and three others of the team were KIA, and everyone else had been seriously wounded.

Oh God! I felt like a spike had been driven through my chest.

Contreros had been Burnell's best friend. The loss showed on his face. He dropped the towel that he had draped around his neck. He sat against a tree staring into the radio's handset, a look of shock and utter disbelief on his face.

The reports continued coming in. We all felt totally help-less. The anger and frustration was clearly visible on the faces of my teammates, who stood waiting, wanting to do something—anything to help our comrades. Our standard procedure was that if a team got in contact, all the other teams in the field would hold their position. That way, the gunships would only have to concentrate on the team in trouble.

Hammond, in charge of the radio-relay team, had moni-tored the entire engagement. He told Burford over the radio that the CO had decided to extract us. We had to get back up to the top of the hill in the next twenty minutes.

Twenty minutes? That was impossible, and the impossible inspired Burnell. We busted ass. As we climbed, I prayed the enemy would show up so we could take them out. Before we reached the top, Looney let the infantry platoon leader know that we were coming in.

When we reached the top, we slipped through the wire, dropped our gear, and tried to find out what had happened. I sat down on a sandbag next to Harris and Meszaros. Smitty and Miller paced back and forth in front of us. Lieutenant Williams was sitting next to Schwartz. He looked over at me and shook his head. Williams didn't try to pretend he was used to this, but he kept his composure, something we had all lost at some point that day.

Burford was sitting on a rubber fuel bladder, next to Burnell. I looked over to see that Burnell was now crying openly. I tried to look away, but shared his pain. One minute he had been fine, the next moment he was in tears. We had been ordered back down the hill.

"Oh God, what for?" Our morale was so low, no one could think straight.

Burnell's sadness over Contreros now turned to anger. He argued with Captain Eklund over the radio. Then we headed back down the hill.

The rain continued. I had never before seen it come down like this. I pulled my poncho over my head and pulled the receiver of my M-60 tight against my stomach. Visibility had deteriorated to just a few feet.

Burnell pulled us into a tight perimeter. He figured that the enemy would hole up in their base camps until the rain was over, and since they couldn't get any choppers in for us, we were going to have to lay dog until the weather broke. He was told that it might be days before they could get a helicopter in to extract us. The Old Man told Burnell to conserve our food and energy, because he didn't know when they'd come get us.

I lost sight of Miller and Smitty, who were less than three feet away. Burnell ordered us to build a lean-to in the dense cover behind. We huddled inside it like a bunch of wet rats riding out a flood. It was the most miserable night I'd ever spent in my life. Our morale had completely collapsed. We were cold and wet, and the mood was gloomy.

Burford, tired of trying to sleep in six inches of water, got up, went outside the lean-to, and sat by the trail in the downpour.

He looked at his watch. It was 0300 hours. As I lay there in the mud, I felt something crawling down the back of my pants. I fought to get unwrapped from that poncho liner but it was wet and difficult to get free of. Finally, I was able to slide my hand down my pants and grope for the intruder.

There! I found something trying to crawl between my legs. It was an enormous leech. He didn't want to let go as I pinched his slimy body.

Gotcha, you little bastard!

"Leech," I whispered to Meszaros, who by this time was watching me with a quizzical look on his face.

The rain came down in buckets all night long. It was bad, but the feeling of losing our teammates made it almost unbearable. My watch fogged up, and I couldn't read it.

By 0500 hours, the rain had slowed to a steady downpour. Every few minutes, I would lift my head and look around for gooks. I shivered in the early-morning cold trying to rest.

Two days later we were still laying dog, which meant we stay quiet and didn't move, and it was still raining. Burnell held the radio under his poncho liner. He had received word there might be a break in the weather. He cupped his hand over the plastic-covered handset.

"The CO wants us back up top. Now! The Old Man is going to try to get a chopper in for us."

It seemed like a bad dream. This couldn't really be happening, but I knew that, once we got back to camp, everyone would be okay. We fought our way back to the top. Then the fog closed in again, and we had to come back down.

Two hours later, we got the word to prepare again to be extracted. One last time we struggled up that muddy slope. It seemed like we'd slide back one step for every three we took forward. Finally, we made it to the top of the hill. We were exhausted, soaked and emotionally drained.

The helicopter above us sounded like it was only a few feet from the ground, but we couldn't see it for the dense fog. Kingsman Two Five called on the radio and indicated that the clouds were beginning to break up and he was coming down. Then our hopes were once again dashed. No sooner had Captain "Wild Bill" Meacham begun to descend when the clouds closed back in around his chopper. He called us on the radio.

"This is Kingsman Two Five. Pop a flare."

"Roger that, Two Five. I copy."

A red flare was popped. From below, it looked like the dense clouds were on fire.

Wild Bill looked down between the pedals and out the chin bubble. He put his ship directly over the glowing red spot below and began his descent. Within seconds, the flare died.

"Give me another flare, same spot."

"Roger that, Two Five."

The chopper continued to drop and finally landed directly on top of the two smoldering flares. We later learned from Wild Bill that he had never felt his ship actually touch down.

After the Huey landed, we ran across the top of the hill and prepared to board. I slid my M-60 across the metal cargo floor and climbed in behind it. Once everyone was aboard, the chopper lifted off and slowly made its way off the edge of the mountain and disappeared into the clouds. The air rifles were gone but the relay team was still waiting for the chase ship to pick them up.

CWOs Dave Poley and W.T. Grant were picking up the reaction force on the other side of the valley. Wild Bill, Grant, and Poley had been flying steady for the last three days. Bill had put in seventeen flying hours on that day alone.

Grant radioed Wild Bill that he had counted beaucoup dead around Contreros's team. The NVA must have thrown everything they had at the LRPs.

Except for the occasional pilot/crew dialogue over the

radio, no one spoke during the entire ride back to camp. I looked out the open cargo bay into a thick fog bank. The clouds seemed to drift right into the ship. I stared at the Snoopy dog painted on the back of Wild Bill's flight helmet.

Grant had painted almost all of the Kingsmen pilots' helmets. But his helmet had a cherry painted on it. It had become a symbol for the other pilots, that they could make it through a tour without getting hit.

An aviator was a cherry until his ship took its first enemy rounds. Before Grant, no Kingsman ever flew more than ninety days without taking a hit. Six months into his tour, Grant made aircraft commander, and still hadn't taken a hit. He wore his cherry with pride. He would walk into the club at night and everyone would ask, "Ya still got it?"

If Grant could keep that cherry this long, they felt they could all make it home.

We flew slowly through the fog for almost twenty minutes. I wondered how the pilots could see anything. Wild Bill practically had to feel his way down to the valley. He managed to keep the ship in a slow descent until he dropped out of the clouds. Once he broke free of the fog bank, he kicked the ship into overdrive and raced back to Camp Eagle.

There was no one on the ground as we set down on the company acid pad. No one met us in the usual way. There was a strange feeling of sadness everywhere.

We went directly to the debriefing at the TOC, still wearing our soaking wet clothes. A major and a captain from G-2 were on the way over to conduct the debriefing. The mood was solemn.

We crowded into the company TOC. I was next to the door, but could still feel the emotion that permeated the room. Captain Eklund confirmed that Sergeant Contreros, the team leader; Michael Reiff; Art Heringhausen; and Terry Clifton were dead. Gary Linderer, Frank Souza, Riley Cox, Jim Bacon, Jim Venable and Steven Czepurny had all been seriously wounded. The only one to walk away was Billy Walkabout.

John Sours had been extracted just an hour before the engagement started, with two broken ankles.

We sat there, silent in shock. Everyone wanted to know the details. Burnell was visibly upset.

We had heard a lot of stories about Special Forces losing teams, but having a heavy team of our own chewed up didn't seem possible.

Captain Eklund was on the verge of tears as he told us about the mission.

"Here's what we think happened. The team initiated the ambush around 0930 and killed nine NVA. When the team checked the dead, they discovered that one of them was an NVA major, and he was carrying a rucksack full of maps and important documents. Contreros radioed the intel in, then pulled the team back into a defensive perimeter and called for a reaction force. I tried for an hour to get him one, but I couldn't get any helicopter support from division. Contreros then decided to move his team to higher ground. He sent his ATL, Jim Venable, out into a clearing to signal my ship with a mirror. The jungle was so thick that I couldn't spot him. The NVA opened up on Venable and hit him three times. The rest of the team returned fire, then pulled Venable back into the perimeter. They had to beat back two enemy assaults. It seemed as if the enemy had given up trying to take the team by a frontal assault, as they were then receiving only sporadic fire. I told them to hang tight; the Cobras had to return to Eagle to rearm and refuel. My ship was running on fumes, so we had to follow the Cobras. Contreros called in artillery fire for about forty-five minutes until we could get back on station. I managed to get hold of two more Cobras, and we all hurried back out to the team. I couldn't get a fix on them at first, then suddenly I saw a huge, bright flash and a large, black cloud of smoke rolling up the knoll."

Captain Eklund paused, and looked at Burnell.

"Burnie, we don't know what it was for sure, but we think

it was a claymore, a forty-pounder. All the Kingsmen chop-pers were tied up in a brigade-size combat assault, and I couldn't get any help to them for several hours. We finally had to put together our own reaction force from the company. Tercero, Coleman, Guthmeller, Bennett, Fadeley, and Bielesch were the first to reach the team. Tercero lead the charge up the hill in nothing but his shorts, shower sandals, and his LBE."

Eklund was having a difficult time. He shook his head.

"I told Contreros to take his team and get out of there. I wanted them to lay dog some place safer until we could get choppers and reinforcements. But he didn't want to leave the ambush site."

Burnell pounded his fist on the table top. "Damn it!"

He stared at the after-action report.

"Sergeant Burnell, I know Sergeant Contreros was your friend. I'm sorry."

Eklund turned and left.

You could have heard a pin drop in the TOC. Just then the G-2 officers arrived to debrief our team. When it was over, Burford and I walked back to the hooch.

"It just doesn't make sense," Burford said. "If they were repelling every attack, how could the gooks move a forty-pound claymore up that hill and not be seen? I think what happened is Contreros called in the artillery a little too close to his own position. But that may have saved the rest of the team."

The rest of the team? There wasn't much left.

The next morning, I opened one eye, then the other. The hooch looked blurry. I got dressed and went to see what I could do. I wanted to stay busy, feel useful, not sit with the sadness and helplessness of the day before.

I walked outside the hooch. The sun was unusually bright. I had to shield my eyes. I walked down to the bathhouse and took a hot shower. That didn't seem to change my mood.

Sergeant Smith came over to the hooch later that day.

"We'll need memorial plaques for their families."

The next day, Meszaros and I walked over to a souvenir shop located in the center of Camp Eagle. We found four small, eight-by-ten-inch wood plaques with a short, but appropriate, eulogy under a metal replica of an American flag: FOR THOSE WHO FOUGHT AND DIED FOR FREEDOM, WE, A GRATEFUL COUNTRY, GIVE THANKS.

Meszaros looked at the plaques, and in a sarcastic tone, said, "Grateful country, that's a laugh!"

The short, brown-skinned Vietnamese behind the counter handed me one of the plaques. I examined it, then told him where to put the names. "You understand?"

I handed him a paper with the names of the four men. He studied the names, then looked up at me.

"I understand. I do numba one job. You come back three day, Okay!"

The Vietnamese shop owner fidgeted with an order form and wrote down each name.

He nodded his head and grinned that patronizing Oriental grin, as if he had done hundreds of memorial plaques and enjoyed engraving the names of all the dead Americans.

As we walked back, I asked Meszaros.

"How do we know whether or not that gook is a VC?"

Meszaros's answer showed his midwestern, small-town wisdom.

"Oh, he's definitely a VC, but only after work hours."

Meszaros stopped, reached down, and pried loose a stone that had wedged in the sole of his boot.

"Think about it. He probably lives in Hue or Phu Bai, right?"

"Right." I readjusted my black baseball cap so the sun was out of my eyes.

"He probably comes from a big Vietnamese family, with beaucoup ancestors buried from here to Hanoi and every place in between. Right?"

"Yeah."

"Well, the odds are that he's related to or is a sympathizer to the VC, right?"

"I never thought about it like that."

Meszaros stood back up and examined the stone he had pried loose from his boot.

"And he probably reports to the local party cell how many plaques he makes each week. That way the enemy gets an accurate body count for their records. It's all very simple."

We walked back to the company area, not saying a word.

Four days later, we had a formal ceremony for our men.

We set up a memorial altar down on the acid pad, with four inverted M-16 rifles, with bayonets attached, stuck into the ground. In front of each rifle was a pair of jungle boots. The toes had been spit shined in the Airborne tradition. It was our way of honoring our dead.

Just before noon we formed up, down on the chopper pad to pay our last respects. The division chaplain was there to conduct the ceremony. We stood at attention as he read the eulogy and said a long prayer.

Captain Eklund looked out over our heads, toward the mountains, as he talked about how much every one of these guys meant to all of us. I had never seen him show any real signs of emotion until now. As he spoke, his eyes welled, and his voice cracked. Several times he had to stop, clear his throat, pause to take a deep breath, and try to regain his composure before continuing. His hands were tightly clenched. It was obvious that he was deeply affected by the loss of his men. So were we.

The mood of the company continued to deteriorate. The hooch where Contreros's team had lived was completely empty now. It became known as the "ghost hooch." Meszaros and I were given the assignment of clearing it out, packing up everyone's personal effects, and sending them home.

Then, almost overnight, two-thirds of the company rotated back home. Since most of the men came to the company together, they left together. Only a few said good-bye to me when they ETSed or DEROSed back to the World. I was still considered a cherry. It was a little frightening. One morning I got up to go to chow, and everyone was gone.

There followed a two-week period when we were not operational. We tried to joke around when the 2d Platoon met for a briefing, and the whole platoon sat on a footlocker. Our company was now down to twenty-three guys from a previous operational strength of over one hundred. I knew it was going to take a period of time to rebuild, and even more time for me to gain the experience and skills needed to survive. The responsibility of leadership was being dumped in my lap before I was mentally prepared. Why were my teachers leaving? I felt like I was going from the third grade straight into college. Still, with all my shortcomings, the lack of experience, and the lack of knowledge about my enemy, I had a job to do. I tried not to think about it, but it was always on my mind.

This shift in mood and responsibility set the stage for the rest of my tour. The next seven missions took on a very serious tone. It was never the same after the Contreros mission.

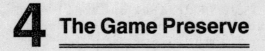

4 The Game Preserve

Christmas had come and gone. Meszaros, Biedron, and I spent an uneventful Christmas Eve on a night ambush outside of Camp Eagle. The gooks had gone home for the holidays. So we spent the night on 50 percent alert, fighting off the mosquitoes and leeches. The best present we received was Gary Linderer returning to the company after getting out of the hospital in Cam Ranh Bay. He was one of the men seriously wounded on Contreros's team the month before. It was great to see him back and in one piece. We threw a big party for him the night he arrived, toasting his physical profile—which meant Gary had limited duty for another six weeks.

While Linderer was gone, a new weapon had been added to the 101st Division's arsenal, and we were about to use it: a helicopter equipped with a thousand-watt loudspeaker, and a two-man psychological team. This team was on standby, ready and capable of being over any spot where an infantry company made contact with the enemy—within ten minutes. Their job was to drop leaflets and play a recorded message promising the enemy safe passage under the *Chieu Hoi* Surrender Program. The tapes were all prerecorded and pretested and approved by the psychological warfare people. The message was supposed to appeal to the enemy's emotions, good sense, and drive to survive. I think we changed all that.

One night Burford came up with a much better use for the equipment. We were at the 17th Cav outdoor movie theater, watching Clint Eastwood's new movie, *The Good, the Bad, and the Ugly.* Honest John went into warp drive. About halfway through the movie, he decided it would be cool to pull an ambush and invite the Psy Ops guys along with a little Eastwood music.

"We'll blow the ambush, fire our claymores, then light our cigars," Burford said with a smile.

I almost fell off the wooden bench seat, laughing. I thought he was just pulling my pud, but I should have known better. We had a score to settle.

As soon as the movie was over, Burford grabbed me, borrowed the movie reel, and walked over to the Psy Ops team tent. The guys came unglued! They loved the idea! We proceeded to coordinate an ambush and battle plan, which now included our two new friends, lieutenants Charley White and Walter Decker.

Those two second lieutenants, White and Decker, stayed up half the night taping the theme song from the Eastwood movie onto their equipment. We had planned it so that the main theme song ran repeatedly and would play over and over for an hour straight. The whistling part, *Oheee-Ohoeooooowah,* was the part of the song we wanted. It was *written* for an ambush!

Burford even got Captain Eklund to go along with our movie-score ambush. I thought we might make the *Guinness Book of Records* for the first combat ambush accompanied with music. Eklund wasn't as excited about it as we were, but he said okay.

White and Decker monitored our frequency for the next two days, on standby, like two kids on the bench, ready and waiting to be called into a baseball game.

Two days later, we were on the Huey insertion helicopter. I was startled out of a half sleep, as the door gunner broke his M-60 machine gun loose from its retainer lock and chambered a round. The chopper began to drop rapidly toward the ground. Like a well-choreographed dance, we fell in behind the lead ship, a hundred meters back. I could feel my heart pounding as the adrenaline rushed through my body.

The CO's command-and-control chopper banked and passed over us. The two Cobra gunships went into a high orbit overhead. They would be in position to make a gun run if we hit a hot LZ.

Every muscle in my body tensed. I gripped my weapon even tighter. We touched down, and I rolled out. I ran to the tree line and set up. We sat quietly waiting for the enemy to show up, but this insert went without incident.

This was to be a three-day mission, so we didn't carry much, just enough ammo and claymores to pull off the ambush, then get out. We were going to move back over to the trail where we had made contact the week before.

On the mission five days earlier, we had found a high-speed trail and had spent two days monitoring it. We had counted almost fifty dinks diddy boppin' down the trail, most of whom looked more like VC than NVA regulars. We were looking forward to bagging us a big catch.

The trail headed in the direction of two villages. We decided to ambush the VC on the morning of the second day. Burford called for the second team, which had been standing by. They inserted at last light and linked up with our team.

Snuffy Smith was their team leader. He carried ten extra claymore mines, and we spent the better part of the evening running a daisy chain that went forever. The gooks were in the habit of moving through in the morning around 0500 hours. But the next day no gooks. We spent all day waiting. Nothing.

Burford was as impatient as a big-game hunter who had been skunked, so he decided to take our team and go looking for gooks. Smith's team stayed back with the daisy chain.

The afternoon sun cast a dark green hue on the jungle floor as we paralleled the enemy's high-speed trail. I took up point, and we moved the team almost a mile into a valley we affectionately called the Game Preserve.

Burford and I broke off from our team to do a two-man re-con. He left the remaining men set up in a tight perimeter at the base of a mountain, in a thick clump of trees. We circled wide around an open field and back into the jungle about one hundred meters from the team.

Burford stopped to check a fresh grave. He had been here weeks earlier and had ambushed a ten-man party of NVA. This must have been one of their casualties.

I decided to check out the rest of the area. I had a strange, uneasy feeling that something was about to happen. Something in the thicker brush attracted my attention; I wasn't sure what it was.

I crept quietly around the right flank of the trail. I'd gone no more than five feet into the jungle, when the shadows of human images moved directly in front of me! I froze and blinked my eyes in disbelief.

A small man holding chopsticks sat in the graying dimness of the jungle. He was not more than five feet away. He appeared to be eating out of a small bag. Ten feet to his right were two more men, also sitting on the ground, eating and talking. The horror of it hit me. I realized what I was looking at. Enemy soldiers! For a brief moment, time froze.

Lucky for me, the enemy soldiers seemed to be doing what every GI did at that time of day—eating. The last thing they expected was an uninvited GI showing up for breakfast.

I stood perfectly still, not sure what to do. My instinct told me to run, my training told me to shoot, but my good sense told me to do neither, not yet. I held my fire, and without taking my eyes off the man closest to me, I slowly backed away.

As my eyes adjusted to the shadows. I could see more NVA sitting among the trees. They looked like ghosts. It was hard to see, even harder to think.

Two of them looked in my direction. I stopped in mid-step. A strange, cold sensation of dread and terror coursed through my veins. I felt paralyzed, unable to move.

I tried to control my thoughts, stay calm, not panic. I knew

I had to get out of there fast. If I had to deal with them inside their camp, where would I start? I would have to kill them all, and that was highly unlikely. I could see even more silhouettes further back in the woods.

If I got into it here and came running out of the woods, Burford might think I was a VC and blow me away.

The gooks continued eating and talking. Step-by-step, I moved backward without making a sound. The man closest to me was talking to the others in his squeaky, high-pitched Vietnamese. I was afraid he would hear my heart pounding.

I quietly raised my CAR-15 and pointed it in the direction of the enemy. I couldn't believe it. No one looked up at me! I felt invisible. I wasn't five feet from the enemy, and they didn't even see me! Tiger fatigues and camouflage paint kept me concealed.

As I moved out of the shadows and into sun, I squinted my eyes until they adjusted. I couldn't see Burford.

Just then he popped out from behind a thicket of trees. He had seen them, too. He took one look at my expression and knew we had a problem. Without a word, we started our withdrawal. The safest thing to do was *di di* south down the wood line and just lay low. If the gooks spotted us they could get in around behind us. We had no radio to warn the rest of our team. We had no time to think. We had no choice but to run for it, or we would be cut off from the team. Our only hope was to run across the open field and make it back to our team.

I went first. I ran ten meters, stopped, then turned back and aimed my rifle at the wood line and waited for Burford to pass me. We ran twenty more meters, set up, and repeated the same maneuver—cover and withdraw. We had to run in the open for almost one hundred meters. As I ran with my back to the enemy position, I expected at any moment to hear shots and feel the bullets tearing into my back. Then I wondered if I would even hear the shots. Nothing. I stopped, turned, and waited again for Burford. Still no shots.

Come on, you long-legged Georgia boy! I prayed. "Come on, John!"

As I got up to run the last twenty meters to the cover, I thought, *Sitting ducks!* We were like one of those duck shoots back in my hometown's summer fair.

We had left Looney, our senior radio man; Meszaros, our tail gun; and Saenz, our demolitions man, in a small perimeter about twenty meters wide, behind a cluster of bamboo trees halfway up the ridgeline.

Setting up in the gloom of early morning haze, it had seemed like a good place to leave them while Burford and I did a little soft-shoe recon. But now it seemed like a major mistake. From the cluster of trees where the team waited unsuspectingly, we had a good fifty-meter climb to the ridgeline above. The only problem was that there was no cover on either side of them to E & E through.

But that wasn't the only obstacle. Our first problem was getting to the trees and rejoining our team.

Burford arrived first and immediately told Looney to crank up the radio and get hold of the Old Man and some gunships, fast!

"We've seen the bad guys!" Burford whispered to Joe Don.

I came in behind Burford, sliding on my butt like I was coming into home plate. Then I looked over at Looney. He looked amazingly calm. I must've looked terrified. Looney got upset each time Burford came up with one of these James Bond-type recon ideas, but when things actually went down, he was unshakable.

Burford asked what I saw in there.

"I think it was Robin Gook and his band of merry men. His *whole* band of merry men. I counted at least ten, John. I was going to sit down and have breakfast with them, then I realized that I had left my plastic spoon in my ruck."

Looney twisted the station dial on his radio. He frowned.

"I can't get any commo. The batteries are dead. Checked them before we left, but they're dead now."

Burford took off his pack, tore it open, and hurriedly looked for a new battery, which happened to be at the very bottom of the pack.

Finally, he handed the battery to Looney and started repacking his ruck.

I crab walked back to see if the gooks were coming out of the wood line yet. Looney attached the new battery and calmly reported in our situation. He told the relay team we had been compromised and that it would be just a matter of minutes before we'd be in contact. "We need gunships ASAP."

The TOC monitored his transmission, but Looney couldn't pick up their transmission and had to wait for the relay team to pass it back. They announced that TOC thought Looney's voice was too controlled for us to be in contact. Looney started yelling into the horn, "What do I have to do to get gunships, start cussing? We got beaucoup gooks less than fifty meters from us, and we have no place to run, assholes!"

The radio was silent for a moment. Then the relay team came back on and told us to "standby" while they went to get the Old Man.

Burford told Looney, Meszaros, and Saenz to get their rucks on and get ready to move.

Meanwhile I had buried myself deep in the vines on the other side of the brush, facing the tree line. I was wondering why the gooks hadn't come out yet.

Minutes passed, and still no movement in the tree line. I sat there watching, with my back to the brush. The rest of the team was on the other side of the cover in a patch of elephant grass.

I stared at that spot where we had left the tree line. It seemed like it had never happened. I could hear Burford and Looney talking as I pushed back inside the cover. It was difficult. The tightly woven vines were almost too thick to pass through without shaking the overhead cover.

Just then Burford stuck his head through a hole in the brush right next to me.

I turned and whispered, "I haven't seen shit yet, John. What do you think?"

"They're laying dog, man; they don't know who or what we are. For all they know we could be a point element of a company. They're just watching. Stay cool, I'll be back."

I moved back through the thick vines and tried to get comfortable. Then the insects got into the act. No matter what was happening, if you stood still long enough in the jungle, the mosquitoes showed up. I tried to keep them out of my ears so I could hear. By cupping my hands behind each ear and aiming them towards the enemy position, the sounds coming from the jungle below were amplified.

Little bastards I know you're in there!

Suddenly, an enemy soldier walked out into the open elephant grass. He came out, looked at the ground where I had been, then stepped back into the woods. I was almost happy to see him. But then that familiar knot began to grow in the pit of my stomach again. I raised my weapon and aimed it in his direction, waiting to see what he was going to do. Then two more NVA came out. I guess they thought we were woodcutters or maybe trail watchers that got spooked and ran. They didn't seem to be too alarmed. In a few minutes, several more enemy soldiers left the cover of the jungle and joined them.

I tried to get Burford's attention without moving my head, but he was busy on the radio, telling Snuffy's team what was going on. My heart was pounding like crazy.

They were not more than fifty meters away, six enemy talking and pointing straight at us. The leader of the group had a PPK-43 hanging at his side. He's waving his hand like he wants his men to flank us.

"Burford!" I was trying to shout in a whisper—it didn't work. I figured they couldn't see me, but they probably had a good idea where we were by the way the leader was pointing. They could surely see the trail we had left as we ran through the elephant grass. One of the enemy troops, who seemed to be giving the orders, pulled out a pair of binoculars and looked right at me.

"Burford! *Bur-ford!*"

The enemy team leader motioned to his men to fan out. I knew that within minutes we were dead meat if I didn't do something. We would be surrounded and have no place to run. Four of the soldiers pulled out what appeared to be pieces of an American camouflage cargo parachute, shook off the dust, then placed the material over their heads, and in an instant they became invisible. I lost them.

I pushed back through the brush as fast as I could. As I did, a stick snapped off and stuck in my neck. Pain darted down my back, but there was no time to worry about it now. I disappeared inside the vegetation while spotting two of the enemy soldiers moving to my right. They were trying to flank us.

I finally got Burford's attention.

"We got beaucoup gooks out there. At least four cowboys are flanking us!"

Burford didn't seem bothered. He turned away from me and gave Looney some last-minute instructions.

"J.D., you take the team to the top of the hill as soon as the shooting starts." He turned back to me, "It looks like it's you and me, dude. We're gonna give cover fire for the team and kill us some gooks! Ya ready?"

I didn't have time to think about what was going to happen next. We both moved quickly back to my OP in the dense vines. Burford could now see the enemy soldiers standing less than thirty meters away.

"Whoa!" Burford nudged me and pointed out across the open field with his weapon.

"Chambers," he whispered calmly. "When you find gooks, son, you find a mess of 'em! Take the bastards on the right. I got the bad guys on the left. On three."

I nodded without taking my eyes off the NVA moving in around us.

"One!"

I moved up on one knee.

"Two!"

I started to stand up.

"Three!"

We both jumped up and opened fire. I looked straight down the barrel at four enemy soldiers who were still in a cluster. I held the automatic weapon low and to the right of my targets.

I held my trigger down and watched as the rounds erupted from my rifle. Because I had loaded every third round a tracer I could see where they were hitting. Dust popped off the enemy soldiers as the rounds stitched them. The first two NVA fell in the initial burst. Then the other two dropped to the ground.

Burford yelled for me to fire at the tree line, which now had opened up on us with small arms fire. White flashes in the green jungle told us that there were more of them. One round just missed Burford's head and burned his cheek as it passed between the two of us.

"Mothers!" he yelled.

I had no time to look. I dropped to my knees and popped out the empty magazine, then flipped the second one in. I emptied the second magazine into the trees across from our position. I could see more flashes coming from the tree line to our right. I caught glimpses of enemy soldiers moving in the jungle.

"Gooks at two o'clock!" Burford yelled.

"Let's go, *now!* Go! Go! Go!"

"To your ten o'clock!" I yelled.

We put a couple more bursts into the woods, then I turned to the right.

Burford was still firing, with his rifle across his chest. I looked up, and saw our guys shooting down at the jungle.

All right! I thought, *We're gonna make it!*

Looney and Saenz were waving us on. We took off in a

dead sprint. After running just ten meters up the hill, my legs started to tighten, and my thighs started to burn.

"Keep going!" Burford yelled. He was almost on top of me. We couldn't stop now no matter what happened. We were committed, in the open, and had to get up to the top of the ridge. I could hear Looney and Saenz firing and yelling at us. They were just above us.

Crack! Crack! Crack!

I could see dust flying twenty feet ahead, where rounds aimed at us were hitting the hillside. I zigged to the right. The gooks were shooting, but they probably hadn't been trained to shoot dumb shits running up a hill. Their training was probably more along the lines of sniping at people behind groups of villagers. They weren't used to shooting at running targets while under fire themselves.

I tried another zigzag maneuver, but my legs had nothing left in them. I gasped for breath. Each step was a fight. The ridgetop was less than ten feet away, when I slipped and fell forward.

Ping! Ping!

Rounds impacted into the hill just ahead of me. I flattened out. The red-hot barrel of my rifle scorched my hand.

"Shit!"

I could see Burford struggling up the open hillside ahead of me. He was trying to stay low.

With one last burst of adrenaline, I climbed to the crest of the hill, then rolled over the top. Without breathing, I slid out of my ruck, opened it and grabbed a fresh bandolier of M-16 magazines.

Looney finally got the radio working. "Chambers, you're trying to get me killed! You leg!" he screamed over the sounds of gunfire.

We all started to yell in the excitement of our momentary victory. The terror disappeared as fast as it had come. Now we felt invincible, as if we had taken on the neighborhood bully and kicked his butt.

By the amount of gunfire, Burford determined that there were about thirty gooks still shooting at us from the tree line.

"Ho Chi Minh sucks and so does the horse he rode in on!" I shouted in between bursts of gunfire.

Looney looked at me. "Horse he rode in on?" he said.

"Okay, water buffalo he rode in on!" I shouted back.

Looney saw the blood running down my back. "You hit?"

"No man, it's self-inflicted. I'm trying to get a Purple Heart!"

Looney reached Captain Eklund. The Kingsmen choppers would be here in five minutes.

We set up a front line. I had the left flank. Saenz and Meszaros were on my right. J.D. and Burford were in the middle. Looney passed word that choppers were coming in.

This was not over yet. We still had Snuffy Smith's team to the north. They were probably wondering if we had gotten the shit blown out of us. Burford got Smith on the horn. He told him to blow the daisy chain and get extracted.

"Don't leave shit for the gooks. Blow the ambush in place. You copy?"

"Roger that!" Snuffy acknowledged.

Moments later someone yelled, "I hear choppers!"

"Hey Looney, take my picture!" I shouted. "I wanna really piss off the REMFs back at the company area. I want a profile shot of me taken during a firefight."

I pulled the small Penn-EE camera from my ruck and tossed it over to him.

"Looney, don't forget to forward the film; I only have three pictures left!" I struck a pose. Looney took two shots, then tossed it back. I took the last picture of him and put the camera back in my ruck.

Just then the first of the Kingsmen helicopters came into view. That unmistakable whacking sound filled the air, but there was also an unfamiliar sound. I couldn't quite make it out.

Burford popped yellow smoke. One of our Cobra gunships made a run over our heads, and we all hit the deck.

Zooomwap! Something ripped overhead.

"Rockets! Stay down!"

As the Cobras unloaded their ordnance, we low-crawled back towards the ridgeline.

The 40 mm cannons tore into the jungle. The miniguns sounded like canvas tearing. I looked back and noticed a Huey setting down about two hundred meters behind us on the level ridgeline to our rear. Through the smoke I could make out one lone figure unassing the ship and running towards us. It was Captain Meacham. We all stood up as a unit, fired one more magazine into the wood line, then started to run back to meet the ship.

Meacham was one of our favorite pilots. He was demonstrating the unwritten code we shared with our pilots. Don't leave anyone behind!

He came running down to help, CAR-15 in hand. He could do some heavy profiling back at the club after killing a few gooks at point-blank range. He wanted a personal closeup, LRP-style body count before he left for R & R. These crazy Kingsmen pilots were not only fearless in the air, but they're not afraid to hit the ground and fight alongside us grunts, either. Of course, Meacham had been a paratrooper himself before becoming a pilot.

"How many gooks did you pile up?" Meacham asked.

"We had so many of them, sir, we had to run up this little hill to let them have a turn at us," Burford drawled. "It only seemed fair to give 'em a shot at us. Hell they can't hit nothin'!"

We all ran back for the chopper. There was that sound again from the other side of the hill but this time closer—the Cobras, I thought.

The pilot was sitting impatiently at the controls of the slick. I could see the painted nose of the Kingsmen helicopter. It was a large, black ace of spades, and with the skids bowed out, the helicopter looked like a giant praying mantis. The blades were whipping at full pitch, ready to lift off as soon as the last LRP boarded the ship.

I headed for the right side of the ship. The bellyman grabbed my hand and gave me a lift in. I sat on the floor with my legs hanging out. Burford hopped in next to me. Then we heard that strange noise again. This time it was closer. From behind the hill, a chopper popped up. It was the Psy-Ops helicopter, playing the theme from *The Good, the Bad, and the Ugly* over their big thousand-watt speakers. It was our little greeting song. A present to Uncle Ho's men from the LRPs.

Oeeoeoooo da da da ooeoeeooo. The foreboding whistle could be heard for miles, and the shouts from our chopper could probably be heard as far.

We had heard that the Psy-Ops pilots hadn't been able to sleep, waiting for the chance to play that song along with their regular propaganda message: *Surrender or Die!* Our plans hadn't gone off as we had expected, but at least we got to enjoy the music.

Our chopper rocked to the right, lifted, then broke to the left. Just then a second gunship made a pass, unloading his rockets.

Zoombamm!

Our slick was starting to gain some speed, and I watched as the lead Cobra made one more gun run on the wood line. Burford pointed to a valley below. I watched a hundred-meter-long funnel of white smoke along the ground.

"Snuffy's daisy chain!" Burford yelled over the chopper noise. "Not a bad job, huh?"

We could see the explosion. Then we heard the muffled pitch of Vietnamese. It was the Psy-Ops bird off in the distance, playing their propaganda tape.

Burford tried to light his cigar in the chopper but to no avail—just too much wind.

I pulled out my cigar and chewed on it. The Psy-Ops helicopter flanked us as we flew back toward Firebase Bastogne.

We came in low, and the whole firebase ran out and looked up. They had heard an LRP team had been ambushed and would be stopping in to debrief. Fresh information about the enemy activity in their AO was always welcome.

As the noisy chopper flared back and landed, we hopped out. The grunts stared at us like we were from outer space. In the background, our new-found friends, the Psy-Ops helicopter pilots, were still having fun playing the Eastwood theme.

Captain Meacham made his flight home to meet his wife. He never told her what happened. The whole time he was in Nam she thought he was just hauling pigs and rice for the government.

5 Earthworms from Hell

Sgt. John Burford was having a cup of the Cav's black coffee and eating a piece of pound cake. He had just walked outside the company TOC and was leaning up against a retaining wall talking to me. It had been hot all day. A twenty-year-old, Shake 'n Bake sergeant by the name of Larry Closson had just arrived with a new batch of cherries. He walked up to Burford and me, trying hard to be friendly.

"Hey, Sarge, how's the coffee?"

Burford looked the new Stateside sergeant up and down and spit some coffee at the ground.

"Well, young sergeant, if you don't mind drinking freshly drained motor oil out of a Cav jeep, you won't mind this shit."

"Not too good huh, Sarge," Closson answered, still trying to be neighborly.

"Nope. It ain't bad, son. It's just different."

A film of perspiration covered Closson's forehead. His skin was fair, and his hair was powder white, cut almost too short even for an Airborne unit. He had a hundred questions, but Burford and I weren't up to answering them. We were preoccupied by our upcoming mission. We had received our preop orders the day before, and we knew that this was not going to be a typical reconnaissance mission. But then, with Burford, nothing we did was typical.

The 101st Airborne Division had changed its tactics. The old reliance on extensive artillery preparation, followed by air strikes, was out. Under the new concept, a minimum of artillery and air power was to be used, and there was to be a new emphasis on surprise. The idea was simple: keep the gooks from feeling safe in their own backyard and take away their freedom to travel from point A to point B.

The local VC intelligence network knew everything that was going on with most American units. Information was easy for them to get. A flight manifest on a clipboard hanging on a wall. Soldiers talking in barber shops, where the local Vietnamese cut our hair. Gooks were everywhere in Camp Eagle. Everywhere except the LRP compound.

I left Burford talking to Closson, and went down to the acid pad to practice immediate-action drills. Burford followed a little later.

Burford thought we should set the ambush positions by order of march, rather than the buddy system.

"We'll drop off the last two men, Boom Boom and Munoz, at our flank," he said. "Then drop off two one-man positions, until we get to Miller. He and McCann will set up the other flank. It's not a big change. Let's practice until we have it perfect."

We ran through the drill a few more times, then took a break to perform our company duties. We were going in late the next afternoon. I thought about my list of things to do. There was to be a briefing tonight. I had to draw special equipment, go over the overflight, help plot our primary and secondary LZs, our route, and an escape-and-evasion route. Then I had to get some sleep.

That night in our hooch, Burford handed me a few extra LRP patches and a handful of tenpenny nails.

"What are these for?"

"Calling cards, son. LRP calling cards. Division wants the gooks to know they ain't safe, so we're gonna send them a personal message from the LRPs—real personal."

As a general rule, Special Forces recon teams liked to insert at last light, while Ranger recon teams preferred first-light insertions. This time, we were scheduled to go in at 1400 hours—two in the afternoon.

Insertion in the middle of the afternoon was always hairy. If you were spotted by a trail watcher, he could alert the local VC or NVA regulars who worked in the area. Then they would come get you at night. The gooks knew it was almost impossible to get a chopper extraction in the middle of the night. It was a very risky procedure.

We were scheduled to take our overflight the morning of our mission, and I wanted to cool off in the shower first.

As I walked down to the shower, I watched one of the new Huey H models getting ready to lift off, full of LRPs. The CO, Captain Eklund, was taking them to Coco Beach for a much deserved stand-down—and though he was not a pilot, he was at the controls.

I walked inside the small field shower, turned on the water, lathered up, and looking at my signal mirror, I started to shave.

Suddenly, I heard a loud crashing sound, followed by an even louder *snap!*

I could hear something flying in my direction, and I hit the floor just as two feet of the main rotor blade came slamming into the bath house. I didn't move, I just stayed on the floor.

I could hear yelling from the helicopter pad below. As I peeked out of my hiding place and looked down the hill, I could see the chopper lying upside down, and fuel and soldiers running everywhere. The pilots were hanging upside down, strapped by their seat belts in the helicopter. JP-4 jet fuel was gushing out from under the fuselage. I watched in disbelief as one of the pilots began to calmly flip off switches.

"Get the pilots out!" Sergeant Johnson shouted.

It was a miracle, but everyone got out okay. I was almost a casualty and hadn't even left the shower.

Despite all this, we still went on our overflight.

On the overflight, we spotted something we'd missed on

our mission the week before. It was a new trail, one klick to the north of our AO.

We inserted that afternoon with a twelve-man heavy team.

After twenty minutes in the air, our chopper banked into a steep descent. Then, as it flared about five feet off the ground, we all jumped out and sprinted for the wood line. Looney and Burford were behind me, as we crashed into the trees and dropped among the cover.

Miller, Saenz and Evans dashed to the other side of the LZ. The chase ship flashed by overhead, as the two Cobra gunships circled in a high orbit.

No one moved, no one spoke. We listened for any telltale sounds that the enemy was around: the rustle of a branch, the snap of a twig, the snap of an AK-47 safety switching to fire, anything that would tell us we weren't alone. After twenty minutes of total silence, we felt our insertion was secure. I reached into my shirt, fished out my floppy hat, and pulled it down on my head.

Looney called Miller on the radio, and they quickly joined us. Burford nodded to Looney to release the gunships. We were on our own.

I looked up to see the choppers heading back to Eagle. The sound of the rotor blades faded in the distance. The sky was a hazy dark blue, and the temperature felt as if it would soon hit a hundred degrees. Looney dialed to the artillery frequency. He asked for a commo check, then flashed Burford a thumbs-up. We were ready to move out.

Burford's radio was set to the main TOC frequency, and Looney's was on the artillery frequency. Our support was only a radio call away.

Burford was one of the few team leaders who liked to carry his own radio. He felt it gave him complete control over the situation. His handset hung high on his left shoulder, next to a smoke grenade and a can of serum albumin. He always wore one oversized leather glove on his left hand to protect him from the thorns and razor-sharp blades of grass that could slice exposed flesh to ribbons.

I went down on one knee as I double-checked our compass heading with the map. Then we started to move out. I took my position at point, and Burford stepped in behind me, then Looney, followed by Miller, Saenz, and Evans.

Our eyes scanned the area as we moved in single file through the jungle. Our camouflage uniforms let us blend into the surrounding vegetation.

We had no sooner begun, when we found something that caused me to stop and turn back to Burford.

I whispered. "Pssst! Honest John, I just found the biggest trail you've ever seen."

It was almost six feet wide and hard packed. When we had inserted, we had failed to spot it, and neither Burford nor I noticed it on the overflight. We stepped away from the trail and moved quickly back into the jungle, trying to leave no sign of our presence.

We moved up to the base of the ridgeline and stopped for the night. Burford moved up next to me. He radioed Captain Eklund for permission to extend the mission, to stay longer, but the Old Man refused, saying that we didn't have enough rations, water, or radio batteries to stay out for three days. He advised us to move back to the other trail, pull the ambush as planned, and get out. But John was curious about this trail and wanted to take full advantage of it.

We had just pulled in our perimeter and started our night watch. I was next to John Meszaros, when I noticed Burford headed our way.

"How would you two like to do a little night gook hunting?" Burford smiled a broad, country smile.

Meszaros and I sat there, waiting for him to say that he was only kidding.

"Whatcha got up your sleeve, Honest John?" Meszaros asked, hoping he wouldn't answer.

"Well, son . . ."

John reached up, grasped his watch which was fastened to his fatigue pocket, looked at the illuminated dial, then looked back at Meszaros.

"The gooks probably have a trail watcher not too far down the path. I'm thinking about lurping on down there."

He pointed down the pitch-black trail. It was almost 0100 hours.

"Let's see if we can catch us a dink a-snoozin'. You been wanting to use that new K-bar . . . well, this is it."

We reluctantly agreed, hoping Burford was just testing us.

We prepared to take off. Burford would carry his M-16, and Meszaros would carry the silenced Swedish K submachine gun we'd brought along. I was to carry my CAR-15, slung, and my K-bar in hand. I was to find the enemy trail watcher and cut his throat.

As we prepared to move out, Meszaros turned and grabbed me by the shirt. "Why did you say we'll go?"

I was still trying to act like I wasn't afraid.

"No sweat, May-Zeus. I've seen this in the movies a hundred times."

"Right! The movies . . . you ain't never grabbed someone in the middle of the night. What if you miss, cut your own hands off instead, just piss him off, and he shoots me?"

We had been trained to take a man down with one hand and run our knife into a kidney with the other hand. But this was for real, and this was at night. I thought over how I would do it. It was like being sent downfield to catch a pass, in the dark. But what if I missed altogether? It seemed like a good idea an hour ago. But now it seemed pretty dumb.

Burford came back over with his gear. I stood up and grabbed my gear. I shook my head as if to say, "What the hell have I gotten myself into?" Then we started down beside the trail. We moved slowly at first, then as our eyes adjusted, we picked up speed.

It was 0200 hours, and the moon cast a faint light that made it possible for us to see the trail. Shadows magnified the outlines of vines and palms and made them look bigger and more like people in the dark.

I led the way, Burford behind me, and Meszaros following as rear security. In a way, this felt a lot safer than following a trail in broad daylight. I was in control, even if I couldn't see five feet ahead of me. The gooks would never think three GIs were traveling at night, intent on a knife kill.

We followed the trail for almost two hours. Burford tapped me on the back.

"Let's go back before we get too far from the team," he whispered. "We can get a knife kill some other time."

I quickly agreed. Meszaros led the way back.

The next evening, Miller took Meszaros, Schwartz, and a radio farther down the trail, near a clump of woods on our right flank. Burford was talking to him on the radio when Miller whispered that he had movement—a lot of it, three meters away. Then he fell silent.

"How many?" Burford whispered into his handset.

There was no reply from Miller.

"Can you talk?" Burford asked. "If you can't, break squelch once."

Miller broke squelch.

Looney got on the horn to Eklund, but couldn't supply any details. When the enemy was past their position, Miller was back on the horn with a report. There were thirty-six of them, all but eight of them visibly armed.

Burford figured that the VC were escorting a group of NVA bringing rice and supplies back to their base camp.

He called for gunships.

The NVA heard the choppers coming before they were in sight. They scrambled for cover along a nearby stream. Burford radioed the gunships to make a gun run down along the stream bed. The spent shells were falling on Miller, Meszaros, and Schwartz.

They dove for cover, thinking they were taking fire from the Cobras' miniguns. Burford called off the gunships.

It started to grow dark. We lay dog the rest of the evening, trying to get some rest. At midnight we moved back down to the trail.

We dropped our rucksacks in the trees and moved out of the jungle about two hundred meters to a cluster of brush overlooking the trail. In the dark of the night, we set up the ambush we had rehearsed two days before.

We set up in three-man positions. Miller, Munoz, and Meszaros anchored the south flank, and Evans, Snuffy, and Saenz held down the northern flank. Then the rest of us spread out in between. Burford, Looney, and I set up along a hillside.

We placed most of the claymores facing the trail, but set one on each flank, aiming down the trail in each direction. When we had set out the claymores next to the trail, we had inadvertently left a trail in the low grass going out and coming back in. I looked down and saw our tracks. I tried to obliterate the tracks, but without much success. The more I did, the more obvious it was. I crawled over and reported it to Burford. He said it wouldn't matter because it would probably be dark when we hit the gooks; they wouldn't live to see the tracks. I sure hoped he was right. It was dark, and I could see them.

We got in position, and remained there the rest of the night. We stayed on 100 percent alert. Our plan was to wait for the gooks to walk by around 0500 hours, then ambush them. Because it would still be dark, they probably wouldn't see us or our path. At least, that's what we hoped.

I had found some brush to hide behind and felt that it would give me good concealment for the morning ambush. But as the darkness gave way to false dawn, my cluster of brush transformed into a very small patch of vegetation that didn't really hide anything except my ass.

An early-morning mist rose from the jungle floor. I could smell the moisture in the air. I couldn't move to better cover, so I tried to stay low to the ground. Still no gooks.

Unnoticed, black-clad figures were walking toward our

team's position. They were VC, and their job was to protect a group of rice porters. The NVA would soon meet them in the wood line, then lead them back to their base-camp area somewhere in the Game Preserve, and the rice might even go as far as the A Shau Valley. What we didn't know was that today they had changed their schedule and were moving later than usual. These black-clad figures were making their way down the trail toward our position.

We sensed something had gone wrong. It was getting later in the morning, and the enemy hadn't shown.

Captain Eklund had decided to send out two Cobra gunships at first light without telling Burford. He felt that it would be better to have them close if we needed them. But the gooks heard the gunships off in the distance and started running down the trail toward us.

Burford sat up, took one last look up and down the trail, then told Looney that the gooks obviously weren't coming today. But as he spoke—almost as if on cue—the first enemy soldier ran into our kill zone.

I caught a flash of movement in my peripheral vision.

As the VC ran by, he spotted me sitting in the open on the side of the hill. He must have realized he was in a kill zone because he ran another fifteen feet and jumped into the large bomb crater in front of Burford's position and started screaming in Vietnamese.

Burford reached over and squeezed his firing device, blowing his first claymore.

Whammboom!

I felt the blast as it tore a path down the trail and mowed down the vegetation below. I looked up, and watched three enemy soldiers come to a complete stop directly in front of me. Burford's blast sent debris raining down just in front of them.

Trying not to take my eyes off the surprised enemy soldiers, I fumbled with my clacker. The electrical firing device had a wire clip that was wedged under the handle to prevent misfiring. With both hands shaking, I flipped back the clip and squeezed on the handle. A jolt of electric current traveled through the wire and set off a blasting cap in the mine. The detonation touched off the C-4 plastic explosive, which sent a hail of seven hundred steel ball-bearings roaring out, killing everything in their way.

The three VC simply disappeared, almost as if they had been vaporized in the blast of my claymore. The sounds of wailing and crying came from inside the crater. The poor gook hoping to hide there was in unspeakable pain.

I grabbed my second firing device and squeezed it.

Wammmboom! I felt it before I heard it.

I was blown back from the blast of my own claymore. I had no cover to protect me from its backblast. The explosion drove debris into my face. I wiped at my eyes and groped blindly for the CAR-15 laying at my feet.

Crack! Crack!

Small-arms fire erupted from the right flank. I returned fire, getting off a short burst, before my bolt locked open—a double feed. Shit! I tore at the duct tape that held my cleaning rod to the barrel.

I took the rod, jammed it down the barrel, kicking out the double feed. I dropped the old magazine and jammed home a fresh one.

I saw the bright flash of another claymore detonation. *Whammmboom!*

To my right, I could see two VC running back up the trail.

Crack! Crack! Crack!

A line of green tracers zipped past, just missing me on the left.

I now had VC on both sides of me. I knew I had to get off that hillside fast because there was no cover around me, just small vines and bushes. I dropped flat as the tracers blew over my head. I could hear Burford returning fire toward the wood line. The NVA had come down to meet the supply party, and had arrived just in time to see us blow the ambush. We had set up our ambush right where they were to meet the supply party. Now we had North Vietnamese on the left flank and Vietcong on the right. There I was, silhouetted on the hillside like a practice target.

Ping! A round hit next to my left foot. I rolled over on my right side and tried to low crawl toward some cover. Dirt, dust, and black smoke filled my lungs as I crawled down to the trail. I could see the body of a dead VC about fifteen feet to my left. I turned back to look for Burford. He was up and firing at the gooks in the crater, then ran down past the dead VC on the trail.

Suddenly, I heard more shots from up the trail behind Miller—on the left flank.

We were surrounded!

Miller, Meszaros, and Saenz were in a firefight with six NVA who had not been caught in the ambush. Boom Boom Evans was trying to pick off the gook porters that had just dropped all their gear and were starting to run back home. One of the VC had stopped and was firing back at us. He was down on the lower end of the trail.

Burford yelled at Looney, "Get Six and tell him we're in heavy contact."

Burford called to the VC in the bomb crater to surrender.

"*Chieu Hoi!* Give up or die, motherfucker!"

No answer. Then a head rose out of the crater. A pale face streaked with mud. His eyes were wild as he looked straight at John then over at me. Burford aimed his rifle. But the gook ducked back in the crater.

As I pulled my rifle up to shoot, I noticed something out of the corner of my eye. It was the "dead" VC who had been lying in the trail. He was reaching for his rocket launcher and was directly behind Burford. I had low crawled to less than six feet from him. He turned and saw me.

Without thinking I clicked my selector switch from auto to semi—I fired one round into his head.

The round tore through his left cheek. His head slammed

backward into the mud. A large gaping hole opened up in the back of his head where the tracer exited.

Burford jumped straight into the air, turned and looked back at me. When he saw what had happened, he grinned.

We could hear the slapping sound of running feet on the wet ground. Burford spun around to follow the sound. I saw more movement to the side. The VC had climbed out of the bomb crater and was running down the trail.

The enemy soldier was hauling ass. Burford put his rifle on semiauto, and took a country-boy aim. He fired five times right at him. The gook never stopped.

He ran right past Miller. The VC was close enough to kiss as he passed him. But Miller was busy firing at three more NVA up the trail. He never even noticed as the gook flew by.

The enemy soldier disappeared where the trail made a bend to the right. Miller followed him through a thicket of bamboo and found him slumped up against a tree. He had two holes in his chest and one in his neck. Burford had hit him all right, but like a wounded animal on the run, he hadn't stopped.

Burford sat down, looked both ways, then duck walked back to the dead soldier. He poked him with his rifle, then reached down and searched him. He quickly found something. His damp pockets were stuffed with maps and papers. I heard Burford yell for me to check the crater.

I got up and slowly moved forward. I expected to catch a bullet with each step I took. I was still scared as hell.

Two more steps and I was there. I peered over the edge and spotted a row of twisted bodies lying in a bloody heap in the mud below. An old woman, a young man, and the two uniformed soldiers.

The young man's face was white and drained of color. The woman was a twisted, lifeless mass of bony flesh; she had a stunned expression on her face. Her bloody, black silk clothing made her look even more grotesque. None of us had seen her before, but we probably wouldn't have hesitated to shoot her if we had. She was with this crew, and she wasn't an innocent civilian—at least not by our lights.

I turned and low crawled back to the dying soldier who had almost wasted Burford. I knelt down on one knee, and reached into his pockets to search for documents. His right arm shot out and grabbed me out of reflex. It freaked me out.

I pulled back in surprise.

I took out my K-bar knife and pinned down his arm.

Burford looked back in disbelief. "What the hell are you doing?"

"He was trying to grab me," I whispered.

"Well, let him die in peace. Go search the bodies in the crater."

I didn't want to go back to that crater, but I forced myself to do it.

I checked each dead soldier, but found nothing. I was satisfied that a further search would be fruitless, so I went back to our perimeter to wait for the Aero Rifle reaction force that was on its way in.

I didn't want to have to search the mangled woman. Now that I thought about it, maybe she was an innocent victim—just some old woman selling rice to the wrong side.

Farther up the trail were the bodies of two more VC lying on their sides. One looked like a rice carrier, and the other was part of the VC cadre escorting them to the NVA base camp.

"Looney, call in the reaction force!" Burford shouted.

Looney was already on the horn to Captain Eklund. The reaction force soon landed on the hill above us, but as the first trooper hopped out he was shot in the chest by a burst of AK-47 fire. He died where he fell.

Burford tossed LRP scroll on each of the dead gooks as the Cav showed up. "Look here, Sarge!" one of the Cav line doggies yelled. He was searching the dead woman in the crater. He reached into the bloody mess and pulled out a plastic bag. He opened it and held up a whole roll of American MPC (military payment certificate). Boy, was I embarrassed! Innocent civilian victim, my ass!

The Aero Rifle soldier took the woman's body and pulled it from the mud and raised her to a sitting position.

Burford turned blood red. He looked over at me. I hunched my shoulders and shook my head from side to side. My job had been to search the bodies in the crater. But I just couldn't bring myself to put my hands in that bloody mess.

"Hey, someone take my picture," the line doggie yelled. "Look at these black teeth. She chews betel nut, Sarge."

Meszaros, Miller, and I exchanged glances. What a jerk!

The Cav swept the wood line as we moved down into the bomb crater and set up a perimeter. Burford suggested a team picture.

The situation seemed fairly secure, so we got up and stood in a line. Burford and I picked up a twelve-foot pole with a tightly wrapped pig secured to it. Schwartz stood on my right, then Miller, Saenz, and Smitty. Munoz grabbed the enemy RPG and walked over and stood in front of us. Boom Boom Evans took the picture.

"The extraction birds are one minute out, pop smoke!" someone yelled.

In less than a minute a yellow haze of smoke boiled out across the hillside. Looney turned to me and told me the story about what happened to him the previous night. I was watching the chopper come in over the crater. As he related the story, he sounded like he was hallucinating.

He told me about his encounter with a two-foot-long earthworm that crawled up under him.

"What?"

The sound of the rotor blast and turbine noise drowned him out.

"What worms? What are you talking about?" I said.

We boarded the chopper, and Looney tried to finish his story. The ship lifted away from the trail then turned east.

Looney continued, shouting over the noise. "I sat in a hole

last night; I thought I could hide in it during the ambush. You know, good cover."

I nodded, trying to humor him.

"I was sitting up behind Burford, when I felt the ground moving under me. I jumped out of that hole. I was standing there just about to fire on whatever it was when Burford grabbed me, and we both watched as a giant worm came out of its hole."

Looney was really upset about this worm, even more than the ambush. He continued. "This worm was as wide as my wrist." He held his wrist to show me.

"It sort of came at me, looked around as if to intimidate me, then turned and went back down into the hole."

Burford told me later back at Camp Eagle that Looney had kept surveillance on that worm all night—so when the gooks showed up that morning he never saw them. He was more concerned about the "killer earthworms" than he was about the enemy.

It was a twenty-minute story, which ended just as the helicopter touched down back at Eagle. We were all afraid Looney would say something about the killer earthworms at the G-2 debriefing, but he never spoke about them again.

6 The Black Box Mission

We all gathered in the early morning hours, waiting for our choppers to arrive.

Our cargo was fifteen black-box sensor devices we were to plant along a series of high-speed jungle trails. We were joking about how this would give the REMFs back in the artillery fire direction center something new to do.

Our team was to infiltrate the A Shau Valley, find trails leading to enemy base camps and staging areas in the vicinity, then bury a line of the sensor devices along the trails. The black boxes were designed to pick up vibrations of enemy soldiers as they passed by. With several boxes placed in sequence, the operator in the rear could supposedly tell the direction the enemy was traveling. The signals would then be electronically transmitted to an American artillery base, where the information would be collected, processed, and acted upon. Then, artillery or air strikes could, within minutes, saturate the area where the sensors picked up the vibrations. This was the intent, but most of us doubted things would work out that way.

These sensors would not only pick up human vibrations but signs of animal passage as well. There was no way to distinguish between elephants, monkeys, and the NVA.

Saenz and three cherries walked up and sat down beside me. Larry looked wiped out as he propped his elbow against a sandbag. He had been with the 501st Signal Company before LRPs, so he was used to starting off tired and packing tons of shit. He looked like he needed a little cheering up, so I called Meszaros over to spin out his scenario.

"Saenz, man, I can see it now. Some Saigon-commando captain monitoring his new electronic black-box sensor device. He measures the ground vibrations to see how many gooks are on the trail. When suddenly, a lost herd of elephants moves through the valley, over their ancient migration route back to the safety of Laos and Cambodia. He picks up their movement on his screen, and cries 'We got gooks!' He gets on the horn to his waiting battery of 155 mm howitzers and peppers the valley below with white phosphorus and HE. The frightened elephants turn and try to run for cover; he looks at his screen, and there is an even bigger reading."

Saenz was perking up, so May-Zeus went on.

" 'Tanks!' cries our REMF. 'They must have an entire division of tanks out there. I've never seen a reading like this before!' He yells to a major puffing on a cigar in the next room. Officers crowd around his monitor. The major gets on the radio. 'Get the air force on the line and set up an air strike,' he says. Colonels and generals nod all around."

Saenz, who was now grooving on the story, nodded. "B-52s."

Meszaros nodded, "B-52s."

The cherries were looking at Meszaros like they really believed this was happening.

"After three days of bombing in the fog-shrouded valley, what's left of a large herd of elephants runs off in terror," May-Zeus continued.

"Our REMF officer's monitor is quiet. He alone has won a great victory against impossible odds. His chest fills with pride; his first combat mission is a complete success. There is no need for a bomb-damage-assessment mission. As the senior officer in charge, our REMF puts himself in for a Distinguished Service Cross, and a Bronze Star for not leaving the TOC for twenty-four hours. Even the second lieutenant who made the coffee gets a Silver Star."

Saenz roared with laughter. "God, what a fight!"

We all laughed.

"Come on you two," Miller yelled, "Quit telling the cherries war stories; it's going to freak them out."

We loaded the lightweight black boxes and ourselves on the lead ship, then tried to find a place to sit.

As we lifted off, I leaned over and yelled, "Hey, Sergeant Champion, aren't you too short to be flying belly?"

The chopper banked to the south. Sergeant First Class Champion was a tall muscular black man, and we all admired him. He laughed a deep, booming laugh, gave me the finger. Sergeant First Class Champion looked like the Olympic champion Rafer Johnson—only bigger and stronger. He was calm and quiet, a Special Forces veteran whose presence assured us that if we got in trouble, he'd get us out.

After forty minutes in the air, Champion pointed down to the ridgeline we would be working. "There's your LZ!"

"What LZ, I can't see no LZ!" I shouted.

Miller pointed down to a small hole in the jungle canopy; it looked way too small.

"Oh, shit!"

As the chopper circled, then came in low, we rolled out the right side. Sergeant First Class Champion quickly handed the black boxes out to the cherries. I ran over and checked the wood line for gooks.

The chopper almost clipped some trees as it pulled up. I asked Saenz if he'd heard about the line doggie who ran around the back of a helicopter and ran into the rear rotor. One of the new guys, Lawhorn, asked what happened.

"Severe migraine, man, severe migraine."

As the chopper left the LZ, we watched it drop as it headed down the steep slope of the jungle-covered mountainside to gain air speed. Then it was out of sight.

We were in high, mountainous terrain, and the choppers had trouble flying that high with a full load. They would have to hurtle down the valley to gain enough air speed to create the lift they needed to climb back out of the valley. I was not looking forward to the extraction when they came back in to get us.

As we sat quietly waiting, I whispered to Miller that I read where President Nixon said we had no troops in Laos. Being as how we just came from there on our last mission, I thought it was pretty funny. Miller smiled and shook his head. He whispered "Map error," then looked back at his map. He directed the team off the LZ, and I took up the point. My job as senior scout was to make sure we didn't walk into any bad guys. I was good at my job and didn't like anyone else doing it. I didn't know anyone else on the team who cared more about my ass than I did, so I was the likely one to protect it.

It was just like a regular recon patrol. We waited a few more minutes, listening for any warning shots. We had been here before, and the trail watchers communicated by a series of rifle shots. There were no shots this trip in.

Good!

This was to be a one-day mission, but it still was a good hump to cover the two klicks we had to move.

Saenz whispered to me, "Wait till one of these mothers breaks or the batteries need to be changed. Who do you think they'll call?" Then he answered himself.

"The guys who planted them, that's who. Did you ever think of that? We're dealing with ten-digit coordinates here. They'll be impossible to find."

"Jesus, Saenz, relax. Go recheck your coordinates."

Saenz was like a brother to me, but sometimes he just worried too much.

Although this was to be a one-day mission, we still packed everything we needed, just in case we bumped into the enemy and had to escape and evade. Still, we had only one claymore each and only a few rations each. If things turned bad, this could quickly turn into a real humbug.

We stayed in close contact with the command-and-control ship flying above. It circled low overhead after we placed the black boxes in order to confirm our coordinates. Miller was worried we would get a "hot" mike (microphone feedback) from the ship being so close, so we had the ship come overhead for a commo check, and there was no problem. As soon as we had our commo check, Miller had the ship move off a ways. He didn't want it directly overhead, advertising our presence.

A Cobra gunship also orbited nearby, in case we got in serious trouble and needed help quickly. It was good to know it was there, but we didn't want it coming too close unless we needed it.

During a break, I whispered to Miller that missions like this one meant the end of the infantryman as we knew him.

Miller frowned and asked what I meant.

"This is the wave of the future—robots and machines. It just doesn't seem fair . . . I mean, I was just starting to enjoy ambushing dinks, and now some asshole in the Pentagon wants to run everything by some remote-control box. It sort of takes the fun out of the whole fucking war."

Miller chuckled. He and I had gotten real close, and there were times I thought we could almost read each other's minds. Our resident psychologist, Peterson, called it pair bonding. You seemed to hang out with one particular friend. I was serving as Miller's assistant team leader and point man this mission, and we were friends.

With the choppers nearby, it was tempting to feel safe. We had to keep reminding ourselves where we were. This wasn't like working for the power company, we were in Mr. Charlie's backyard.

Finally, we found a trail junction. Miller stopped the team and placed Saenz and the three new cherries on security. I got out my K-bar and started digging. We planted one of the boxes, then the others in its series. Each box cost Uncle Sam the price of a new Rolls Royce, and there were three to a series. After burying the boxes, we pulled the safety pin from the self-destruct device and very carefully covered them until only the thin, green, wire antennas were visible—just barely visible, even to us. Then we camouflaged the excavation with leaves and transplanted vegetation. The ground cover was thick near the ground, so it would be impossible for the NVA to spot the short antenna. It would be pure luck for the enemy to stumble across one of them.

I marked the coordinates—ten-digit coordinates—on my map. The command-and-control chopper came in overhead. The pilot spun his tail boom around and hovered directly over the tree tops until the Old Man got a fix on us. None of us liked having the helicopter right overhead where it could give our position away.

The slick settled down as if he were sitting on top of the tree.

Even fifty meters away, we could feel the rotor blast come through the trees, and it felt good.

We verified our coordinates, and moved on to the next spot. It looked as though a good number of enemy troops had walked down this trail in the past few days.

We put in our next series along the cross trail first. We were all expecting an encounter with the enemy, but we were in luck—and so were they.

By 1700 hours, the last box was in the ground, and it was time to head back to Camp Eagle. Miller had one of the cherries, a sharp Guamanian kid named McCann, call for extraction. Sergeant First Class Champion would be flying bellyman again, and the bird would be picking up at 1745 hours. The command-and-control ship and Cobra were gone, and we were alone—three vets and three cherries—deep in the enemy rear. Miller and Saenz and I were very pleased with our cherries. They were holding up well and doing their jobs like they'd been doing this sort of thing for months.

When we reached the LZ, we set up a circular defense perimeter around it and lay quietly waiting for the choppers. Maybe things would get easier now. Maybe the sensors would set the stage for a new type of high-tech warfare, where the combat soldier would no longer be needed. Perhaps we were

the last of the gladiators. But then, someone still had to go out
and place them where they would get the job done.

Miller was breaking McCann in on the radio, and McCann
was taking right to it. He acknowledged a transmission, then
whispered that our extraction ship was inbound.

"We got inbound choppers."

Rolle, the copilot, came in over the radio speaker. "This is
Kingsmen One Eight. Pop smoke. I will identify. Over."

Miller pulled a yellow smoke grenade from his web gear
and tossed it out in the center of the clearing. The dirty yellow
smoke hugged the ground as it poured from the canister until
a light breeze caught it and lifted it up through the jungle
canopy.

"This is Kingsmen One Eight. I got yellow smoke."

"Roger yellow smoke," McCann answered.

The mountains began to cool as the hot afternoon sun set
low in the west. Mr. Roach brought his chopper in from the
south. Both sides of the ridgetop broke off sharply to the valley floor some one thousand feet below.

As Roach held the Huey in a hover a foot or two above the
ground, we sprinted through the rotor wash and climbed up
onto the chopper floor. Sergeant Champion, the bellyman,
announced over the intercom that we were all on board.
Roach pulled pitch, and the helicopter started to lift. The
Huey had just cleared the ridge when the engine suddenly
stopped. We had no way of knowing it at the time, but we had
just taken an enemy hit and the bullet had lodged in the fuel
control unit (FCU).

A loud warning buzzer started beeping like crazy. Roach
slammed the collective down, yelled something to his copilot, then pulled the starting trigger. Almost instantly the engine came alive.

"What happened?" I yelled to Staff Sergeant Champion.

"We lost the engine, I guess?" he yelled back.

Beep, beep, beep, beep.

We came down in the middle of the saddle then started back up, but just as we were about to clear the ridge, our main rotor blade hit a tree. We heard a loud *schwap!* The chopper began to vibrate violently, and a second set of high-pitched warning beeps started, indicating low rotor speed. We had just sheared off three feet of the main rotor blade and it felt like we were inside a huge washing machine out of balance.

"Blade strike!" Roach yelled into his mike.

Beep, beep, . . . beep, . . . beep, beep, beep, beep, beep.

The vibration was beyond anything I had ever experienced. But even with all the shaking, our pilots managed to keep the helicopter in the air. They cleared the ridge and got us away from the mountainside. But then we really started dropping. Roach screamed over the intercom at Champion and the two door gunners, "Brace yourself, we're going down!" He flattened the collective to enter an auto-rotation.

None of us in the cabin understood what was going on, or what the pilots were doing, but from where we sat it seemed that we were in an uncontrollable fall and, any minute now, we were going to bite a big chunk of jungle.

Roach knew he had to keep the airspeed up. Too much collective, and the blade would stall and stop turning. Too little, and we would come down too fast.

This was the cherry mission for Lawhorn, McCann, and Thomas—and it looked as if it might be their last. They looked as terrified as I felt. I looked back at them and yelled, *"ALLLL RIGHT!"*—the way members of the Polar Bear Club yelled as they jumped into subfreezing water. They thought I was giving emergency instructions. They looked shocked. I hoped that it might ease their tension. It didn't!

I was seated next to the open door. Champion grabbed hold of my pack and pulled me in tight to keep me from bouncing out when we hit. I grabbed the back of the crewman's seat and braced myself. We were now falling like a brick, and the vibrations made the ship feel like it was coming apart.

I turned my head to see what Miller and the rest of the team were doing. With their striped faces they looked like frightened tiger cubs huddled in a cave. The copilot, Rolle, was calling over the radio,

"Mayday! Mayday!"

The ground was coming up fast—two hundred feet, one hundred feet.

As we got to fifty feet, Roach pulled back the stick, then jerked up on the collective as he nosed forward. The rotor blades bit hard into air, and it seemed to slow us down—a little.

Ka-Bamm!

We hit hard and bounced up in the air, then down again with a thud. I slammed against the ceiling of the helicopter.

All I could think about was unassing the Huey. Champion was talking to the pilots over the intercom, then relayed the message to us.

"Pilot says don't leave the ship until the main stops turning!"

"What?"

"Everyone hear me!" Champion repeated the message in a deep, booming voice. "The pilot's afraid the main will disengage."

We waited anxiously until the rotors stopped turning. I looked out. We were in the middle of a large valley, with a narrow tree line less than twenty meters to our three o'clock. It was getting dark fast. We had no idea where we were or how close the enemy was to us.

Mr. Roach unbuckled his seat belt with one hand and tried to work the electric circuit breakers to cut power to the downed bird with the other. Miller tapped on his window.

"Come on sir, we are sitting ducks out here. Let's go!"

The ship's radio didn't work. Miller got on our Prick-25 radio and called the Old Man. Roach unsnapped his holster and pulled out his .45 automatic. "Sir, follow Champion to the wood line," Miller shouted.

The door gunners were unlatching their M-60's as we fanned out to pull security.

"Chambers, twelve o'clock, fifty meters. Go!"

I ran out about fifty meters, and set up security on my side of the perimeter. I thought about what had just happened. My God! We had just survived a chopper crash! I tried to get my mind back on the present situation.

It was starting to get dark, and a dense ground fog was rolling in.

Champion kept the chopper crew from clustering up. They were not used to being on the ground in Charlie's backyard.

He then directed the crew to set up along our small perimeter. We were at all four points of the compass encircling the downed chopper. Since we were in the open, we could only crouch in the elephant grass and wait.

One of the Black Widow helicopters picked up the Mayday call on its way to Firebase Evans. After about thirty minutes, the Huey landed and picked up the flight crew of our downed chopper.

As the ship lifted away, I watched the right-side door gunner manning his M-60. He was scanning the distant tree line to the east, ready to suppress any unusual movement. The CO radioed and told us that we would have to stay in and secure the crash site until a Chinook arrived on the scene to salvage the Huey.

Half an hour passed, then an hour. Time dragged, and the waiting was starting to make me a little nervous.

A Cobra appeared overhead, and I felt a little more at ease. We would be a choice target for any local NVA with a mortar tube. We were sitting ducks.

Finally the CH-47 showed up. A CH-47, or Chinook, was a big twin-rotor, cargo helicopter, affectionately called a "Shithook." I was on Firebase Bastogne once when a Chinook landed. Its 130 MPH rotor wash blew three guys over. I grabbed my boonie hat and shoved it inside my shirt.

The ship hovered overhead while Miller and Champion rigged a lift harness and hooked the cable to the downed Huey. The Chinook lifted the crippled bird up like a toy airplane hanging from a string. We tightened our perimeter and waited another twenty minutes for a slick to extract us.

"Finally!" Miller shouted. "We gotta bird coming in! Pop smoke!"

"Roger that!"

I had found a large thigh bone of some dead animal and stuck it in my web gear as a souvenir of the mission.

A lone Kingsman slick touched down in the clearing. We ran for the open doors and scrambled in. The ride back was much better than the one that had deposited us here. The helicopter was cranked up and traveling about a hundred and ten knots, barely fifty feet above the trees.

It was pitch black now, and we could see the lights of Hue off in the distance. As we flew over the city, we could see people moving through the streets.

By the time we arrived at Eagle, it was nearly 2300 hours. The acid pad was completely dark when we set down, but there waiting to greet us was Jeff Ignacio, who everyone called Pineapple because he came from Hawaii. It was good to know someone cared.

"Hey, you guys gotta go see Lieutenant Williams. You missed getting paid."

"You gotta be joking, Pineapple," said Miller. He shook his head and shrugged, then lit a cigarette.

I guessed the guys didn't have any idea what we had just been through.

"Oh, well," said Miller. "Let's go get paid."

Saenz caught up to us. "Did you say get laid?"

"No, but that's certainly not a bad idea!" Miller's eyes lit up.

Up at the TOC, First Lieutenant Williams sat behind Top Walker's desk. He had just finished a cup of Top's panther-piss coffee, which had been brewed on a hot plate thirteen hours ago.

"Top must make this coffee with napalm and JP-4." Lieutenant Williams smiled. "Well, you guys okay? I heard you had a little problem on the way in."

"You might say we got sidetracked, sir."

We all laughed.

Lieutenant Williams then told us about this experimental claymore the army was developing and how one of his buddies had just completed a field test. These were the latest in sci-fi toys that the R & D boys had concocted. They could be fired by a wireless, remote-control device, but they were designed by people who had never been in combat. In order to detonate the mine, you had to hold the remote firing device in direct line of sight to it. Great for a desert, but we were fighting a war in jungles clogged with vines, shrubs, and trees. The next problem was the range of the remote control device and the placement of the operator. Lieutenant Williams's buddy told him that you had to be directly behind the mine, and no more than twenty feet away. This might sound great in some Pentagon R & D department, but those people had obviously never fired a claymore in combat. The backblast alone from that type of mine exploding that close would kill you—if you didn't get shot first, standing up and trying to get a line of sight on the device.

Williams related the story as he counted out our pay in MPC (military payment certificates). I picked up my money, recounted it, and took ten dollars out. I put the rest back in my envelope, and gave it back to the lieutenant to put in the company safe.

"Thank you, sir," Miller said. He took twenty dollars instead of his normal ten. It must've been Saenz's comment about getting laid.

"Hey, you guys sure you were not hurt?"

"Yes, sir," I said. "We're sure. Miller's ego was damaged a little in the crash. He thinks he's shorter."

Miller didn't laugh. He only appreciated jokes about his height when they came from Linderer, not me.

Later that night, back in the second platoon hooch, the

action was just about to start. The wind was blowing and we could hear the rain start pounding down. It sounded like a cow pissing on a flat rock.

The roof of our hooch was an army squad tent. A two-and-a-half foot opening, about shoulder high, ran around the hooch. It had been covered with plastic to keep the rain and wind out.

A blast wall made of sandbags was stacked three deep and four feet high around the hooch, except for openings in the front and back. A few feet across each doorway stood three fifty-gallon drums, filled with sand and topped with a couple more layers of bags. The blast wall would absorb shrapnel from a rocket attack and even turn the buildings into a fighting position in case of a ground attack.

Inside, Anderson, Bennett, Peterson, Passmore, Meszaros, Biedron, and Ricky "New Guy" Lawhorn had just returned from a beer run. They were singing a bastardized military song as we walked into the hooch. We tried to join in, even though we didn't know all the words.

> She's the yellow Rose of Saigon
> And I think she banned the twist,
> But she's a real cute dolly
> She's one I think I've missed.
> You can talk about the president
> And about his brother Nhu,
> But don't talk about my yellow Rose
> If you know what's good for you.
>
> My little Rose of Saigon
> Is just a refugee.
> She fled down from Hanoi
> To make jobs for you and me.
> She's snowed old Maxwell Taylor
> And Ambassador Nolting too,

Now Johnson's her big buddy
And gives her money, too.

She's angry at the Buddhists
And she hates the *New York Times*
Because they always rib her
And accuse her of war crimes
I look for many changes
When she meets with Mr. Lodge
Cause it's said that he's a sucker
For eastern camouflage.

Yes my yellow Rose of Saigon
Is a veteran through and through.
She's careful with her money
In case there is a coup.
She's bound to salvage something
For all her local enterprise
Before the VC win their fight
Or America gets wise.

It was a much more sophisticated song than "Boom-Boom," or "Your Son's Coming Home in a Plastic Bag, Doo-dah, Doo-dah," our more usual favorites. Miller grumbled something about how it wasn't appropriate for LRPs to hang around CIA whorehouses, learning spook songs, but I think he liked it.

Everyone had to drink to us and to our first helicopter crash landing in a public place. Then the stories started. First Miller told his side of what happened. I didn't agree, so I told my side.

"No, we must have had five hundred gooks on three sides of us."

"No, it was only two hundred!"

Miller began to ham it up, as the beer started to take effect.

"Hey, Chambers, show them your water buffalo bone."

I tossed it to Miller, who started doing an American Indian

war dance. After a few more beers, Miller started to describe how it happened again.

"Six gooks opened fire on us and cut five feet of blade off."

I jumped in.

"Miller you are so full of shit! It was ten gooks and a RPG round that took out the blade, and it was more like ten feet."

The cherries were hanging on every word, as if their very lives depended on the outcome of this story. They couldn't believe how cavalier we were about almost getting greased. Ricky New Guy, who was not quite buying the bullshit, having been with us, protested.

"Hey! Come on, you guys."

Miller, who had just bit into an apple, left over from lunch two days before, spit it out then challenged anyone to a shooting contest.

"You can't knock this apple off my head—not a one of you can!"

He adjusted his half-eaten apple so it balanced on the top of his head.

"Go for it!" Someone egged me on.

I picked up a half-full, metal canteen and did my best Sandy Koufax wind up. I let it rip. Everyone started cheering as I cut loose, but the canteen missed its intended mark and dropped two inches. It slammed into Miller's forehead.

A gash opened, and blood started streaming down his face. Everything got quiet.

"Sorry, man, I didn't mean to take out your eye."

Miller, who was three sheets gone by now, was acting like a ceremonial Indian warrior and began rubbing the blood all over his face. The three-inch gash above his right eye was wide open and bleeding heavily.

He grabbed the heavy, water-buffalo leg bone and started to swing it in rhythmic circles, dancing around with it.

He took some blood and smeared lines down his nose and along the sides of his cheeks. Then he drew a line down the center of the bone and started grinning. I knew I was in trouble now!

"Come on, man, I'm sorry!"

I tried to reason with him, but it was too late for that. The one thing you couldn't do with Miller was reason with him. He's insane most of the time and unreasonable the rest of the time. The man is barely civilized. He began chanting in tongues.

All the cherries looked as if they were going into mild shock. Anderson's mouth dropped open. They thought Miller had gone nuts. I couldn't hide. I had to take whatever was coming.

With a wild follow-through and a loud Indian yell, Miller flung the bone as hard as he could in my direction. End over end it came. My left hand went up to protect my face. I closed my eyes, hoping for a glancing blow.

The water buffalo bone smacked into my left hand and fell to the floor.

"Fuck, I think you broke my arm, Miller." I yelled out.

Then the pain started. A mad throbbing set in. I reached for a real weapon, my K-bar. Miller looked stricken—not by my K-bar, but by the thought he'd really hurt me.

Just then, our platoon sergeant, Sfc. Milton Lockett walked in. He took one look at my hand, and then at Miller's bloody head.

"I should give both you yahoos an Article 15 for damaging government property," he said, shaking his head. "You had both better get your young paratrooper asses down to the aid station, *now!*"

When Lockett said "move," we moved. Besides, we needed medical treatment.

We were feeling pretty drunk as we walked down to the dispensary. I carried the bone as a souvenir. Miller had a bandana tied across his forehead and most of his right eye. He looked like a pirate—a drunken pirate. It took about fifteen minutes to get to the 85th Evac. When we got to the door of the hooch, we could hear a very badly wounded trooper screaming in pain. We entered the reception area. The surgeon and his medics were struggling to save the life of a horribly maimed trooper, and it shamed us so much we left. The orderly at the door told us that the man had stepped on a land mine that afternoon. It had blown pieces of metal up through his feet, legs, and into his spleen and abdomen.

Miller and I took one good look, and we turned and hauled out of there.

Miller, wearing his bloody bandana, looked over at me with his one good eye, shook his head, and said, "No way, man! I'm not going back in there."

We turned around, and headed back to the company area. We found Chet "The Jet" Losinger, who gave us a handful of Darvon and told us to take at least six. We did, and in thirty minutes, I couldn't feel or hear a thing except the sounds of that wounded soldier screaming somewhere in the back of my mind.

The next morning, after the Darvons had worn off, we both awoke feeling like we had been spread-eagled across that clearing when the chopper slammed into it.

7 Recondo School

Two months after my hand had healed, I found myself seated on the floor of a steel, airport-terminal building, just outside the city of Phu Bai. We crowded under a huge, jury-rigged fan, waiting to board the C-130 that would fly us down to the resort city of Nha Trang and MACV Recondo School.

The city of Nha Trang is located one hundred and forty miles north of Saigon on one of the most beautiful stretches of seacoast in the world.

Ron Reynolds, Harry Duty, Dan Roberts, and I were on our way to Recondo School. We'd waited over seven months to get a shot at it. Recondo School was graduate school for an LRP. It usually meant you would be given a team shortly after graduation—if you graduated.

After several hours, the big transport plane still hadn't arrived. Reynolds went over to check the manifest but couldn't find my name or Duty's on it.

"Now what?"

Reynolds and I found a REMF who looked in charge.

"I'm not on the manifest," I told him.

"That's Nam, man." The REMF sergeant answered in a sarcastic tone. He didn't even look up.

I just knew the asshole was going to get his ass kicked right there. Reynolds pushed me out of the way and turned back towards the NCO.

"Listen, you rear-echelon piece of shit, you'd better figure

119

out how to get my men on that plane, or you're going to spend the rest of your tour in a full-body cast!"

The REMF sergeant stared hard at Reynolds and realized that he was fortunate to have received the warning. He looked down at the papers shaking his head, then looked back up at Reynolds. Reynolds was six feet five and weighed in at a muscular 225 pounds.

"I see . . . uh, I must'a made a mistake, Sergeant. There are two extra seats here." He shuffled the papers, stamped the copies, and hurried away.

Duty yelled over to us, "Did you get us window or aisle seats, Reynolds?"

Just then we saw the plane on final approach. The big C-130 taxied straight for the reception area. At the last moment, the pilot gunned his left engine and swung the big plane almost completely around.

The large cargo ramp in the rear of the plane lowered, and I could see the gaggle of American soldiers. We watched as they deplaned, a contingent of fresh new troops. As they walked down the ramp and onto the hot tarmac, their eyes flashed as they took in their surroundings. When they walked past the four of us, they eyed our tiger fatigues and scoped them out for some type of military insignia.

As the last of the green troops stepped off the plane, Duty yelled, "Sixty-two and a wake-up!"

"Duty, you're such an asshole!" said Reynolds. "Leave the cherries alone! Let's get on board."

Duty had shattered my vision of the cool, confident LRPs heading out on a new adventure. Duty had a way of making a unique situation seem quite ordinary. We were too elite to go harassing cherries. That was the way legs and REMFs made themselves feel superior. We were supposed to be too hard-core and cool to even care how many days we had remaining in country.

We climbed in, and everyone bitched as we tried to get comfortable on the plane's hard, cargo floor. We slid under the safety straps that were lying across the metal floor. We sat there with our knees drawn up like a bunch of first graders, waiting to hear a fairy tale. The floor was as hard as a metal, cargo floor could get. Duty did a poor impression of a stewardess.

"Fasten your seat belts, please. Coffee, tea, or clap."

It wasn't that funny. Duty had a previous tour as an LRP for the 1st Infantry Division, the Big Red One. He had a way of embarrassing us.

The plane started down the runway, banging, bouncing, and gaining speed, then climbed heavily away from the tarmac. We braced ourselves to prevent us from falling over backward. This had to be the noisiest aircraft in the air force. The roar of the engines was so loud, we couldn't hear ourselves think.

As the big plane banked to the east, I got that old familiar knot in the bottom of my stomach. I enjoyed jumping, but I hated to fly.

An hour passed. Without warning, the pilot put the aircraft into a steep bank.

"I hate the leg air force!" Reynolds yelled.

"What?" I shouted back.

The combination of the plane's unexpected drop and Reynolds yelling in my ear scared the shit out of me. "Man, I was half asleep!"

"Air force."

"What?" I shouted again at Reynolds.

"Air force assholes never tell you shit. They think we're just cargo on the floor."

We touched down minutes later. As the noisy plane taxied up to the concrete apron, the large cargo-bay door dropped as we attempted to stand. The effort was next to impossible since we were all suffering from numb-ass syndrome.

Some air force general must have worked overtime figuring out that by removing the seats and putting long cargo straps across the floor of the C-130 Hercules, you could get

25 percent more cargo space or some bullshit like that. It never made any sense to us. The plane had over 425 square feet of floor space, which could easily seat fifty-five troopers with full combat gear. Take out the seats, and it would hold sixty. I hated air force generals, but almost as soon as I stepped off the plane, I decided that I liked Nha Trang.

The city of Nha Trang's central location made it logistically ideal for training special op personnel from all over South Vietnam. It was headquarters to 5th Special Forces Group (Airborne), which also had subordinate units spread all over the country.

It was a beautiful Saturday afternoon, as we rolled into town. We were on our own until Sunday morning. We'd decided to see the city and try to get laid. We hurriedly flagged down a pedicab.

"Ah, numba one GI!" said the driver. He gave us the thumbs-up sign, and the four of us tried to sit down on the front bench seat. A pedicab, as they called it, had one bench seat up front, with the driver riding behind. You sat astride the front axle of the three-wheeled contraption.

"What a piece of shit," complained Duty-Pie. He had cause for complaint because he had to sit on Reynold's lap.

"Hotel Nha Trang!"

The driver rattled off some rapid Vietnamese mumbo jumbo, and off we went. Moments later, we were driving through downtown Nha Trang.

The sidewalks were overflowing with people in traditional Asian straw hats, loose-fitting white shirts, and black pajama-like pants. The vendors seemed to outnumber the shoppers, as they displayed piles of slogan-covered T-shirts and sequin-and-oil paintings on black velvet. I commented on how amazing it was that such classical art could only be found here and in Tijuana, Mexico.

Old, rickety tables lined the sidewalks, covered with every kind of black-market, army-surplus item possible. The more traditional storefronts displayed ivory, jade, and Indian rugs of all kinds.

We arrived at the Hotel Nha Trang. Reynolds gave our driver two hundred piasters in Vietnamese money, about two dollars U.S. After we checked into the hotel and learned about the nightly curfew, we decided we had better hurry to find out where to get laid. The curfew took effect at 2100 hours. We were all sore from the day's flight.

Carrying weapons in Nha Trang was a no-no. So we broke our weapons down and hid them in a duffel bag behind the bathroom door that opened into our room.

After dropping off our weapons, we moved down to the hotel restaurant and ordered everything on the menu. I mean everything.

"Chow! Nothing better than gook food," Duty said.

We ate, and kept eating. Chicken fried rice, ham fried rice, noodles, bamboo shoots, soup, and Coke—lots and lots of Cokes. Reynolds ordered a plate of *bo nuong la* and wolfed down the chopped beef wrapped in grape leaves. He was using chopsticks, and Duty and I were using the large spoons the hotel provided.

We all ordered more food. We all agreed that it was great.

After dinner we went to a nearby bar. There was no band, only a World War II–era jukebox and a collection of records just shipped over from Tokyo. A waitress played the newest hit by the Beatles, "Get Back." I kind of liked it.

A beautiful Vietnamese girl walked over to our table.

"Hi, GI," she said. "You want me good time? I be numba one girl, I no be with other GI in all of Vietnam. Only you."

"God, I love an honest woman. She's mine!"

She was a real Vietnamese beauty. She wore a bright, flowered ao dai of pure silk. Her collar was closed tightly in the Chinese fashion. But in the Vietnamese fashion, her gown had a slit along the side from the floor to her waist. It revealed her black satin underwear. Underwear! I'd forgotten what real females looked like. She had silken, jet black, Oriental hair, the kind that always looked clean. It dropped past her shoulders, almost to her waist.

I told Reynolds I thought I was in love, this time for sure.

"You buy me drink," she cooed.

"Yes! Yes!" I reached for my wallet.

Reynolds broke out three big Cuban cigars. I asked where in the hell he got those. He just grinned and winked at me.

On a small stage, two Vietnamese women danced topless to the beat of the new Beatles tune. There was a huge speaker in each corner of the club, and the music was blaring at max volume. We noticed two Special Forces NCO's sitting at a table near the door. The Green Beret closest to us wore his beret tilted cockily to one side.

I ordered a pitcher of Ba Muoi Ba and asked the waitress to take it to their table. They both turned and gave us the high sign. One shouted, "Airborne," when he noticed the subdued jump wings sewn on our cammies. We shouted back in unison, "Airborne!"

In many ways, the Vietnamese women looked more sophisticated than American round-eyes. Besides, I'd had it with Western girls, especially after my girlfriend stopped writing me.

These girls were different. There was a certain respectability about wartime prostitution. Besides, they had great-looking legs. At least they were honest about who they were boom-booming.

After several hours of drinking, a second Vietnamese girl showed up. They soon invited Duty and me to follow them home. I started to get nervous. Duty said he had something for my nerves. I followed him to the bar and had three straight shots of whiskey with him. It seemed like we were there for hours. We walked back inside, and the girls were gone! Reynolds was sitting with two bar girls. I asked him where our dates had gone.

He said they had just walked outside to get a pedicab. I told Reynolds the two girls he was with were a waste of time.

"No boom-boom man, just play you for drinks," I said.

"Man, I'm from Texas, and we ain't never seen girls like this where I'm from," Reynolds said in his slow, Texas drawl. "Besides, I'm too drunk to care!"

It was almost 2100 hours, and Nha Trang had a strict curfew. Duty and I walked outside. I wanted to follow the girls, but the alcohol was taking effect. I was stoned. We just stood there while the open pedicab with our dates rolled away.

"Man, look how beautiful they are," Duty said, wistfully.

They seemed to be headed down the street toward the center of town, but we had no real idea where they were going.

"They sure are great looking, man. Where are they going? What's the address?" Duty looked at me.

"Address? I thought you had their address!"

Just then, a Vietnamese "cowboy" pulled up on a Honda motorbike and asked me something in Vietnamese.

"What? I can't understand you. No *bie!*"

He said something that sounded like give ride, and I hopped on and told him to follow those girls. Off we went.

As I held on, I started tripping on the scenery.

It was beautiful, really beautiful. Everything was peaceful. The whiskeys had taken hold—big time. I was out of it.

I forgot all about the girls and the war. It seemed as if time was passing in slow motion. I noticed the scenery had begun to change from residential to rural. I could feel the warm night air in my face. I had committed the LRP cardinal sin; I'd let down. Then it struck me.

Rural, shit! We're headed for the fucking jungle.

I tried to desperately recover my senses.

This guy could be working for the VC. He's got me, and I am going for the long ride to some VC camp.

The VC would pay a five hundred dollar bounty for a dumb-shit GI's head. *Wait till his gook buddies see the 101st patch and the LRP tab on my shirt. They'd pay him a hundred thousand piasters for a LRP. I just made this guy's career.*

I yelled for this guy to stop, but he didn't pay any attention to me. He started going faster. Nha Trang City was just a glow in the night behind me—there were no lights ahead.

I sobered up fast. I reached for my belt and found my K-bar. I pulled it from its scabbard.

"Turn around!" I commanded. Then I held the edge of the ten-inch blade in front of his face. That got his attention and really pissed him off.

"Humph!" He straightened up, then slowed down and turned the little motorbike around. I almost fell off when he did, but I held on for all I was worth. I had the gook by the shirt, and he was yelling at the top of his lungs.

"You crazy GI! You numba ten asshole GI!"

Maybe so, but I was going to be a live asshole GI.

I held on until we got back to Nha Trang City. When I jumped off, he pulled away calling me every kind of gook insult he knew. I set off in the direction of the hotel.

By now there was no one left on the streets. I was alone. I started to get a little concerned but was too damn mad to be scared.

I don't know how I found the hotel. I must have walked for an hour. I thought of several interesting ways to kill Duty.

This is the shits! I thought. *I will definitely kill Duty-Pie when I find him. Shit! I was almost a POW, and I haven't even checked into Recondo School yet. Duty's dead!*

After finding the hotel, I found my way up to the room, put the key in the old French lock and opened it. I had no idea how I'd found the hotel, let alone the room. A small electric lantern was glowing pale orange above a small vacant bed. I crawled in, still half-drunk, promising myself that I'd kill Duty in the morning. I was too tired to do it now.

The large ceiling fan turned lazily above me as if nothing had ever happened. I drifted off to sleep.

Bang!

I woke with a start. Was that a gun shot?

Bang!

"Sounds like a .45 round. Get down!" Reynolds yelled.

Reynolds rolled to the floor, and I followed suit.

"Sounds like it's in the hotel."

I low crawled over for our weapons.

Duty was still asleep when the third shot rang out. It sounded as if it were in the room next door. We were all lying motionless on the floor.

Soon there was a knock at our door, and someone hollered, "Military police!"

Reynolds got up to open the door. I quickly returned our CAR-15s to their hiding place. The door went flying open, and in stormed three White Mice, Vietnamese MPs—guns drawn and in a bad mood. They had us line up against the hotel-room wall. In walked the captain of the Mice. "Thuan" was sewn on his breast pocket.

"You are Americans, 101st?"

"Yes, sir!" we said in unison.

"Do you have guns?"

"Oh, nooo, sir!" I pushed the bathroom door back to hide the exposed CAR-15s, as the nasty-looking group walked right past them.

"Wake up, wake that man up!" Captain Thuan ordered.

"Duty! Duty! Get up, we're about to go to jail."

Duty woke up in a daze. He got out of bed and stood next to us as the gooks looked around the room. Duty, still half-drunk, walked into the bathroom. He started to close the door behind him. I thought, *Duty, No! Don't shut the door, the rifles are behind it.*

As he pulled the door shut, he saw the four rifles through the crack of the door frame. He quickly pushed the door back and walked over to us. The three MPs looked puzzled by all this activity but never spotted the weapons.

Since Reynolds was the senior ranking NCO, he was questioned by the captain outside the room while the three ARVN MPs stood guard over us. They searched our rucksacks, found some C-4, det cord, a lot of M-16 magazines, and some leftover gook food.

"Where are your rifles?" the Vietnamese captain demanded.

"We checked them in at MACV Recondo School this morning," said Reynolds as he walked back into the room.

"What happened? What did he tell you?" I asked.

"Somebody shot a whore down the hall. They thought it was us. They were looking for guns."

"What? I hate this place!"

After the MPs left, we tried to sleep but couldn't. I would have felt safer back at Camp Eagle—or even out in the jungle.

We checked into the Recondo School at 0800 hours and compared stories with Dan Roberts, who'd just showed up.

"Where you been, man?" I asked as he walked up to the three of us.

"Getting laid, how'd you guys do?" he asked.

"Just great, we all got laid," I lied.

As we stood in loose formation that first morning, the whole compound was buzzing with rumors about the Special Forces camp up in the Central Highlands that got hit the night before.

Dan told us he had heard that as many as ten Soviet-made tanks and at least a battalion of hard-core NVA troops hit the camp before dawn. The SF advisors and their Montagnard minions had kicked some ass while driving back the assault. He told us that they even destroyed several of the Russian light tanks. The SF advisors had suffered some pretty heavy casualties themselves. He told us that he had heard that we might be used as a reaction force to relieve the camp if they needed one. We weren't that far from the Central Highlands, and we were already in a Special Forces camp. I told Reynolds that maybe this school was not such a good idea after all. He told me not to worry.

I guess I wasn't ready to hear about Russian tanks. We noticed a lot of chopper activity and a very nervous SF cadre.

Suddenly, the screen door of the Recondo School head-quarters building flew open and out came a burly-looking E-7 wearing a green beret and extra large, tiger-striped jungle fatigues.

"Welcome to Recondo School, I'm Sergeant First Class Roberts. I will be your principal instructor during your stay here."

Then, in a louder voice: "I would like to go over the rules here at Recondo School. Should you violate, stretch, or disagree with my U.S. Army Special Forces rules, you will be dismissed and ordered to return to your unit.

"Rule one: This is my U.S. Army, and my home, and you will be expected to keep your AOs clean and orderly. You will not smoke that dope here, and you will stand inspection every morning after your run. Chow is at 0730 hours. Understood?"

"Yes, Sergeant!" our group of sixty men shouted in unison.

"Rule two: During the instructional course work, you will not smoke, talk, play grab-ass, and you will not fall asleep on my fellow SF instructors, and yes, gentlemen, it is ninety-seven degrees under those tin roofs. Understood?"

"Yes, Sergeant!"

"Rule three: During the run, you will not stop, talk or take any sand out of your rucksack, or you will be asked to return to your unit. Understood?"

"Yes, Sergeant!"

"Rule four: During each course of instruction, you will be given a new set of safety rules. If you break any of my safety rules, you will be returned to your unit. Is that understood?"

"Yes, Sergeant!"

"Rule five: During the swimming part of the course, you will be given an inflatable life vest for emergencies. If you are a weak swimmer, and you do not tell us, we will let your sorry ass drown. This is no summer camp. Nothing gives me a case of the ass more than having some sorry straight-leg drown while attending my Special Forces Recondo School—I have to fill out six forms in triplicate, and I hate forms—do you understand?"

"Yes, Sergeant!"

"Rule six: During the training mission, you will be operating in enemy territory. There will be no sleeping on watch, talking on patrol, or pill popping during the mission. We do lose people here at Recondo School, especially when they don't follow my simple six rules. Is that understood!"

"Yes, Sergeant!"

"We have representatives from two of our allied forces going through the course with you. You will be training with the Royal Thai Special Forces. They are good troops, and you can learn from them. But you will not fraternize with the Korean ROK units. You are to stay away and have no—and I mean no—contact with them. Is this understood?"

"Yes, sergeant."

"Classes will begin at 0900 hours. That will be all, men."

8 Recondo Training

Ron Reynolds, Harry Duty, Dan Roberts, and I sat in the classroom's second row. The assistant commandant walked into the formal training building, a plywood structure with a sheet-metal roof. He made his way toward our classroom.

"Ten-hut!" someone called out.

We stood at attention as the young major walked to the front of the room.

"At ease, men! Take seats."

He wore his beret at a rakish angle but took it off and stuffed it into the side pocket of his jungle fatigues.

He had to walk around a large, varnished table in the center of the room. An oversized MACV Recondo School patch was painted on its surface. The room was set up classroom style, with a walkway down the center.

I didn't notice the Koreans or the Thais. I mouthed the words to Reynolds, "Where are the gooks?"

He put his finger to his mouth. "Shhhhhh . . ."

The Special Forces major stopped and turned to face us. He was short and stocky, about five foot nothing. Directly behind him was a dark green curtain. Another huge Recondo emblem was painted on it. There was also a Special Forces patch. He walked over to the three-foot logo, as if he were inspecting every detail. To his right, allied flags hung from varnished flag poles. The United States, Australia, South Korea, Republic of Vietnam, and the Kingdom of Thailand were represented.

"I'm Major Bob Lunday, assistant commandant of the 5th Special Forces Recondo School. I want to welcome each of you. I would like to familiarize you with the mission, standards for selection, and the program of instruction that we adhere to here at MACV Recondo School."

We were all listening.

"First, I would like to give you a brief explanation as to how the school was established and why Special Forces is conducting the training.

"In September 1965, detachment B-52 of the 5th Special Forces Group (ABN), known as Project Delta, began a unit training program on long-range, reconnaissance-patrol techniques. This program was initiated for the purpose of training Project Delta replacement personnel. The conventional U.S. forces in country learned of this training program and requested that they be allowed to send selected personnel to attend these courses. As its potential value became apparent to major unit commanders, interest in reconnaissance training progressively developed."

The major glanced at the four of us seated in the second row. We all wore the 101st Screaming Eagle Patch on our left shoulder. Then he continued.

"The school started with ten troopers from the 1st Brigade, 101st Airborne Division, in September of 1965. In mid-1966, General Westmoreland directed that a study be made of the long-range, reconnaissance-patrol capabilities of U.S. units in Vietnam. As a result of the study, General Westmoreland directed that a three-week program of instruction on long-range reconnaissance patrolling would be conducted and that the instruction would be based upon the Project Delta concept of operation. The 5th Special Forces Group was asked to organize and conduct the school, and the commanding officer of the 5th Group was designated as the commandant.

"The school was officially opened by General Westmoreland on 15 September 1966. The title given the school, Recondo, was coined by General Westmoreland and is a derivative of three terms long associated with soldiering: *Reconnaissance, Commando, and Doughboy.*"

I couldn't help frowning. Doughboy?

"The mission of the school is to train selected personnel from LRP combat units in specialized techniques and skills necessary to conduct successful long-range, reconnaissance operations in South Vietnam.

"The school presently has an authorized cadre strength of six officers and forty-eight enlisted men. In addition, one Australian and three South Korean liaison personnel are assigned duty as staff members at the Recondo School. We also have assigned, as school and support troops, one quasi-military CIDG (Civilian Irregular Defense Group) company. This unit is used for camp security and as an immediate-reaction force during the combat-operation phase of the student training program.

"The standards for student selection are set forth in USARV (United States Army Republic of Vietnam) Regulation 350-2. We consider the proper selection of personnel the most critical aspect of the long-range, reconnaissance-patrolling program.

"By direction of the USARV Commander, *no* person is accepted for the training at this installation except a volunteer. In General Westmoreland's words, 'A Recondo must be skilled, smart, tough, confident, and courageous.'

"We assume that you, as a volunteer, are smart, tough, and courageous before you arrive at the school, and these traits will be tested. The other two traits, skill and confidence, you will develop throughout the training program.

"The program of instruction for the school lasts twenty days and consists of 260 hours. The capacity for each class is sixty-five students. Quotas are allocated to all Free World military forces in Vietnam, based upon their requirements and requests.

"The first week of training consists of academic subjects taught in the classroom and adjoining outdoor training areas.

During the second week, practical exercises in helicopter operations are conducted in conjunction with a four-day, field-training exercise on Hon Tre Island, located five miles off the coast.

"This field-training exercise enables you to put into practice those techniques learned during the first week of your classroom instruction. During the third and final week, you are deployed as six-man teams on four- to five-day reconnaissance patrols in hostile areas west of Nha Trang.

"You will be given a standard Airborne physical-training test the second day of this course. This will give you and the cadre an indication of your physical condition. In addition, you are given a confidence test on the forty-foot tower. This consists of climbing a rope ladder, without equipment, and descending a forty-foot, knotted rope.

"This test is to mentally prepare you for rappelling, rope-ladder, and emergency-extraction training involving helicopters during the second week. Also, in conjunction with small craft training, a swimming test is administered."

I started to squirm in my seat. He had mentioned my Achilles' heel, swimming. Two summers ago, I almost drowned, trying to surf the waves in Hawaii. I barely made it back to shore after getting caught in a riptide. I could swim, but I wasn't exactly a candidate for the underwater demolition team.

"Daily PT begins at 0430. You will do eight repetitions of Army Drill One and start the course by running a two-mile road march with equipment, consisting of a forty-pound pack, patrol harness, and individual weapon. The runs get progressively longer each day. On the seventh day, you conduct a nine-mile run, with equipment, in ninety minutes. The second week continues with Army Drill One and road runs.

"When this course was originally established, we used to also administer a map-reading examination on the first day, and those who failed were returned to their units. The percentage of failures was so high, that instruction on map reading was increased to fifteen hours of study prior to being tested. Those students who then fail receive additional instruction during the second week. Those students who pass are used as assistant instructors during this additional examination.

"Basic first aid, survival, medicines and drugs, life-saving steps, treating special wounds, and the use of the albumin blood-expander unit will be taught to you. You will also be taught how to give both muscular and intravenous injections."

I had heard about this part of the course. I grabbed my arm as if I had just gotten an injection and could feel the pain of the two-inch needle.

"During the communications part of the course, we teach characteristics and operation of the PRC-25, HT-1, and URC-10 radios. You will become familiar with field-expedient and aircraft antennas, SOI and message writing, communications procedures, and guidance of aircraft.

"Intelligence training will consist of combat-intelligence principles, terrain analysis, basic photography, handling of POWs, captured documents and equipment, and VC military organization, operations, and tactics. You will learn Special Forces patrolling techniques. We will also be covering preparation, organization and security, special equipment, helicopter infiltration and exfiltration techniques, survival, immediate-action drills, and the grid system and point-of-origin methods for reporting information and location."

Then he handed out several sheets of paper describing patrol techniques and tips.*

MACV RECONDO SCHOOL
5TH SPECIAL FORCES GROUP (AIRBORNE),
1ST SPECIAL FORCES
APO SAN FRANCISCO 96240

PATROL TECHNIQUES AND PATROL TIPS
HANDOUT 707-1 PATROL PLANNING STEPS

*See also appendix.

1. PLAN USE OF TIME
2. STUDY SITUATION
3. MAKE MAP STUDY
4. COORDINATE (CONTINUOUS THROUGHOUT)
5. SELECT MEN, WEAPONS, AND EQUIPMENT
6. ISSUE WARNING ORDER
7. MAKE RECONNAISSANCE
8. COMPLETE DETAIL PLANS
9. ISSUE PATROL ORDER
10. INSPECT AND REHEARSE
11. BRIEFBACK

The major continued.

"During the weapons training portion of the course, you will have the chance to zero your personal weapon, fire an M-79 grenade launcher, and all the common VC and NVA weapons. You will also participate in jungle-lane and instinctive-fire exercises and receive instruction in the installation and removal of booby traps and mines in addition to three hours of artillery fire adjustment.

"During the air-operations block of instruction, you will learn the capabilities and limitations of the HU-1 series helicopter, loading and unloading procedures, landing-zone selection, infiltration and exfiltration methods using rappelling ropes, rope ladders, and the McGuire rig. The forward-air-control procedures will be taught by an air force liaison officer. During this class you are required to direct an airborne forward air controller to an actual target.

"During all training, we consistently stress alertness, attention to detail, discipline, and a few tricks not in the book.

"Your course culminates in a four-day, long-range, reconnaissance patrol to gain enemy intelligence in the mountainous jungle areas west of Nha Trang. The mission requires you to apply all the skills and techniques acquired during the previous two weeks. Your teams will be assigned a reconnaissance zone to conduct a map study of this area. You will then

go on an overflight to select infiltration landing zones and exfiltration landing zones.

"Under the guidance of the school's team advisor, you will
conduct patrol planning and preparation, briefbacks for teams
and aircraft commanders, and will then be infiltrated into
your assigned reconnaissance zones. You may be required, at
any time, to call for and adjust artillery fire or air strikes,
guide in reaction forces, or undergo emergency extraction.

"Your assigned school advisor accompanies and evaluates
each team through the combat operation. Only those students
who have achieved the required academic points and have
demonstrated overall proficiency as potential reconnaissance
soldiers in all practical work during the first two weeks are
permitted to participate in the third-week combat operation.

"Since the school opened, 2,951 personnel have attended
Recondo training; 1,801 have graduated. The attrition rate
has been approximately 36.8 percent."

He took a moment to let that statistic sink in.

"Even though it will be apparent by the fifth day of training
who will not pass the course, no students are released until
the end of the second week, in hopes that they can assimilate
as much of the training as possible. The only exceptions to
this policy are medical or disciplinary problems who require
immediate release.

"Graduates of the MACV Recondo School provide the
unit commander with the following distinct capabilities:
They may be infiltrated into enemy-controlled territory for
periods of up to seven days without being resupplied. Once in
the area, they will be able to detect enemy infiltration routes,
cache sites, base areas, way stations, and identify VC and
NVA units. They will be trained to direct air and artillery
strikes and to receive and guide reaction forces to a target.

"As a Recondo, you can provide your commanders with
the most current and accurate intelligence about the enemy
and their area of operations, prior to commitment of his
combat-maneuver elements. This can save the lives of your

men and avoid wasting your unit's time and energy trying to find the elusive enemy we are fighting.

"As a graduate of this school you will be authorized to wear the Recondo pocket insignia while in Vietnam."

He turned around and pointed to the black patch on the curtain.

"The arrowhead, pointing downward, symbolizes the air-to-ground methods of infiltration into enemy territory and is further representative of the American Indian skills of field craft and survival.

"The dark pattern with a light background indicates the capability for both day and night operations. The V stands for both Valor and Vietnam. I want to congratulate you for being here, and I wish you luck."

He then came to attention. We all stood and saluted. He returned the salute. We stayed at attention as he walked past us and out the door.

Our class of RS-17-69 had Thai Special Forces, ROK Koreans, U.S. Marines, navy SEALs, and representative LRPs/Rangers from every unit in Nam. We were told we would learn more in three weeks than some commanders would learn in an entire tour.

Just to be cadre you had to be on your third or fourth tour. To Special Forces NCOs, it was perhaps the best assignment the war had to offer. The cadre instructors took their jobs and training very seriously. The school was designed to instruct and share the years of experience these Special Forces NCOs had acquired, and they were totally committed to sharing their experience. Still, Recondo School, with its nonstop training crammed into three weeks, was the best-kept-secret training school the army had.

I looked at my watch. It was 0330 hours, the first full day of Recondo School.

"Get up! Hit it, outside for PT."

A burly, redheaded NCO named Franklin stood in the PT

pit and led us in the exercises. He looked more like a minia-ture version of Charles Atlas than a Special Forces instructor. After he was through with us, he had us line up, grab our gear, and get ready to race each other through the streets of Nha Trang.

The runs were killers, each one longer than the first, build-ing up to the torturous nine-miler. Each one was with full combat gear: rifle, six quarts of water, sixteen magazines—and one small additional item, a measured, forty-pound sand-bag placed in the rucksack.

I was still trying to catch my breath after the exercises, when I saw Sergeant Franklin head for the main gate to start the run. I stood next to Reynolds and Roberts. My heart was pumping so fast I felt like a jackrabbit. Every time I com-peted, I felt this way.

"Go!" Franklin shouted.

We all started to sprint, through the gate, down the gravel road, and past the bunker that guarded the Special Forces compound, then outside and down the isolated road that led to the city of Nha Trang. As I moved in behind Roberts, I could feel my heavy rucksack shifting on my back as we turned and headed down the main street. There was not a soul on the streets, as if we were running in a ghost town. Am-Nuay and Somnuek, my new Thai friends, blew past us like we were standing still. I knew they were good, but I had no idea how fast they were. I finished, exhausted and gasping for air. I had thought that I could stay with the leaders the whole distance, but no way. I finished in the middle of the pack.

A sure way to recognize a Recondo graduate was by the burn marks under his armpits and on his lower back. Running with that forty-pound rucksack wore the skin right off. I thought the run would never end—and this only the beginning.

What I was really worried about was the swim the next day, especially after a three-mile run down to the beach. We would have to swim against the current out to a raft, approximately one hundred meters offshore, swim around it, and return without resting on the raft. If you failed, you washed out of the school.

On the morning before the dreaded swim, we had finished PT and our run, and I was walking to the chow line when someone grabbed my hand. It was Am-Nuay, the Thai Special Forces sergeant I had befriended in the commo class. I looked down, and he was holding my hand like I was his girlfriend. I jerked it away, and he looked at me funny.

Reynolds, who was behind me said, "He's okay, man, you are his friend, and that's how these people show friendship. It doesn't mean he's queer."

I think I hurt his feelings, and I felt bad, but no one had warned me about these different customs.

Finally the day of the swim test arrived. I knew what was coming. If I could just get through this part, everything would be great. I had faked being brave in jump school, but soon I'd be facing my biggest fear—drowning!

"I want to be an Airborne Ranger," we sang as we ran. Hell, I was an Airborne Ranger! If I could only keep my mind off this swimming, I could probably even believe it.

Before long, we'd run to the beach, and I could see the ocean.

"Take your boots off and line up," ordered one of the instructors. "You will swim in groups of four. As soon as one group gets out to the raft, the next group jumps in."

I watched as the first group put on deflated life vests.

"This vest is only used if you get into trouble."

Yeah, right, I thought. *If I get into trouble, I'll just stop and blow it up.* This was getting scary to me now. The stupid vest had to be blown up, but only if you were drowning.

Forget it, I wasn't going to use it. I'd just drown without it, rather than with it.

I saw the first guys take forever just to get to the raft. It looked like they took three strokes forward and the current pulled them back two. I wondered if I should tell someone I don't think I can make it.

We stood in line at the foot of the shore. It was our turn.

"Go!"

I ran out as far as I could, then dove out flat and coasted for a few feet. The other three guys were already ahead of me, but I didn't care. I was already tired, and I had barely traveled ten yards. I lay on my side and did a kick stroke. It was working, but I was taking too long. I could hear the instructor yell at me to get going. I started swimming, one arm over my head, then the next. I lifted my head and tried to breathe; salt water filled my mouth. I looked back and couldn't see the beach. Then I saw it was only twenty feet to the raft and safety. I reached out and started to stroke again.

Ten feet, I'm almost there. My legs were cramped and my arms felt as if they were rubber. The raft! I reached out to grab it. Salt water washed my eyes as the ocean swells rolled over my head. I went under, then popped up with a loud gasp. I reached out from under the water and was met with a push in the face. I slid back under. More water in my lungs. I came up fast.

"Touch this raft and you are out, troop! Go for it, man! Hang on! Swim, just swim!"

I still had to go all the way around the raft. I was terrified and exhausted. I came back up and tried to blow water out of my mouth and find the tube to inflate the life vest. Each time I tried to blow into the vest, I would go under water. I popped up again as a swell swept over my head. I was getting nowhere, and now I was drifting out past the raft.

"Hey, 101st, this way!"

I dropped the life-vest tube and started to swim. I passed the raft and knew it was sink or swim. I still couldn't see the shore. Each time a wave came in, it lifted me up and then down.

"Keep going. Don't stop."

I could faintly hear the guys on the beach yelling, then I blacked out. The next thing I remember was clawing the sand with my hands. I was still swimming, but I was on the beach.

I tried to stand up but fell back into the ocean. I could hear voices over the sounds of the waves.

"You made it, man, you made it."

I crawled the rest of the way, then collapsed and just lay there like a fish, gasping for air. I rolled over on my back as a wave broke over my head. I looked up at the sky.

"Get up, troop, or I will make you do it again!" said the SF instructor.

I stumbled up the steep, sandy beach to the top of the knoll where the rest of the guys were. I lay down next to three guys from the 173d. I couldn't talk. We still had rubber-boat training. After surviving that, we rode back to the compound in trucks. I knew I had made it now, the rest was downhill. Two of the navy SEALs who did the swim were both complaining about how hard it was—I just grinned. Of course, they had to clarify that it wasn't that *hard*. Just harder than the army had a right to demand.

Hon Tre Island—The second week

March 20, 1969, we all headed down to the waiting choppers for the ride over to the island. Our Special Forces NCO yelled at us over the roar of the turbines as he moved from ship to ship.

"Don't cluster up when you unass the ships. Move up the hill and meet by the tree line."

The three choppers lifted up, and we were off. I watched from the open door. The pilots seemed to be having fun, flying in formation.

We had been in the air for about twenty minutes when I saw the island. As we approached, I looked down and saw a beautiful sandy shore that formed a giant U-shape around the island. The jungle followed the steep hill straight down to the bleached-white beach. The ocean was breaking right up on the sand and was less than twenty yards from the jungle. The color of the water was a milky light blue, and as you looked farther out, it got darker. What impressed me was the lack of civilization. There were no hotels, resorts, or people. A place like this anywhere else in the world, and some asshole real-estate developer would have a string of hotels down there.

The pilot put our ship into a steep bank. I held onto the tran-som support behind me. As we landed, I noticed that CIDG strikers were already on the island, pulling security, setting up camp. It reminded me of a scout camp when I was a kid.

We hopped out of the chopper and moved toward the trees. It lifted up and circled back toward Nha Trang for another load of students. We went right to work. There was no time for grab-ass in this school.

Reynolds and I walked past a group of strikers. They had brought along a bag of live ducks for dinner. Later, on our way back to our bivouac area, we walked past the same group of strikers. One was preparing a meal.

I stopped and watched as he pulled a cute little duck from his gunnysack, set the bird on his lap, and started gently pet-ting it. Then, with what seemed the sharpest knife I had ever seen, he reached under the duck's throat and cut it wide open. The bird remained still, as the striker continued to stroke its back.

A second soldier held a pan under the bird, and soon all of the duck's blood had been collected. It was not the least bit cruel to watch; you could almost see the respect these people had for their animals and the honor in such a simple ritual. Still it was repulsive. The second cook made a sauce from the blood, to be poured on the nightly rice ball that was a striker's main diet.

The next morning, I asked Reynolds what he'd like for breakfast. Spaghetti, or beef and rice? Disgusted and still half-asleep, Reynolds pointed to the beef and rice? I took out a ball of C-4, brushed the leaves away on the ground, and set the ball of plastic explosive in the center of three rocks. Reynolds handed me his matches. I lit the C-4 and placed my canteen cup over the flame. Within seconds, the water was boiling hot and ready for a LRP ration.

Duty walked over with a chili-con-carne LRP open, ready for the boiling water. As I poured the water over the dehydrated ration, I noticed that none of the strikers were anywhere around. Reynolds handed me his canteen cup for the cocoa. It began to warm up. I loved this time of day, because it reminded me of hunting trips in the mountains with my uncle Floyd.

Duty found a leech balled up under his arm. It was almost two inches long, and he was excited over the opportunity for a little revenge. He set the leech on the ground and field stripped his claymore. He looked around, then opened it with his knife and took out a small piece of the C-4 explosive from the mine.

He then wrapped a small piece of C-4 around the leech and lit it. The leech stood straight up, then disappeared, as if it never existed.

"Some fun, huh, Duty-Pie?"

He put the two pieces of his claymore back together.

"You'd better not let these Special Forces guys see you do that, Duty."

Duty ignored my comment.

"Better not count on that claymore when the gooks come," said Reynolds.

"I love to roast leeches, the little bastards!" Duty had a problem coexisting with other life forms.

"And you can always get another leech," said Duty.

The rest of the day was spent shooting almost every rifle the North Vietnamese and Vietcong had. The next day we ran tactical drills and called in a FAC (Forward Air Control).

"Heads down!" Reynolds shouted. "Here she comes!"

It was an air force F-4 Phantom. The jet fired its rockets up on the side of the hill.

Directing those jets was the most fun I ever had—Reynolds agreed.

After leaving Hon Tre Island and returning to the Recondo School compound, we spent the next day relaxing and planning our mission. By being isolated with other recon men from other units, we had the opportunity to talk shop and exchange new ideas. It also gave us a chance to focus on the mission at hand.

This was the day before our graduation mission. We tried to relax and take a few pictures. The mood was lighthearted. I had pictures taken with my team, and our Special Forces instructors, and my new Thai friends. The day ended with a trip into town. I almost missed the trucks when they came to pick us up. I ran out of the hooch and grabbed one of the last seats in the waiting deuce-and-a-half. One of the cocky Marines wasn't so lucky. He saw there was no room in any of our trucks, so he walked over to the ROK Korean's truck. Reynolds told me to watch.

"Watch what?"

"Just watch."

The young Marine climbed up into the back of the truck with eight Korean ROK Marines, all sitting at perfect attention. He sat down as the horrified soldiers watched.

Just then a ROK sergeant came around to the back of the truck and started shouting in Korean and motioning for him to get out.

"He's in the sergeant's seat."

"So?"

"Watch," said Reynolds.

The Marine didn't budge. He had just made the Korean sergeant lose face, and to lose face, for a Korean, was considered worse than dying.

The ROK sergeant pulled the American from the truck, and as we all watched in shock, he came after the Marine wielding an entrenching tool. He was going to kill him in front of his troops to regain his loss of honor.

The young American rolled to the right as the tool came down next to his head, then ducked under the truck. Just then one of the Special Forces NCOs, who was behind the truck, ran over with his pistol drawn.

He started to yell in Korean. The sergeant calmed down. The Marine ran over to the American truck and climbed in over the rail and disappeared into the group. We drove off as the Korean sergeant was getting an ass chewing in front of his men by his Korean lieutenant, who looked as if he would kill the guy.

We heard later that he got the shit beat out of him. The event reinforced my belief that we would never understand any of these Asian people.

9 Graduation Week

During the third week of training, the school sent out six teams: sixty men, not counting the two Korean Marine teams and one team of Thai Special Forces troops. Our ground support would come from the Recondo School cadre and one company of strikers—about two hundred CIDG mercenaries.

In the area where we'd be pulling our training mission, there were no villages, no civilians, and no friendlies. We would be in Indian country. Our graduation mission was to search out, locate, and then outguerrilla the NVA.

At first light, 0500, we lifted off from the chopper pad and swung around toward the east. This was new terrain for all of us, except for Msg. Louis Lepage, our Special Forces Recondo School team advisor.

Last week was for fun, four days of field-training exercises on Hon Tre Island. This week would be for real. No more school, this was it. I was excited and scared at the same time.

This was unlike most of the missions I'd been on back in I Corps. For one thing, I didn't know my teammates well.

Prior to Recondo School, some of the teams I had been out with had allowed guys to smoke cigarettes on missions, as long as they kept it concealed. Wearing insect repellent was taken for granted when the bugs got too bad. Some of my non-Recondo-trained team leaders even cooked in the field.

Not this mission! Smoking was not even up for discussion. The gooks didn't wear insect repellent, and neither did we.

The enemy could smell it on you and locate your position. Cooking was out of the question. Rations were eaten cold.

Some team leaders back at my unit, after a few days in the bush, would relax patrol discipline if it appeared to be a cold AO. They assumed that, because there was no sign of the enemy, they could let up.

On one such mission, on the last day out, we had a grenade-throwing contest a few hours before the choppers came in to pick us up. I threw a WP grenade and started a fire on the LZ, so I had to diddy bop out in the open and put it out. Not too smart.

Of course, that was at our loosest, most slack. And not all SF—or Recondo School—recon teams were so strict as to do without insect repellent. We had Master Sergeant Louis Lepage, and Lepage was something of a Recondo School legend. Miller had gone through a year earlier, and he still talked about him.

Our chopper picked up air speed as it leveled off at nine hundred feet. I looked over and saw the pilot's airspeed indicator registering ninety knots. The ride lasted about as long as our trips to the Game Preserve back in the mountains west of Hue but not quite as long as our deep patrols on the far side of the A Shau Valley.

My mind raced, thinking about the SF camp that had been overrun by Soviet-built PT-76 tanks. I had never even thought of the gooks having that kind of shit.

I was more nervous about this mission than any previous patrol, even though this was *only* a routine training mission.

The Huey made a sharp turn toward the west, my mind drifted back to Camp Eagle and my first contact with Special Forces.

Ray Zoschak and I had been visiting MACV-SOG's FOB-1, having a few beers with the Special Forces NCOs who ran CCN (Command and Control North) missions out of FOB-1— some of them into Laos and North Vietnam. We had heard that CCN operated with indigenous tribesmen, Chinese Nung mercenaries and other exotic types, on their teams. Our missions must have seemed like Girl Scout cookie runs to them.

We'd been drinking and bullshitting around. I noticed several glass cases set up around the combination hooch-bunker drinking facility. One, in particular, caught my attention. I walked up for a closer look, and inside the case was a blood-stained green beret with a rather large bullet hole through it. I couldn't believe someone had made a display case for this dead guy's beret.

The SF soldiers made it seem like a big deal, like these guys really cared for each other. When someone got killed in any other unit, it was about as personal as filling out a subscription to *Sports Illustrated*. You didn't keep their gear around to bring back the bad memories. That would have made them seem like real human beings. They were just cherries or old foul dudes or lifers. Anything but people.

I about shit when I discovered that Zo loved the idea of these death shrines. He couldn't wait to get back to Camp Eagle so he could go to work making his own glass case. I thought I was bad, but Zo was a little too gung ho for me.

My thoughts of Camp Eagle and FOB-1 disappeared as I noticed the two Huey gunships flying up behind us. I could only catch a glimpse of them every so often. The copilot of our slick turned back toward me, his dark visor reflecting my green-black face. He raised one finger acknowledging that we were almost there. I wondered if I would remember everything we had learned in the last two weeks. I really wanted to do this right.

A small hole in the dense jungle became visible as the Huey neared the LZ. I could feel the adrenaline pumping as the two escorting gunships began to circle the landing zone. One of them pulled in close to our slick, and I saw the pilot's face.

I reached in my shirt and rubbed my Thai Buddha. Am-Nuay, my Thai buddy, had given it to me three days before we left.

"VC no can shoot you now! Buddha protect you," he said. I sure hoped he was right.

Our pilot eased forward on the control stick, and the nose of our helicopter dipped toward the jungle below. All of my senses went on red alert. I felt like I had to shit! I tightened my stomach so there wouldn't be an accident.

I was to be the first one out. As I said a silent prayer, the chopper surged forward, then flared. I was outside on the skid, and I could see the ground coming up fast. Thirty feet, twenty feet, ten feet. It was time to go.

I pushed off, and all one hundred pounds of web gear, ammo, and rucksack propelled me forward. As my right foot hit the jungle floor below, I felt my leg buckle with the weight I was carrying. I fell, almost in a controlled run. Almost.

The sound of the chopper was deafening. The weight of my pack was pushing me down. My right knee hit the ground, then my right shoulder, and finally my face, headfirst into the ground.

After medical training last week, I had decided to redo my ruck and put all my medical supplies in an extra claymore bag, jury-rigged to the top of my pack. It was just enough weight to throw me off balance.

I fought back to my feet and moved off the LZ and into the jungle. Blood was trickling down my face, but I was more embarrassed than hurt.

I wasn't a cherry. I'd been in the bush for seven months. Twelve LRP missions, and I'd pull an idiot stunt like this? Sergeant Roberts, who'd seen me fall, just shook his head, turned, and disappeared into the brush.

Within seconds the helicopter was gone, and it became deathly still.

"Team six is on the ground," Silva, the floppy-hatted U.S. Marine had called in the first sitrep.

"Commo check. Over," . . . *buzz*. The sound of static filled the silence between communication.

Buzzz . . . "Roger that. Lima Charlie out."

We quickly moved about one hundred meters off the LZ and set up in a tight perimeter. Our advisor had designated me as point man of the ten-man team. Ten men was too big for a recon team, too small for a good heavy team. Still, I would have been confident with any sized element, as long as Msg. Lepage was our advisor.

Sfc. Cliff Roberts, 5th Special Forces, commanded respect before he even opened his mouth. This was his fourth tour in Nam and second assignment at Recondo School. Mistake was not a word in his dictionary.

Lepage was along only as an observer. The plan was that each member of the training team would take turns at various jobs, from team leader to point man. He would be grading us.

Harry Duty, originally from a small town in Tennessee and more recently from our own 75th Rangers, was packing a LAW and walking slack behind me. Sp4c. Santiago Serna, a 173d LRP from N Company, 75th Rangers, was the number four man, behind me, Duty, and Lepage. He had the artillery radio in his ruck.

Lt. Richard A. Korey, one of the two officers on the team, was a SF lieutenant. The other was a REMF SF captain, just out to earn his Recondo patch. The lieutenant was headed up north to FOB-1 and, man, was he gung ho! Funny, he didn't look the part. Korey looked more like a CPA. He'd spent the past week trying to convince me to 1049 to Special Forces for assignment to a SOG team. We became good friends. He would later be listed as MIA.

Don "Hooch" Caldwell started out as tail gunner and was the tenth man on the team, one of the most important people on the patrol. A good tail gunner can sterilize your trail so no one knows you were ever there. He would often remain behind for fifteen to twenty minutes to make sure no one was following. Tail gunner was as important a position as point.

It didn't bother me much that a SF instructor was only a few meters behind me watching every move I made. I was good at walking point. It was a lot like deer hunting, and

I was good at that. Even so, Lepage was the type of Special Forces soldier who would even make John Wayne feel uncomfortable.

I got out my map and compass. My team leader and I shot a heading through the mountainous terrain. After we verified our coordinates, we set off on our patrol route. Working for the Forest Service during the summer had made map reading a snap for me.

The first day, we humped for ten hours and found no sign of the enemy. We took turns at different positions, took one meal break in midafternoon, tightened our equipment, and shook off the leeches. Without cigarettes or insect repellent, getting rid of leeches seemed impossible. Then Lepage passed back a taped-up shaker of salt. It killed the leeches quicker than insect repellent.

Late in the afternoon, we stopped and took a short rest break, waited for dusk, then started up again. We had a point on the map that we wanted to reach before it got too dark. After a ten minute halt, we started off again.

We covered only five hundred meters that first day. Sometimes, we covered a lot of ground. But most of the time we traveled at a painfully slow pace. If we suspected the presence of enemy troops in the vicinity, we would slow the pace down to a crawl, concentrating on noise discipline and movement control.

Slow motion patrolling was more tiring than busting brush and hauling ass—a lot more tiring.

One of the tactics we used to check if we were being tailed was to set an ambush on our back trail. Once we felt clean, we moved the team of ten men slowly up and along a sidehill into the thickest cover we could find. I noticed how the green canopy above became denser, while the valley floor below opened up and made it easy for us to observe any enemy movement. I'd been in areas exactly the opposite. Vegetation patterns were the result of drainage patterns. I remembered that from class, but I guess I'd figured it out before and just didn't know that I knew it.

We moved into a thicket, and spaced ourselves out about five feet apart, close enough to be able to touch each other in the pitch-black of a triple-canopy night. Then we went about the task of stringing out our claymore mines.

I crept down about thirty feet from where I planned to sleep and spread the legs on my claymore mine. It read THIS SIDE BACK. The blast from a claymore would throw out seven hundred steel ball bearings like a shotgun blast, except that this shotgun blast would level everything in a 120 degree arc for up to fifty meters away. The backblast could kill, too, so claymores couldn't be placed too close in.

In total darkness, if you held the claymore to your belly, and it curved around your body, you knew it was pointed out toward the enemy and not back at you. If you screwed up, got in a hurry, set your claymore facing the wrong way, and detonated it, there wouldn't be enough of you to send home in a letter. This knowledge made me extra cautious when setting out my claymore.

I was concerned about my weapon jamming.

The CAR-15 was a shorter, cut-down, commando version of the M-16. It was nearly perfect in size and capability for recon operations. The only problem, other than the extra noise and the muzzle flash it produced, was the shorter internal piston. It was no problem unless you fired it on full automatic. Then, the CAR-15 might get out of sync and feed two into the chamber at one time, causing it to jam—and I had an older CAR. Sometimes it would chamber two rounds at the same time. This was a common problem. A lot of LRPs wouldn't have anything to do with CAR-15s, and others distrusted the standard M-16 even more. I carried a cleaning rod, duct-taped to the CAR. If my weapon jammed, I would pull off the rod and push it through the barrel, until the jammed round flipped out. I got pretty fast at clearing a jam. I wrote my uncle Floyd about it, and he wrote back that he would send me his Winchester 44-40 if I wanted it. What I wanted wasn't Uncle Floyd's 44-40.

Setting up a claymore ambush the way I learned it back at L Company was not something you would ever see in a Special Forces training manual. Chet the Jet taught me to crimp the metal blasting cap with my teeth.

I carried a wooden box full of blasting caps. I took one from the wooden container and had just slipped the female end over the electrical cord. I bit down lightly, thinking, *I hope I can still do this right.*

The sight of an LRP crimping a blasting cap with his teeth was considered real macho but very dangerous. Lepage almost had a cow when he saw me do it.

"Didn't the army issue you any brains, or were you just born stupid?"

I stopped. Lepage had a way of whispering that sounded a lot like yelling.

Some of the bad habits I'd picked up before Recondo School were coming to the surface. After the whispered tongue-lashing by Lepage, I moved back to my spot on the perimeter. Only two men were permitted to eat at a time, the other members of the team pulling security. After an hour, it was my turn to eat.

I pulled the tape from the spaghetti LRRP ration I had prepared the day before. I ate quietly and was ready for my night watch shift. All nature calls were done Special Forces style. You had to relieve yourself by kneeling down to piss, and you had to piss directly on a leaf or a bush so that it made no sound. If you stood up and just pissed on the leaves like guys in line units did, any NVA or VC within a hundred feet could hear you. We also had to stay in close to take a shit and bury it with the paper.

I had just returned from burying a pile, when it suddenly dawned on me where the term "case of the ass" had come from. The paper! I would like to personally castrate the asshole who sold the army that number ten-gauge, one-and-a-half-inch-wide toilet paper we had to use.

Larry Chambers in uniform at different stages of his military career.

Chambers with
his CAR-15.

Chambers with
captured NVA
barbecue supplies.
(rice, a pig and
a rocket launcher
—what more could
you ask for?)

Linderer (L),
Chambers (R), and
Miller (C) after
black box mission
—Chambers and
Miller inflicted
each other's
wounds.

The opening ceremony for Recondo School.

Rappelling down tower 1st week of school.

Dan Roberts (L), Somphorn (C), and Chambers (R). Giving us Buddhas to wear for protection.

After killer run, Somnuek (L), Duty (C), rest of company behind.

Thai soldiers practicing American radio procedures.

Maps and captured enemy radio from Recondo School missions.

Helicopter landing on Hon Tre Island.

The one tree on the island, everyone struggling for its shade.

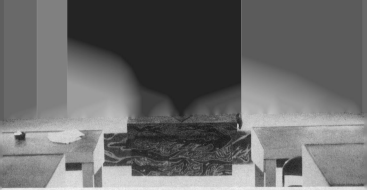

Graduation photo of Somnuek, Charee, Am-Nuay and Chambers.

Larry Chambers' hard-won Recondo School graduation certificate.

Chambers, Closson and Linderer a few days before the lightning strike mission.

Boom Boom Evans (L), Reynolds (C), unidentified, Zo holding radio on right.

NVA trail markings as listed in the notebook of an NVA soldier.

No one I knew back home had the constitution to use that stuff. No one had fingers that small. I would like to have a dollar for every time I got shit on my hands trying to use toilet paper designed for a hamster. The only real nonwar use it could possibly have served would be as fine-grade sandpaper for smoothing doll furniture. I wondered if Nixon ever used this stuff. I guess that's what you get when you accept the lowest bid.

After six days in the jungle, the combination of stale sweat and plain old body odor made us all stink. But the smell could actually be an advantage. Your diet gave you a distinct aroma. The gooks smelled like rotten fish. We had been eating Vietnamese indigenous rations for the past two weeks, just to pick up their smell. If any trail watchers got downwind from our team, they would just think we were another VC unit. Besides, smelling a little ripe was considered the mark of a veteran.

With the last bit of evening ritual behind us, we settled in for the night. The watch was passed from left to right, and once you turned over your watch, you could catch a few hours of sleep. If you fell asleep during guard duty in Recondo School, you were out—if it didn't get you killed.

This was also critical on a Ranger team. Falling asleep, or making any loud noises such as snoring, on a mission was reason enough to be kicked off a team and transferred that same day to a line unit.

Caldwell, a Shake 'n Bake sergeant from the 173d Airborne was about five feet to my right. Duty was five feet to my left. I had set up my sleeping spot on a narrow animal trail, so I could stretch out. I was twenty meters above the main trail and as far away from Sergeant Lepage as I could get.

To complicate matters, we were sleeping on the side of a hill. From this position, we could monitor the trail throughout the night and still remain undetected. Since we were such a large team, we only had to pull two one-hour shifts, instead of the usual three shifts that a smaller Ranger team had to pull.

My first watch started at 2200 and lasted until 2400 hours. My next shift was six hours later. It would become a real test of endurance just to stay alert after thirteen hours of humping the jungle with a hundred pounds of water, ammo, hand grenades, and other explosives on my back. Fortunately, I was used to it.

There were advantages and disadvantages to being on a Ranger team before you came to Recondo School. You already had a lot of jungle smarts. You could function under all kinds of conditions, and you had highly developed methods of keeping yourself awake, such as jabbing yourself in the leg with your knife and planting sharp rocks under your ass. The disadvantages were the bad habits you'd picked up. A GI is basically lazy, so you learned how to do things the easiest way.

The purpose of Special Forces Recondo School was to teach you to be better than your enemy. This meant taking advantage of his weaknesses and not allowing yourself to become complacent. Recondo School stressed things like not using insect repellent, even if the mosquitoes were driving you crazy, and not traveling down open trails.

Even in choosing a camp site, we learned to take a little more time and be a little extra crafty. We would always choose two NDPs a hundred yards apart. At the first site, we would go through the motions of setting up our perimeter, even sitting down and eating. After it got dark, we would sneak away to the second site, where we would spend the night. In Special Forces a shortcut was never the right way. It was the same among LRP/Rangers, but the SF instructors at Recondo School didn't trust us to do the right thing. They made us do things right.

During my first watch, I found myself thinking of old girlfriends, wild parties, and all the good times I'd had back home. I also thought about coming face-to-face with the enemy. The same old questions ran through my mind . . . again.

How would I react if they came tonight? Would I open up on them? No, that would give our position away. Blow my claymore? No. Well, maybe . . . Alert the team leader? Sure . . . but I couldn't see my hand in front of my face, so how would I even find him to alert him? Would I freeze? What if they just walked right in?

Six hours passed, and it was my watch again. It had gotten a little colder and a little damper, and the jungle had become pitch black. Every sound was amplified.

"Chambers, man!" Duty was shaking me violently.

"Yeah, what?" I murmured, trying to open one eye to see.

"Take the watch and don't kill any gooks tonight. I've got this wet dream planned with two round-eyes, and I don't want to be disturbed."

I was already bored. I tried to stay awake. Some teams pulled forty-five minute watches, and even thirty-minute shifts, depending on how tired they were. An hour could seem like an eternity now.

I wondered what was my old college girlfriend doing tonight? Probably getting laid. What were all those war protesters I read about in California doing tonight? Possibly getting laid. Everyone was getting laid—everyone but us. I hadn't even been able to get laid on my free night in town.

I could barely see my watch. I had to hold it right in front of my eyes to see the greenish glow that illuminated the numbers on its face. To keep awake, I did multiplication tables in my head. Anything to keep awake.

My mind wandered back again to northern California, Corning High School, and girls. I had tried not to develop any serious feelings for any one girl—feeling can get you killed here.

But you couldn't stop all the feeling all the time, especially at night. God, I would kill to be with a girl. Just to feel for someone. I went back to dreaming.

I pictured myself driving up to school in a '62 white Corvette, top down, Credence Clearwater blasting on the radio. I'd be wearing new Converse, low-cut, black tennis shoes on my feet—no jungle boots. My friend Bedillion's new GTO is parked behind me. I'd pull up, and there is Vickie Barbo . . .

I was dreaming with my eyes open—a dangerous thing to do.

Suddenly, I looked up and saw a pair of green eyes staring back at me from no more than ten feet away. My first thought was that it was a gook. But gooks were human, and human eyes don't glow.

It started moving toward me—whatever it was. It came slowly at first, then faster. I had no time to react. The thing tried to run past me, but my position on the trail blocked it— so it jumped in my lap! The thing was doing a wheely on my groin. I slapped at it, and it jumped three feet in the air, then made a sound like a small mountain lion. It landed on Duty, who had been asleep only a few feet away, right on Duty's head with all four feet outstretched!

Duty jumped up, wearing the thing over his face, and ran into the jungle.

Lepage jumped up. With his rifle in hand, he headed toward the commotion.

I realized now that it had to be a mongoose.

Duty ran toward the trail, with the creature holding on. He tripped over Sp4c. Emanuel, who was sleeping, wrapped up in his poncho liner. Now he was rolling on the ground, desperately trying to get free.

"Get that guy down and quiet!" Lepage whispered harshly.

By now, the mongoose was as terrified as Duty. He released his hold on Duty's face and ran down his back. Fortunately, it didn't bite him, or Duty would have gone into cardiac arrest. Duty-Pie scrambled to his feet and took off again.

Caldwell put his foot out and tripped him as he went by. Then we both jumped on top of him. We rolled down the embankment in a cluster. I put my hand over Duty's mouth, and Caldwell tried to restrain him.

"It's okay, Duty—you ain't shot. It's okay! It's gone. It was only an animal."

"Yeah," Caldwell said. "It was just a fucking little critter. You know, a gook beaver, or something."

We climbed back up the hill to our positions. I was fighting to hold back my laughter.

"Chambers, this is your fault!" Duty whispered.

"What are you talking about? What am I supposed to do about animal attacks? I must have missed that part of the course," I retorted.

"Shhhhh." We could hear Lepage hissing in the background. He had settled the team down. He was not very amused at the whole affair.

When we got back into position, Lepage decided to pick up and move to a new location, just in case we'd been compromised.

Caldwell got on the radio and told C & C we may have been spotted. We picked up our claymores and put them in our rucksacks. Since we slept with our web gear and boots on, all that was left was to ruck up and move out.

I hoped the dinks hadn't heard all the commotion. If they had, they would be all over the area by first light. We moved for nearly an hour before we found a spot that Roberts liked. This had happened to me once before on Burford's team, when we had accidentally bedded down among phosphorescent vegetation. I remember waking up and seeing the outline of every member of the team. The whole AO was full of the stuff. It was dangerous moving a team to a new location in the middle of the night. We sometimes carried a night-vision Starlight scope, but you could hardly walk and look through the scope simultaneously.

I told Duty to keep his eyes open for dinks, animals, and anything else that came his way. He didn't find my comment amusing.

The next morning Duty and I shared a breakfast of cold, beef-and-rice LRP ration. I had prepared the next day's breakfast the night before. By pouring water in the plastic pouch, then slipping it into my pants' pocket, my body heat would warm it during the night. It was a long way from a hot meal, but it wasn't really that bad. We sterilized our NDP, burying any debris and trash left in our NDP. We made sure that there were no signs of having been there.

"Boy, am I glad that the night's over!" I whispered to Duty. "Rumor has it that Lepage is going to nominate you for soldier of the cycle and personally present you the Recondo honor-grad dagger."

Duty was not amused.

The weather started to turn sour, and it began to rain. Everyone had taken his turn as team leader, point man, radio operator, and tail gunner. We were beginning to show signs of fatigue. There were more frequent short water stops and rest halts. The three weeks of nonstop training in the intense heat had taken its toll.

We found a high-speed trail and decided to parallel it to see where it led.

I never told Duty, but this was a dream come true for me. My dad had been a career man, twenty years in the army, a real war hero. He had enlisted in the U.S. Army at seventeen and was an infantry officer and proud as hell of it. He had volunteered for the Alamo Scouts during World War II, and he and his platoon had been sent into Jap islands they hadn't even mapped yet. I really felt like my father's son now.

The rainy mist sapped the color from the jungle vegetation. Everything turned from lush green to dull gray. I stopped the team, listened, then started slowly moving again. I was watching for any telltale signs of the enemy. I scanned the trail for any likely NVA ambush sites.

I liked point. It fit my personality. I had to know first what was going to happen. As a kid, I used to hunt down and open up my Christmas presents while they were still hidden about the house, days before Christmas. There was also a certain respect a team gave a good point man. I wanted that, too.

We were spaced five meters apart and headed up a muddy hill. I noticed a lot of overgrowth in the valley on the right. The slope was very steep there. The fourth man back was carrying the M-79 grenade launcher and was trying to push through the overhanging wait-a-minute vines, when a vine caught on the trigger of his M-79. I heard the soft *tooop* as the weapon fired.

Two or three seconds elapsed before the round impacted about three hundred meters down the hillside. Everyone froze. The echo of the explosion seemed to last forever. I thought Lepage was going to kill us all. The soldier must have had his safety off. Lepage shot us a look that demanded a body count.

We waited ten minutes. Everyone was getting real nervous. Lepage motioned me with a hand signal. Move on!

We moved off the hill silently, down into the valley below.

It had rained the day before, and the ground was getting very slippery. It was difficult to keep your balance. With all the weight on our backs, it was almost impossible not to leave a trail moving downhill.

The enemy may not have known what had happened, but they had to know we were here. That M-79 round had certainly alerted them. Our risk factor had just quadrupled.

We moved off the hill. Suddenly, I spotted something down the trail and halted the team. As the team stood frozen, I moved closer as the team waited motionless behind me. A tree in the ravine below appeared to have some type of markings on it. I decided to check it out. I could see that there were signs on at least two sides of the tree. They were man-made and could only be some type of signal for any NVA in the area. We set up a circular perimeter around the tree as Lepage sketched each marking in his notebook.

At 1500 hours, we started slowly down a side path. This

time I crossed back and forth to throw off any possible ambush attempts that may have been waiting ahead.

The radio buzzed. "Team Six. Sitrep. Over!" Caldwell, the RTO, called in our situation report.

I started getting nervous after seeing the fresh signs of the enemy.

I soon found another tree with similar markings about four feet above the ground. Lepage stopped to record each new enemy sign. The markings were like road signs on a major highway back in the States. I wished that I knew what they meant. For all I knew, we could have been standing in a minefield.

I didn't like it a bit, especially being down in a valley. We were just too damned vulnerable. If we were going to get in a fight, we would be better off on high ground.

Lepage must have been reading my mind. He motioned for me to continue the patrol.

We soon entered a clearing, the kind you often spot deer feeding in back home. I circled slowly around the open clearing, then picked up the trail again on the other side. It took a full twenty minutes to complete the maneuver.

I reached for a tree limb as I started to duck under some overhanging vegetation. I felt something damp and slimy. I stopped and looked at my hand, then studied the object on the other side of the limb. There, just inches from my face, was the biggest wad of green snot I had ever seen. It was fresh, and it was human!

I held up the trophy goober, and I alerted our team leader and pointed to the trophy goober. He grinned—that kind of proud grin a father gave a son when he did something good. I wiped the slime off, onto the side of a tree, and pointed at it for the rest of the team to see. We were getting closer. Then he motioned for me to continue. I moved out, thinking to myself that Lepage really liked this shit!

The tension was building. I could feel my heart pound. I prayed that the gooks wouldn't hear it.

I carefully lifted one foot then the other. I could sense that something was about to happen. I just knew it.

I searched for the outlines of people in the trees ahead. My uncle had taught me how to spot deer in my mind and then look for that image in the woods. Most people did it wrong. They would walk right past a deer standing in cover and never spot him. You have to expect to see your prey. The majority of hunters just see the trees.

I was determined not to lead us into an ambush. For almost an hour, we moved through a mass of tangled vegetation.

Then, it happened—thirty meters ahead I saw the form of a man outlined in the mist. He seemed like a ghost. One minute, he was there; the next minute, he was gone. I raised my weapon as he suddenly rematerialized before me. I blinked once to make sure I wasn't seeing things. He was still there, trying to confirm that he, too, had spotted something.

He was on one knee. He turned his head back like he was talking to someone behind him—that was his mistake!

I fired, putting three rounds into the side of his head. It exploded like a melon with the impact of the rounds. He spun around and collapsed.

There was movement to our ten o'clock and more movement behind the dead NVA. I caught a glimpse of people running down the trail. My ass slammed shut when I heard the high-pitched popping of an AK-47 firing on full automatic. The unforgettable sound of 7.62 mm rounds passing within inches of my head encouraged me to take some kind of action.

I dove for the ground. Limbs were falling all around me. My body seemed to be functioning at half speed. Everything else had gone ballistic.

More rounds cracked overhead. I flipped my selector switch to rock 'n' roll and sprayed the area to my front. I emptied my magazine into the enemy position.

Rounds were now coming in from both sides. I emptied my second magazine into the jungle ahead. Then I turned to run for the rear of the patrol, as I had been taught.

My slack man was not there to back me up. He had lit out along our back trail with the first shots. I was alone. This was not my Ranger team—I didn't really know these guys, and they didn't know me. We had been taught to fire, then leapfrog back to the end of the patrol line. Each man in the column would cover the man to his front as he withdrew. In this manner, there was a continuous hail of fire keeping the enemy at bay until the entire team had broken contact. It worked when each man did his job, but in my case, my slack man had failed to perform. I looked back toward the tree line, fired what I had left in my magazine, and dropped to the ground. Well, if I couldn't retreat, then the bastards weren't going to shoot me in the back. I knew I was about to die.

I looked over my shoulder and saw some of the teammates running to the rear, thirty meters back up the trail. Where in the hell's Duty? Where's Lepage? Where's my fucking back-up? This was definitely not the way we rehearsed it back in training.

I jerked open my ammo pouch, and grabbed a full magazine. Then I heard someone yelling down the trail behind me.

"Get your cherry asses down!"

Lepage was headed to the front. He nearly knocked the Special Forces captain on his ass, trying to get to my position.

He was a sight to see! Lepage burst on the scene like John Wayne, firing the M-79 grenade launcher and screaming at the top of his lungs, "Get down! Get out, out of my way!"

One of his rounds impacted twenty meters to my front.

The next round hit a tree ten feet away and bounced back over our heads. When the round hit, it had not traveled the necessary distance required to arm it. So it didn't explode. Our luck had taken a definite turn for the better.

I was now on my fifth magazine. I flipped open my second ammo pouch. Shit, this was it! The rest of my ammo is in my ruck.

Seconds later, Duty-Pie showed up with guns ablazing. He had charged up from the fourth position to help Lepage and me deal with the situation. This was Duty's second tour as a LRP/Ranger, and he knew his shit, and he was fearless!

There we were—Duty, Lepage, and me, out front, earning our combat pay. Lepage maneuvered toward the enemy position, firing the grenade launcher as fast as he could reload.

Funny, once the action started, it seemed almost like a game. Duty and I started lobbing frags on the enemy position.

As the first grenade exploded, the entire North Vietnamese Army opened up on us. We had pissed somebody off. We began to pull back. We had no idea how many enemy soldiers were in front of us, but it was becoming obvious that there were at least a couple hundred more than we could handle.

For all we knew, we could have been in a fight with the point element of an entire NVA regiment. It was time to confuse the enemy by changing tactics.

We ran like hell!

We caught up with the rest of the team, fifty meters up the trail. Still on the run, Lepage called in our coordinates over the radio.

"Contact, contact!" Lepage called on the run.

"Team six in contact with unknown number of November-Victor-Alpha. Request fire mission. Over!"

He was running, dragging the radioman's cord—and the radioman—behind him.

"Fifty meter Hydra-burst, Willie-Pa pa! Grid coordinates, five Lima three Roger! From my last sitrep! Fire for effect. Over!"

Lepage kept moving.

Within seconds, we had arty screaming in overhead. We could hear the 155 round bursting in the air as we sprinted up the trail.

Twenty minutes later, we stopped to catch our breath. Sixty seconds later, Lepage started barking orders.

"OK, get your butts up, and let's move! They know we're here now! We got to cover some ground and find a good place to lay dog. We can't put the strikers in until first light."

"Man! If we hit the point element of a battalion, we could be history by morning," Duty whispered to me. He didn't seem too upset at the prospect—just excited.

Finally, Lepage pulled the team into a thicket that provided some decent cover. If they hit us in the darkness, we would blow all our claymores and E & E to the top of the mountain.

We decided that our best course of action would be to stay put and wait until dawn. No one ate. No one talked. No one got much sleep. We put out only two claymores, trying to be as quiet as possible. We heard movement all night. The gooks were busy looking for us.

At 0315 hours, I was on watch—as was everyone else. Lepage slid over next to me to discuss what would happen if we got hit. He was noticeably pissed off at some members of our team, and so was I.

"You guys did a hell of a job out there today. I owe you one. I'm buying the beer when we get back," he whispered.

First light found Lepage in a foul mood. HQ wanted to know what we hit, and we were supposed to go back. Lepage wanted me to take point, with Duty on slack, and him right behind to cover our asses.

It was very dangerous retracing our steps, and we knew it. But there was even greater danger in not knowing what, and who, we had run into. Sometimes I forgot how expendable we were. MACV-SOG wanted to know more. And as paratroopers, we were earning fifty-five extra dollars a month to find out.

Our simple training mission had turned into a real Recondo adventure, with the possibility of discovering an entire NVA battalion less than a klick away.

Lepage briefed us. He told us what to expect. The training mission was over. There were no reports of enemy units in the AO before our mission. MACV hoped that we had discovered the reinforced NVA battalion that had hit the SF camp up in the Central Highlands.

"No more trade-offs!" Lepage whispered. "Chambers goes

to point. Duty at slack, and the rest of you stay in your same position as yesterday. This time, if anyone forgets procedure and runs, your shit will not be worth taking home. Do you understand me?"

Everyone nodded in agreement.

Each man on the team carried six quarts of water, three frags, a compass, a pen-gun flare, a strobe light, gas mask, one pint of serum albumin, food for six days, an indigenous ground cloth or poncho liner, and two pairs of socks. I usually packed two smoke grenades, one white phosphorous, three frag grenades, and anywhere from sixteen to thirty magazines of M-16 ammo. But that was yesterday. Today, I was down to nine magazines and one grenade. It was not enough to last through a good firefight.

At 1030 hours, the morning rain dropped off to a drizzle, just enough to make the humidity unbearable. For the second time, I sensed that something was about to happen. I was developing a sixth sense. I don't know how to explain it, but when I got that feeling, I paid attention.

I moved slowly back down the trail. An hour later we were back in the area where we had made contact the day before. As I moved closer to the point of initial contact, an NVA in a green uniform stepped out from behind a tree and stood directly in front of me.

For a split second, we both stood there looking at each other. He stared at me, as if he didn't realize who or what I was. I jerked my rifle up, aimed, and started to squeeze the trigger, but at the last second, held my fire.

I suddenly realized that this was another human being looking back at me eye to eye. Some of the Old Foul Dudes used to say that you should never look a man you intend to kill directly in the eyes. Now I knew why! I slowly lowered my rifle.

"Dung lai! Dung lai!" Duty shouted from behind me. "Halt! Halt!"

I knew Duty was covering my slack, and Lepage was behind him, so I decided to take this guy alive, if possible.

Maybe my motives weren't so pure. Maybe I was just afraid to kill him after looking him in the eyes.

The man turned and started to run. I took off after him. Lepage aimed his rifle to blow him away, but I was in his line of fire.

The overhanging branches whipped my face as I chased him off the trail. I reached him just before he disappeared back into the jungle. I nailed him with a flying tackle and came up on top of him.

My body weight smashed him face first into the ground. He cried out in pain. We landed in tall elephant grass alongside the trail and began to wrestle and fight. I heard Lepage and Duty yelling as he reached up and tore my shirt as he struggled to get free. I tried to hold him down with one hand and grab for my rifle with the other. He began to yell for help, and I tried to get him to shut up by putting my hand over his mouth. I couldn't quiet him, but I didn't want to kill him.

Finally, I grabbed his hair, yanked back his head, and jammed the barrel of my rifle down his throat. That did the trick. The man didn't make a peep after that.

While I kept my rifle barrel stuck in his mouth and my legs wrapped tightly around his waist, Duty ran up and searched our prisoner.

"Shit man! This gook's an NVA officer, look at this!" Duty said, pointing at the man's belt. "We just snatched an NVA officer!"

I looked for a weapon and tried to help Duty search the man without loosening my grip. Then I spotted something. A shiny, brass belt buckle, with a bright red star in the center. I had to have it. Nothing else was important. I reached down and jerked the buckle from the terrified NVA. I think he thought I was going to rape him.

"Man, that buckle alone was worth more than five hundred dollars to any REMF," Duty announced.

"Fuck a bunch of REMFs, that baby's mine." I answered, holding the trophy above my head.

It was the trophy of trophies, the crème de la crème—an NVA officer's belt buckle! And I had just liberated it.

Lepage shouted for the team to fan out in a circle and set up security. He ran up to Duty and me and the NVA officer, and looked down at the three of us.

"What the hell do you clowns think you're doing?" he announced in a gruff voice. "You trying to kill him, or are you just trying to scare him to death?

"Chambers, that's not the way to take a prisoner. I almost shot through you to kill that fucker. Don't ever pull a stunt like that again! I couldn't understand what you were up to."

Lepage smiled. "Oh, by the way, Chambers, I wouldn't pull that trigger. You'll blow off your own nuts."

The way I was contorted, my rifle was pointed back at my groin.

Now, our young NVA captive started to go into shock. I tried to talk to him in a calm voice, but he didn't respond. He must've thought we were going to kill him, Korean style, especially after that flying tackle. Rumor ran through the NVA ranks that Korean troops who worked this area loved to take prisoners so that they could use them for Tae Kwon Do practice.

After I pocketed the buckle, Duty and I tied his hands behind his back with his own belt. Lepage taped his mouth shut.

We yanked him to his feet and moved him into the perimeter, as Lepage called for reinforcements. A reaction force from Recondo School was on its way. We were told to hold on to our prisoner, it wouldn't be long before help arrived.

Lepage told me that he was going to try to get me in the Recondo School record books for the first POW by a student.

A short time later, we heard helicopters a few miles out. They were approaching from the southeast. A company of CIDG strikers from the Recondo School were on their way in. The helicopters landed one after another. The strikers set up a perimeter and made a quick sweep of the area. We were all exhausted. I told Duty that finally this mission was about to end. *Boy was I wrong!*

Our perimeter grew, as more reinforcements arrived. Gunships and slicks were circling everywhere. I think it was the first time I had actually felt secure in my seven months in country.

After the last ship came in, Duty and I turned our prisoner over to a rather villainous-looking CIDG captain and his Nung interpreter. The captain was a real badass. No smiles, just pure hatred. His Nung sidekick really had a hard-on for the NVA. Lepage told us that the Vietcong had murdered his whole family five years ago. He now lived only to kill VC and NVA. He did a real efficient job of getting them to talk, too.

Captain Hoang, the CIDG captain, was not quite as crazy, but he, too, was adept at getting information. He took great pleasure in interrogating prisoners. He had been known to connect electrical leads to certain sensitive body parts and then throw the juice to it. Barbaric, but guaranteed to make a deaf mute speak.

Rumor was that he once took two POWs up on a chopper ride for a little early-morning questioning. It seems there was a high-ranking Viet Cong general who had moved into the region. The Captain wanted some fast information. He pushed the older of the two prisoners out the door of the aircraft at nine hundred feet; he fell to his death. Then he turned to the younger prisoner and asked him the same question. The frightened man told him he was the general's aide.

"Where can we find this VC general?" Captain Hoang demanded.

The terrified POW just pointed out the door to the ground below with his chin.

Captain Hoang stopped using that particular technique soon after. But he did have other ways of getting the information he wanted.

Lepage, the CIDG captain, and his interpreter moved

across the perimeter with our badly shaken prisoner, who was just starting to get friendly with me and Duty. The interpreter told me that he thought I was a Korean.

"He very scared of Koreans. Koreans kill everything. Kill old men, women, water buffalo. Then put all the bodies in pile and burn the whole place down. Very glad you no Korean," the interpreter translated.

After about an hour they returned. Lepage announced that they had hit the jackpot. The captured prisoner told them his name was Dinh Thuan and that this was the start of something big. They were not part of the group that had hit the SF camp, but they were down here in preparation for a major offensive. We'd broken up the lead party of a medical-supply unit carrying fresh supplies from the North. A bunch of fresh NVA troops were headed this way.

The enemy we killed the day before were part of an escort of new recruits. Most of them had never before been out of North Vietnam and had never even seen American troops.

"Except for Jane Fonda," Duty added sarcastically.

All U.S. and ARVN bases would be put on alert. Over one hundred bases had been targeted, but we'd screwed up their game plan.

"He thought we were Koreans?" Duty seemed amazed at that.

Roberts told me I was going to walk point for the strikers tomorrow.

"You'll lead the strikers back to where you made contact. I'll take a platoon, drop off the ridge, and move up the valley to link up with you."

I told Duty that we were being set up for the slaughter. He agreed.

"This mission ain't over till it's over," Duty said. "And it seems far from over."

"We'll move out at first light," Lepage added and walked off, smiling at our plight. He had an evil sense of humor. That's one of the things we admired most about him.

Duty tried to sleep but didn't have much luck. Neither did I—at least not at first.

At 0500 hours, on day four of our mission, Duty and I awoke to the sight of smiling Asian Faces. They were everywhere, doing all kinds of shit. It looked more like a Boy Scout Jamboree than an army encampment.

Wet uniforms were drying in the trees. Rice was bubbling over cooking fires; this was the first time I had ever camped with a company-sized unit before. I hoped it would be the last. I could see how people got that false sense of security. I looked around, and there were good guys everywhere. In the Rangers you usually looked around to find bad guys everywhere.

When I volunteered for the Long Range Patrol, all my paratrooper buddies thought I was nuts. Six men, alone, sometimes beyond artillery range and radio contact. If you got your ass in a sling—you were history. *No thanks!* But the guys headed to the line didn't think it through. Sure, they may have had a hundred or so guys stomping around close by. But they were still just a piece of meat. With only six men, we knew we were outnumbered, so we kept alert—the entire team stayed razor sharp—the entire time in the field. But a night with all those indigenous troops, you would have thought Duty and I were at the Holiday Inn. Duty even joked about calling for room service.

Getting started that morning was a real freak show. The noise was unbelievable. By morning, everyone knew that Duty and I had snatched that NVA officer. As we made our way up to the front of the column, several of the strikers gave us the victory sign.

I had dreamed of this moment. I played army when I was a kid, visualizing myself going into combat, leading hundreds of men. Now it was actually happening.

When I was growing up, other kids played cowboys and Indians. I played army. My dad had pulled some real hairy missions on Luzon, and he got wounded on Okinawa. He won a

Bronze Star, and a chest full of lesser medals. He even got wounded again in Korea.

Moving along with all the strikers, I had time to think. Maybe most of what I was doing was really to win my dad's approval, to make him proud of me. In his letters, he never said anything, but I knew he knew what I was doing. I knew that he was bursting with pride.

We moved on. It was very foggy. We couldn't see fifteen feet in any direction. I led a zigzag pattern to avoid any ambushes the NVA might have thrown up along the trail during the night.

As we moved closer to the contact point, everyone seemed to sense the danger and voluntarily kept the noise to a minimum. I slowed the pace down. We moved down the trail, through the valley, and past the opening. It reminded me of an early-morning deer hunt. We passed a rock outcrop.

Wait! What rock outcrop? Rocks? There were no rocks around here! Shit, I don't remember any rocks. Now what the fuck do I do?

You could turn an LRP team of six men around pretty easily, but how do you turn around a company of a hundred or so men, strung out for two hundred meters, particularly when those men don't speak English?

I stopped the company for a five-minute break. I checked my compass then the map. I knew this was right! I just didn't remember those rocks.

We moved another one thousand meters and somehow linked up with Lepage and the rest of the strikers. I was surprised and relieved to run into them. I didn't even tell Duty that I'd thought we were lost.

The sun was now thinning out the fog. We watched as it began to lift out of the valley. I knew we were close. I'd spotted familiar trees and recognizable terrain features.

Duty and I went on ahead, maybe fifteen meters from the strikers.

I slipped my selector switch to full automatic. We were close, real close.

I had taped a double magazine together the night before with a piece of duct tape. This time I would have a backup magazine handy without reaching into an ammo pouch.

As we got closer, I could see something in the trail ahead. I stopped the patrol and moved in for a better look. Bingo! We had hit the jackpot! There were ten packs, and numerous blood trails ran off in three different directions. The gooks had been hurt bad but had plenty of time to carry off their dead, set booby traps, and dig in.

Lepage stopped the column and put his men to work. Strikers were everywhere, picking up NVA packs, medical supplies, and searching for bodies. They didn't seem to worry about booby traps as they policed up all of the NVA gear.

Duty and I were part of the security force, protecting the strikers while they finished searching the area.

I got nervous after a while. We were spending too long in one spot. It was getting late in the afternoon, and I was beginning to feel the fatigue of three-weeks', nonstop training and four days of constant stress.

This Recondo School training mission had been as rough as any LRP mission I had been on back in I Corps. I could barely keep my eyes open whenever we took a short break.

I tried to joke with Lepage, asking him if I could bring that forty-pound sand bag next time we went out. He didn't think it was very funny.

I overheard Lepage talking on the radio about getting extracted. But the nearest LZ was so small that only one Huey at a time could set down.

I saw Lepage and the CIDG captain talking.

The fog was beginning to creep back in, and I was getting really worried that we'd have to spend another night in the bush. No one wanted that. But Lepage seemed to be gaining new strength, and he was at least fifteen years older than any of us.

Surely he would call for an extraction soon.

We spent a good part of the afternoon pacing back and forth in the triple-canopy jungle. I saw Lepage with my captured NVA officer. The prisoner looked terrified. Lepage had him in a STABO rig, sitting there on his ass in the center of the clearing. A STABO rig is a harness worn into combat that could double as an emergency extraction rig.

I walked over and sat down beside him. He looked up and tried to smile. He was afraid and somehow knew what was going to happen next. Our interpreter sat with me and the young NVA officer. The prisoner started crying; he told the interpreter that his men would shoot him out of the sky as he was lifted to the chopper.

A lone chopper soared overhead. A rope dropped through the right skid. The POW was going up alright, but he wasn't going to be winched into the helicopter. He was going to get the scenic route back to Nha Trang on the long end of a one hundred-foot rope.

Lepage ran over and grabbed the rope, clipped it to the STABO rig, and the NVA officer was bye-bye!

The helicopter lifted its load clear of the trees and sped away, with the POW dangling one hundred feet or so beneath the chopper. He was on his way back to Nha Trang and the Kit Carson training school for turncoats and traitors.

Lepage told me there was a three-ship LZ at grid coordinates Lima 10 Uniform 5.

I looked on my map, and from the center grid, all I had to do was count to the left ten and up five. *Oh great!* I could tell by the contour lines that we would be traveling uphill all the way to the LZ. I had a theory about recon missions—the last day was always uphill. I could never understand it.

Hours later, we had reached our limit. Our graduation mission was almost over, and it had been one that none of us would ever forget. The lack of sleep and the excitement had left us physically, mentally, and emotionally drained.

"Here come the slicks. Birds inbound," Lepage informed us.

The choppers looked like bees in a swarm as they moved over the ridgeline.

As the second ship touched down, Duty and I ran for the right side. I pulled myself into the chopper cabin. I took a seat on the floor next to the door gunner and faced out.

I grabbed hold of the troop seat behind me and held on. The Special Forces bellyman stepped on my right hand as he helped Duty in, but since I was safely aboard, I didn't really care. I flashed him a peace sign. He was speaking into his helmet mike as the chopper began to lift off.

The chopper vibrated and rocked to one side. The shrill, high-pitched whine of the turbines was reassuring after four days out in the jungle. We climbed up slowly to about fifty feet, then the pilot nosed her down and tore across the valley.

The pilots contoured the terrain, hugging the ground fifty feet off the deck. We were heading back toward the city of Nha Trang and the safety of MACV Recondo School.

As we flew into the darkness, all we could see was the glow of the green cabin lights. It was almost pitch-black outside. After twenty minutes or so, we saw the city, and it was beautiful. We must have been cruising at max speed.

I was on the right side; when the pilot slid the chopper around to the left, it gave one the sensation of flying sideways. I loved it. I could feel the warm air as it rushed into the cabin. I was not the least bit tired. Not now! I was too busy enjoying the exhilaration.

I thought about what had happened the past few days. *I captured an NVA officer, and I got his belt buckle to prove it. I can't wait to show the guys back at Camp Eagle.*

We set down on the Recondo School tarmac. I jumped out and spotted my two Thai Special Forces buddies, Sergeant Am-Nuay and his sidekick, Sergeant Somnuek. They were there to meet us. Was I glad to see those guys! As we walked back to our hooch, I couldn't keep the smile off my face.

Everyone had to see the NVA officer's belt. The news of

our success had preceded our return. All the other teams had come in the day before. We were like heroes returning from the hunt. But this was Recondo School, and this was the army. We had a debriefing at 2100 hours, to go over the entire mission in detail. This was just another day at the school—Recondo School!

Lepage announced there would be no morning formation, just a private graduation party at the Playboy Club later that night.

I asked Lepage if Duty and I could stay and go out with him on the next cycle's training mission 'cause we had so much fun. He just grinned and walked into his hooch.

Reynolds, Duty, Dan Roberts, and I graduated and returned to Camp Eagle. Our new Thai friend Sgt. Sookpool An Nuay was awarded the honor grad's dagger, and I had a new NVA belt buckle.

10 <u>All Lit Up</u>

I was startled out of a sound sleep. It was Tubby Closson, shaking me. I tried to pull the poncho liner over my head, but he kept pulling it off.

"Closson, get out of my face, and leave me the hell alone!"

But the big, baby-faced sergeant stood there—fucking with me until I got up.

"OK! What?" I said.

"Be at my hooch in fifteen minutes," Closson ordered, then turned and walked out the door.

I got up, dressed, and sat around for twenty minutes just to piss him off. When I opened the door of my hooch, I was hit with a searing blast of morning heat. It was going to be another scorcher. I walked over to Closson's. Gary Linderer was sitting on his cot, reading a letter from his girl.

"Hey, Linderer."

"Hi, man, sit down." Linderer sounded serious. "I've got some bad news." He proceeded to fill me in on our next mission. "The A Shau Valley, man! We might as well be going into Hanoi."

There were so many NVA living in the A Shau that they had their mail delivered there. Linderer told me the last two Special Forces SOG teams that went in had reported unidentified choppers. SOG had two other teams simply vanish in that same area over the past eighteen months.

"Vanish? C'mon Gary, I hate that word—*vanish*. Don't use it again!"

I told Gary that I wasn't crazy about this kind of shit.

"When I signed up to fight the VC, I was told they used homemade crossbows, old rifles, and pungi pits."

"Not anymore they don't!"

Gary was not in the mood for jokes, but I needed to lighten the mood.

"Are you still having that crazy dream where we all get killed?"

Linderer had a premonition back in March. In a dream, he and I were on the same team in the A Shau Valley, and we get killed in a huge explosion during a firefight. Closson, Sours, and Rucker get maimed in the explosion. This dream had been haunting him for almost eight months. And now the events seemed to be playing out right on cue. What was so damned eerie was that we hadn't pulled any missions in the A Shau since 1968, and to top it off, I had never gone out on a mission with him before.

"Look, Gary, don't worry, with all those trail watchers on every fucking hilltop, we'll probably get shot out before we ever get on the ground."

"Thanks! That really makes me feel a lot better, dickweed!" Linderer seemed very agitated, as he paced back and forth the length of the hooch.

In the northwest corner of the A Shau Valley sat an abandoned Special Forces camp that had been overrun by NVA three years earlier. A lot of people had died trying to defend it. The NVA threw everything into holding the A Shau because it was located along the Laotian border and provided a natural conduit between their sanctuaries in Laos and the heavily populated cities along the coastal plain in northern I Corp. They had demonstrated time and time again that they intended to hold on to the valley at all costs.

"We have the honor of being among some of the first Americans to reenter the valley since the 1st Cav got their asses shot off last year. That ought to make you feel that your life is not being sacrificed on some humbug patrol."

Linderer shook his head and walked out of the hooch, headed for the TOC. I followed close behind, still trying to cheer him up.

"OK, Gary, if a plane crashes on the Missouri border, where would they bury the survivors?"

"Jesus, you don't give up, do you, butt-wipe?"

"OK, OK, just trying to help. Have you been to confession yet?"

Gary opened the door, and we walked in. The briefing was already under way. I found a seat next to Rucker. First Lieutenant Guy, the new executive officer, was reviewing intelligence reports with Closson and Sours.

"We've located the 9th NVA Regiment in the vicinity of Base Area 611, in the northern part of the valley. The 6th NVA Regiment is also suspected to be somewhere in the vicinity. Last week, elements of the K3 Sapper Battalion attacked Firebase Berchtesgaden. And the 29th NVA Regiment is bivouacked somewhere in the vicinity of this mountain, called Dong Ap Bia, at coordinates YD 3296."

He pointed to the oversize map that hung on the wall behind him.

"Agents report that several other battalions have recently infiltrated the valley, bringing total enemy strength in the region to approximately thirteen or fifteen thousand combat troops."

Lieutenant Guy told us that aerial reconnaissance indicated that the safest place to insert was in a small clearing next to an old 1st Cav minefield.

I looked over at Linderer, his eyes were the size of silver dollars.

"Jesus! Whose brilliant fucking idea was that?" he asked.

Captain Cardona spoke up. "It's my idea, Sergeant."

"Excuse me, sir, but don't you think that old highway just to the north, or anything but that minefield, would be a little safer?"

"No, Sergeant, G-2 agrees with me," said Captain Cardona. He was Eklund's replacement. "The enemy has radar-controlled 37.5 mm guns ringing the valley. You can't just fly in the front door like the 1st Cav tried to do."

"Great idea," I whispered to Rucker, "the gooks would never think of looking for us in one of our own minefields."

Rucker nodded. Linderer slumped down in his chair, and put his head in his hands, as if he couldn't believe what he'd just heard.

Lieutenant Guy wrapped up the briefing with some good-news/bad-news humor.

"The bad news is . . . no one has the maps to the old mine-fields. But the good news is . . . our first sergeant knows the old SF camp and figures the mines won't blow because they're so old."

"That's it? Too old?"

Linderer got up and stormed out of the TOC. He was speechless. Now he knew the source of the explosion that was supposed to kill us. Gary looked as if he'd just stared death in the face. I felt sorry for him. He had gone through some hairy shit back in November, and now this. It was more than any-body should have to face. I must admit that his premonition was beginning to give us all a bad case of the willies, espe-cially since all five guys in the dream were going to be on this patrol.

My position as senior scout put me out front, walking point. If Linderer's premonition came true, the odds were that I would be the first to die. My overactive imagination kicked into high gear. *Well, I could step on an old land mine. Better yet, with so many dinks out there, I would step on one of them.*

The A Shau Valley was like the valley of the Little Bighorn—big time Indian country. Now I knew how Custer must have felt. It would just be a matter of time before we waltzed into something too big to handle—and we all knew it.

I walked into Linderer's hooch and found him writing an-other incredibly long letter to his fiancée, Barbara. He told me I should write a last letter home, too. Maybe he was right.

I decided to write to Kranig, an ex-101st trooper and one of my best friends at Shasta College. He had gotten shot up a couple years back with the 1st Brigade. I told him to use my ten-grand insurance money to have me stuffed like a mule deer, dressed out in my class A uniform and jumpboots, and mounted on display where all the girls would see me.

I showed the letter to Linderer, but he didn't think it was funny. I told him I was going to get him good and stoned that night.

"What the hell, man," I reasoned. "What can they do to us? We're going to get stoned down on the bunker, and enjoy our last night on earth. If they bust us and send us to Long Binh jail, they'd be saving our lives!"

Gary appreciated the logic in my reasoning, even though he was a typical midwestern farm boy who had never even tried marijuana. It was the first and only time I ever smoked any dew with Linderer. He was so funny, I almost split a gut!

He would hold the pipe like General MacArthur, inhale it, then say, "Six thousand NVA, huh!"

I'd interrupt, "At *least* six thousand NVA, and that's if we get past the minefields."

We sat on that bunker line and killed three bowls of May-Zeus's best dew. This was special dew. May-Zeus kept it in a bag stuffed in his pillow. Mother Rucker came down with a full bottle of Jim Beam. He unscrewed the cap and threw it as hard as he could out into the concertina wire. We killed it in twenty minutes.

"You know this company has gone to the dogs. When Captain Eklund was company commander, he would have never pulled shit like this mission. He cared about us."

Everyone showed up that night. Chet-the-Jet and Miller came by to wish us good luck. Closson started down, then turned and left when he smelled our smoke. I felt like we were at a samurai ceremonial party, the kind the Kamikaze pilots had before taking off.

Gary was worried about being taken prisoner, so that

night, we made a solemn pact. If either of us got all fucked up, the one who was left would make sure the other was not taken alive.

"But don't shoot me in the head." I reminded him about my last request to Kranig.

Linderer finally laughed, and said he would try for a neck shot. That way, I would be presentable for my memorial display. I felt a little better, but still full of apprehension. At least my life was in good hands. I figured that a farm boy from Missouri could easily make a neck shot, so I didn't have anything to worry about.

Closson and Sours went on an overflight the next morning and returned around noon. We sat with them at the mess hall and discussed what they had seen. Closson told us that they had spotted the wreckage of an old Jap plane near the LZ.

"What!"

"Yeah, a real Jap Zero from World War Two, complete with the rising sun painted on its tail section."

"Jesus, that sucker must have been out there for thirty years or so."

"I didn't know the Vietnamese had fought the Japs."

Miller showed up and gave us a complete history lesson on Indochina. He said, "The Vietnamese have fought everybody in Asia—particularly each other." That's what he liked about them.

Everyone was in a very sober mood. I packed my gear Recondo style, even down to the smallest item. That way, if I was killed or wounded at night, my teammates would know where to look for my equipment.

Let's see, left leg, lower pocket: SOI, map, and notebook. Upper left hand pocket: signal mirror. Small pocket, lower leg: mosquito repellent. Right top pocket: compass. Right bottom pocket: pen-gun, flares, and signal panel. Right rear pocket: twine. Upper left, arm pocket: pill kit. Next to my binoculars, I put my Penn-EE reflex camera with its split prism range finder.

I pulled out my Recondo School notes and looked them over.

Hmmm, point-of-origin patrol grid system breaks down into four equal parts, and keeps breaking down. False easting and false northing means right and up. An azimuth is a horizontal, clockwise angle, measured from a baseline . . . I'll never remember this shit.

As I got off my bunk, I was in deep thought, reciting the four lifesaving steps in my head. *One—clear the airway, stabilize the head and back and elevate shoulders. If unconscious turn on stomach . . .*

Two—stop the bleeding. Direct pressure on wound. Pressure points; one, temple; two, jaw; three, clavicle; four, brachial bicep; five, femoral, groin . . . Constricting band is to be tightened only to slow down bleeding when all else fails . . . Protect and dress the wound; if fractured bone, splint above and below the break . . . Prevent or treat for shock . . . If shock has started, do not give morphine . . . Do not inject near wound . . . Replace fluids . . . Use blood expander . . . For sucking chest wound, lay person on wounded side, no morphine, no elevation, check for exit wound . . . Abdominal wounds, do not put organs back inside . . .

As I recited this over to myself, I decided to do a last-minute check fire of my rifle. I got Mother Rucker to go with me. This was not a normal mission, and everyone in the whole company knew it.

We had a good team. Everyone was experienced except for Hillman. He was a quiet kid, but he seemed to have a good head on his shoulders. Larry Closson, our team leader, was the guy I was worried about. He seemed to be a little too gung ho and operated by the book.

Linderer had been a team leader and had seen a lot of shit. Rucker was as crazy as me. Rucker would handle our commo as senior RTO. Sours, too, had been a team leader, and an honor graduate at Recondo School. Everyone but Hillman had at least fifteen missions under his belt.

I was not feeling very confident. I was really worried about this one. I kept reading over the orders for my R & R, just to occupy my thoughts. Australia . . . and I was trying to get an extra leave for capturing that NVA back at Recondo School so that I could go to Hawaii. When I returned, I would be a real short-timer. I intended to pull another mission or two, go on leave, then pull a few more missions. Instead of DEROSing, I would extend my tour and try to get a ghost job in the rear until my ETS. I didn't really want to risk fifteen months in Nam, but I wanted to be a civilian when I left this place. Hell, I was just a draftee.

I put on the NVA belt buckle I had captured at Recondo School. I strapped my K-bar to my leg, then slipped into my tiger fatigue shirt.

Just then Closson showed up and told me that we had twenty minutes to get down to the chopper pad.

"Lift off at 1715."

I grabbed my web gear, rucksack, and rifle, and walked down with Linderer to the acid pad. We arrived before the choppers, so we had some time to go over last-minute checks. Our fears were lessened by the excitement of the mission, but you could still feel an unusual tension in the air. This mission was different.

I watched as Linderer touched up his camouflage. Mother Rucker looked over. His face was dark green, fading into light green, with one brown strip across his chin. My face paint was not as perfect as Linderer's or Rucker's. I just sort of smeared it on. I had two black lines under my eyes like a defensive halfback. Linderer took one look at me and shook his head.

My tigers were faded and worn, Rucker's looked dark and tailored.

"Rucker, where'd you get the brown?"

He had a whole story about some captured NVA camouflage paint he got from a SOG guy in Phu Bai.

I tried to perk up the other guys, but no one was in the mood. Closson was getting final commo checks on both radios. Hillman stared off into space. There was a fatalistic mood that had settled over the entire team. I could tell Linderer's thoughts were on his premonition.

We heard the Hueys warming up across the valley. The sounds grew louder as they lifted off the Cav chopper pad. They circled around the compound and landed in front of us.

I stood up and walked toward the lead chopper. Then I heard someone speaking from behind me. It was Captain Cardona.

"Men, we'll be landing on Firebase Blaze for a few minutes before we insert you."

I guessed the gunships would rendezvous with us there for the final leg of the flight.

"You'll be going in a half hour before dusk. You'll have time to find an NDP before dark."

Then he walked over to the slick and told the pilots about the change in plans.

Looney, Meszaros, and Lawhorn wished us luck. They would be pulling our relay on Firebase Blaze. They were boarding the chase ship for the flight to the firebase.

Linderer and I posed for one last picture, as Schwartz leaned back and tried to get both of us in one shot. My stomach knotted; it was time to get on the ship.

Linderer kept his eyes fixed on the chopper as he walked. He shouted over his shoulder as he climbed aboard, "C'mon, Chambers, the fuckers want gooks? Let's get 'em some gooks." I climbed in behind him.

I felt our pilot pull power; the helicopter lifted up a few feet, then jerked forward.

I felt the rush NVA sappers must feel before they hit an American base.

I stared out the open door. Looking down at the rolling hills, I could see endless graves that dotted the countryside outside Camp Eagle.

From twenty-five hundred feet up, the graves resembled fish ponds, open at one end, with a large gravestone at the entrance to keep out the evil spirits. By the number of graves, they must have been burying people here since the beginning of time.

Within minutes, we were across the Perfume River and flying past Bald Mountain. Linderer pointed out the door toward a solitary mountain peak. "Nui Khe," he shouted.

I knew that place well, the first mission I had was there . . . Linderer had been wounded near there . . . We sat, deep in thought, thinking about the improbability of surviving the next four days.

We flew over Firebase Birmingham, and headed toward Firebase Bastogne. I recalled those first few weeks after I arrived in Vietnam—the restless nights, and the self-doubt about my ability to perform. I was happy during those early days with Burford and Byron as team leaders. But then things changed, and people moved on. I felt abandoned, even though Linderer, Looney, Meszaros, Rucker, and a few others were still here. I knew they, too, would be leaving soon. They all had forty-five days or less. Miller was still here. He'd been here forever, and as far as I knew, he had no intention of ever going home.

Twenty minutes later, we landed on a newly built firebase on a mountaintop, just east of the A Shau. Closson jumped down and ran toward the C & C ship. As the pilot torqued down to idle speed, Linderer, Rucker, and I stepped out onto the PSP chopper pad. Sours and Hillman walked around from the other side to join us, as we waited for the Cobras to arrive. I held onto my boonie hat as the CO's ship lifted off and headed east to pick up the gunships.

I looked around and noticed the 155 battery in the center of the firebase. We waved to Looney as he and his team walked over to set up their radio-relay base in a perimeter bunker. Linderer took a map out of his waterproof case and held it up to take a closer look.

"If we get too far on the back side of Dong Ap Bia, we're not going to be able to get any artillery fan, at least not from our people. Matter of fact, we won't even be in Vietnam, man, that's Laos."

That was just what I wanted to hear right now.

I pulled out my own map and noticed that I'd folded it wrong and couldn't find our AO.

Closson walked back with two artillery officers and a hard-looking staff sergeant, who were trying to figure out how they would get support for us in the no-man's-land where we were headed.

A small American flag hung from a pipe outside the command bunker. I'd rather be on a mission than in that sandbagged death trap.

Rucker grabbed my arm and pointed to the chopper. The pilot was signaling us to get back on board.

We would be approaching the A Shau from the eastern side, and these redlegs on this pissant hill of a firebase would be our closest friendlies.

"Next stop, A Shau," Rucker shouted.

Just then two mean-looking Cobra gunships passed high overhead.

In a few minutes, we were airborne and flying west. After ten minutes or so, I could see the mountains to the west of the cloud-shrouded A Shau—where the NVA were waiting.

Suddenly, the chopper dropped toward the ground. It was the first of a pair of false insertions our pilot would make to throw off any NVA LZ watchers who might be watching our chopper. As we came in closer for the first fake insertion, I watched Linderer prepare to jump.

Had he forgotten that this was a false insertion? He must have been preoccupied with that damned premonition.

Closson grabbed his web gear and shook his head. Linderer looked embarrassed. I was worried that Gary was taking this dream shit too seriously. It was breaking his concentration—and making me nervous! I pulled myself closer to the right door.

We pulled one more fake insertion, then headed for our LZ.

I looked down at the small clearing and noticed that the

weeds were very short, almost as if they had been mowed. It was like we were landing in my parents' back yard. I thought I spotted a makeshift bamboo fence as we came in. This was someone's vegetable patch, complete with a barrier to keep the animals out.

The chopper came in fast and low. We rolled out. I hit the ground first, got my footing, then ran toward the tree line. It was only a matter of seconds from the time the chopper skids touched down until it was airborne again.

As I ran, I caught a glimpse of a metal disk, partially exposed on the ground. I stopped and looked back. Closson and Linderer were looking at the same thing and signaled the rest of the team of its location. They ran up to my position.

As I searched for cover at the edge of the tree line, Closson tapped me on the shoulder and pointed his thumb over his shoulder. "Mines back there," he said.

I got a knot in the pit of my stomach when he said the word mine!

We pulled up in the thick tree line, where the jungle seemed dark and foreboding. Rucker made a quick commo check, and my worst fears were realized. We were in the old minefield, and we couldn't get the relay team on the radio. He finally got the C & C ship and was told to head to higher ground. Shit, we had just run through a minefield!

My adrenaline was pumping with every step. This was the edge, and there was no way back.

I stood still, listening for anything that sounded human. I noticed a ditch directly in front of us and moved along it toward the northwest slope of Dong Ap Bia (the mountain that later was to be called Hamburger Hill).

We were in the area where G-2 reported that a sapper battalion was located. The vegetation thinned as we climbed the slope. I felt more secure in the cover of the jungle, and out of that damn minefield.

We were engaged in a strange game of Monopoly, and we had just passed "Go." Closson was back conferring with

Linderer. They seemed somewhat confused. I pulled out my map but couldn't make sense of it.

Soon our fearless leaders had figured out that we had inserted on the wrong ridgeline. Closson came up to me, pointed toward the southeast and whispered that we were three hundred meters off course. Fucking great!

The chopper had mistakenly dropped us off in the middle of the minefield instead of on its flank. In defense of our pilots, a chopper crew coming in fast, into a strange place, can easily get mixed up. Closson pointed to a steep slope on the northeastern slope of Dong Ap Bia. He wanted me to move out and swing in a wide arc to the southwest, which would put us on a course to scout the entire base of Dong Ap Bia on the Vietnam side of the border. We knew that if we didn't find the enemy, we would have to cross the border. The foliage seemed a darker green on the Laotian side.

Dark clouds rolled in. It looked like it was going to rain. I lead the way up the slope. I stepped lightly, looking for mines, booby traps, and gooks. Looking down, I turned back to Closson and pointed to my boots. They were caked with soft mud. The moist soil made walking almost impossible. I continued on, but for every three steps forward, I would slide back two. It took almost two hours before we reached the crest of the ridge. By then it was almost pitch-black.

I stopped behind the cover of dense thicket, which blocked my vision. I moved around the tangled vines and froze when I spotted the high-speed trail at my feet. I raised my hand to halt the team. The trail was dark from recent rains and seemed to run parallel with the ridge and just off the crest. It was chopped up with fresh tracks.

We backed off the ridge and into an overgrown thicket under the jungle canopy. I found a level spot between several tall trees that looked like an ideal NDP. The spot was about eight feet wide and well concealed. Even if the gooks knew we were here, they would play hell trying to find us during the night. We were only twenty meters from the trail.

Linderer looked at me with a satisfied smile and nodded his approval.

Rucker called in sitrep and gave the coordinates of our NDP. "Windyguard Two Two, commo check. Over."

Looney came back immediately, "Windyguard Two Two, this is Windyguard Three, I read you Lima Charlie. Over."

Linderer took off his rucksack, untied the flap, and pulled out his claymore. I'd left my ruck on the ground and was checking out the surrounding area, but went back to it now.

I untied the top flap. I had a hard time getting the straps loose. But one last hard tug, and it came free. As I opened the canvas cover, I saw my claymore lying right on top.

Sours and Linderer crawled out under some thick brush and set up their claymores facing the trail. I took Hillman and set our two mines out, covering each flank. Closson took care of our E & E route downhill.

In less than ten minutes it was pitch-black. Closson called in some artillery preplot on the trail and back on the minefield.

We pulled fifty-percent alert. I had the first watch with Sours and Hillman. At about 2100 hours, we heard movement out on the trail. The NVA seemed pretty casual as they passed our position. We estimated thirty or more. We could only see the shadows of men as they walked past us, less than twenty meters away. An hour later another group came by, moving toward the peak of Dong Ap Bia. They obviously didn't suspect that we were there. Their noise discipline was poor. I tried to relax once my watch was over, but with so many enemy troops moving through the area, I found it extremely difficult to unwind.

Suddenly, I was jarred out of a half sleep by the sounds of a gasoline engine starting up a couple hundred meters away. I looked at the greenish glow of my watch. It was midnight. Linderer appeared in front of me. There was no expression on his face. He whispered, confirming my fears, "They've got a base camp up top, complete with electricity." No one slept that night. We unconsciously pulled in tighter.

Linderer prevented Closson from calling in a fire mission on the generator, arguing that it would alert the enemy of our presence.

"They'll come looking for us, and we don't need to attempt a night extraction out of that minefield," he said, convincing Closson to hold off.

Rucker called Looney and reported that we had beaucoup gooks on the high ground and they were having a party at the top of the hill.

A thunderstorm moved in from across the border and soaked us. I started shivering from the dampness and the sudden temperature drop. We spent the night trying to stay warm. Staying dry was impossible.

The sun was just coming over the mountains across the valley when we heard movement in the valley below. I bolted upright. Linderer and Rucker were already standing, looking over the brush. They counted more than a hundred enemy soldiers.

I could see them as they climbed the steep trail now. It looked as if they were carrying bags of rice. Several were carrying RPGs, and others had AK-47s. All of them wore dark green uniforms and floppy hats, with what looked like shredded camouflage material sewn on top. Many of them appeared to be wearing branches and leaves tied to their backs as camouflage. It was the sort of camouflage a man would wear to hide from aerial observation, not from observers on the ground.

I looked over at Hillman, who was fiddling with his canteen. I snapped my fingers silently to get his attention. He looked up, and I mouthed the word gooks. He froze.

The enemy column passed within twenty meters of our position. When they were gone, Closson motioned for us to move up the ridge to the trail. I looked back at him.

"Follow them," he whispered.

I watched Sours and Linderer nod in agreement.

Rucker was having a hard time getting commo, as we

picked up and moved out slowly. I stayed low to the ground in case another enemy patrol showed up.

Sours followed me up the ridgeline to the trail. I stopped at its edge, then stepped out and looked both ways before crossing it. Sours followed quickly, covering my rear.

I was very nervous, traveling right behind what appeared to be a full company of NVA. Silently, five meters apart, we moved another twenty meters before I halted the team. I could hear the jungle birds calling up ahead. Those little bastards could give you away, but they would also warn you when company was coming. Their calls were normal, unexcited. The enemy column had continued on up the crest of the ridge.

We waited for a few moments, listening for any sign of the enemy, then moved farther back away from the trail. I looked at Closson and mouthed, "Let's stay off the trail."

He nodded in agreement.

I moved about twenty-five meters away and stopped the team in a cluster of large boulders.

The new location gave us some concealment and better cover than our previous OP. We stayed put for the remainder of the day, watching and listening for the enemy patrols.

Suddenly, Linderer cupped his hands to his ears and looked up the ridgeline. He turned back toward me, his eyes wide. He pointed up the hill, so I cupped my ears and turned my head in the direction of the sounds. I heard chopping.

"Hear that? They're building bunkers," Linderer whispered.

Lightning flashed to the west. We were about twenty-five hundred feet above sea level, so when the regular afternoon thunderstorms moved in, out of Laos, we were actually right there in the clouds with the storm. Thunder and lightning crashed around us for about thirty minutes, then the storm moved out as quickly as it had come in. At least it dissipated our scent and deadened any sound. The price of safety was getting soaked and staying wet all night.

I pulled out my indigenous poncho liner and wrapped it around my shoulders and head.

Linderer signaled that he was going to chow down. He had a spaghetti LRP ration in his left hand and a canteen in the right. He poured the cold water over the ration and stirred it with his finger.

I leaned over and asked him if that was how they taught you to eat in Missouri. He took his finger out of the plastic container and licked it, then flipped me the bird with its neighbor.

After the team finished eating, we set claymores around our perimeter. We kept them in close to prevent any wandering NVA from discovering them and propped them against large trees to protect us from the backblast. It was pitch-black when we heard the enemy moving up the trail. They illuminated the trail with filtered flashlights. We had to be close to a major base camp. Rucker reported the sighting.

As my eyes adjusted to the darkness, I made out the faces of our team members. Hillman seemed terrified by all the enemy activity. His dark face was strained, and his youthful look was gone. What a way to lose your cherry.

Two other groups passed our position during the night. I couldn't help notice that they were all going in the same direction.

The damn generator kicked on a few minutes after midnight. I guess they felt safe running it in their own backyard. But it sure kept us up all night.

With the morning of April 22, 1969, Linderer seemed to be in better spirits, as if he sensed that we might survive this mission. We had survived the minefields and several large NVA patrols. We knew where the enemy was, and he didn't have a clue that we were nearby.

I took out a beef-and-rice LRP ration I had prepared the night before. It was warm from my body heat, and the water had rehydrated the meal. It tasted better than any steak I had ever eaten.

Closson gathered us in close for a conference. He said we needed to go up to the mountain and find out what the gooks were up to. I was shocked. It was insane to try to climb higher than we were. What was the purpose? Hell, we knew where they were. We could almost hear them farting.

Linderer came unglued, and I was afraid he and Closson were going to get into it right there in the field. Linderer told Closson he wasn't going anywhere until it was time for the extraction.

"I'm not going anywhere except back to the LZ. I'm too fucking short to start playing John Wayne," Linderer whispered.

Closson's ears turned red, as he snarled a threat of court-martial if he refused an order. All we needed was an argument now. We'd be killing ourselves.

Closson looked at me, and I shook my head. No way. Closson turned and looked over at Sours and Rucker, who both shook their heads. Hillman shook his head. Closson was out-voted. Even though Closson was a Shake 'n Bake, he had enough good sense to agree. Besides, Sours had twenty-eight days left, Mother Rucker thirty-five, and Gary was going home after this mission.

We were as close as you could get to an enemy unit without asking for trouble. There was no point in getting closer. We knew that there was at least a battalion above us, and they weren't building picnic tables. We had accomplished our mission and had remained undetected. No one could expect any more.

We had pulled off a perfect mission in the middle of the whole damn North Vietnamese Army, and he didn't even seem to appreciate it.

We spent the rest of the day laying dog. The enemy seemed to be using the trail only at night.

As the daily afternoon thunderstorm rolled in, I watched from under my poncho liner as lightning struck again and again on the surrounding hills.

Just the summer before last, I was fighting forest fires. Lightning strikes meant double overtime. Now they meant sleeping wet.

In the middle of the rainstorm, Closson decided to make us pay for disobeying him. "We are moving to a new location." I could tell that Linderer was working up his own storm, but this time Closson got his way.

I didn't like moving. It was risky in a heavy downpour. It took away sight and sound and pushed the odds in the enemy's favor. Closson wanted to move to the other side of the ridge. I led the team up to the trail, hesitating momentarily as we stepped across it and disappeared into the jungle on the other side.

We found a good spot just off the trail and moved into some thick cover to wait for the coming darkness. We set out two claymores facing the trail and one facing our back trail, in case we needed a quick exit. We didn't hear any movement during the rest of that night, but I don't think anyone slept much.

I didn't sleep at all. The disagreement between Linderer and Closson had rattled everyone. We were no longer on a team wavelength.

Four of us were team leaders, and a full half of the team was short. This was not a good combination in any situation.

Early the next morning, we spotted a twenty-five man patrol in the valley below. They were far enough away that Closson decided to call in artillery. As Linderer and Closson were busy trying to plot the enemy coordinates, Rucker was calling in the fire mission.

"Redleg Seven, Redleg Seven, Windyguard Two Two, fire mission. Over."

The sound of static filled the space between transmissions.

"This is Redleg Seven, go!"

More static.

"Five zero November-Victor-Alpha in the open moving to the grape two three. One zero zero zero mikes from our last position."

Rucker was at his best. The grape was two for north, and three for west. They were moving to the northwest.

"Give one round willie peter, air burst, then HE, full battery on the deck, fire for effect. I will adjust. On my command!"

"VT (Veritable Time). Fire!"

"Shot!" came back over Rucker's mike.

"Shot out," Rucker whispered.

"Splash."

"Redleg, add a hundred right, drop five zero, fire for effect!"

The rounds impacted in the valley below us. We stayed down because we were too near the gun-target line. Since we were above them, a short round could drop right in our laps.

Linderer had his topo map out and was plotting a course to the LZ. He had one thing on his mind. We had accomplished our mission, and he wanted to get out in one piece.

Then came the regular afternoon thunderstorm, right on schedule. I looked at the back of my claymore mine and wondered if it was too close.

I signaled to Closson that I was going to move my claymore farther out. I duck walked the short distance to the edge of the ridge, picked up my claymore, and let out some more wire so that it would extend another ten feet down the hill.

As I climbed back up the hillside, I noticed that everyone was getting ready for the storm. I waved to Linderer, then sat down, facing out, on the south edge of our perimeter. I opened my rucksack, took out my oilskin NVA poncho, and put it over my shoulders, then moved the small, hand-held, firing device for my claymore out from under me and set it to my left. I laid my CAR-15 across my lap and rechecked the safety. It was off.

I watched the storm moving over the ridge toward us. This looked like a bad one. You could already smell the brimstone in the air. The rain came down in sheets. It began to hail. I looked back toward Linderer and Closson. Linderer was playing grab-ass with Closson and had dropped a few hailstones down the back of Closson's pants. It was beginning to look like we would be able to wrap the mission without those two killing each other.

Sours looked up from his position, just off the edge of the hill. He was trying to open a can of C-ration peaches. Hillman sat quietly, peering over his weapon into the gloom.

I pulled a leech from under my right arm and tossed it down the side of the hill. I wondered how long it would take the little bastard to crawl back up here to find me. I was gazing out from under my poncho when another heavy downpour started.

Here we go again, I thought.

Closson whispered for Rucker to call the relay team and check on the time for extraction. Rucker keyed his handset. Suddenly there was a tremendous white flash—no sound! Then a blast of hot wind hit me like a freight train.

I was flying through the air, engulfed in white light, for what seemed like several seconds before the sound of the explosion rolled over me. It happened so fast that I lost track of where I was and what I was doing.

I hit the ground, flipped, and rolled down the side of the ridge, flattening everything in my path. Then I came to a jolting stop. I had landed faceup. My head pounding. Rain drops stung my face. I couldn't see. I couldn't tell if it was from the blast or the rain. I lay on my back feeling nothing, conscious only of the ringing in my ears. My eyesight returned after a few seconds. My mind screamed questions that my senses could not answer. I had no idea where I was, or what had happened. I was paralyzed—unable to move.

Then the numbing pain came, weak at first, but growing stronger. I tried to get up, but my legs wouldn't respond. I reached down and touched my legs, but I couldn't feel a thing—so I prayed.

I expected NVA soldiers to find me any moment, then cut my throat to finish me off. I smelled something burning. It smelled like hair and wiring burning. I knew it was coming from me.

Where were the gooks! Why hadn't they come to finish us off?

I noticed the rain had stopped, but water still dripped from the branches overhead. I looked up the slope. I didn't recognize anything. *Where in the hell am I, and how did I get here? Where's my weapon?*

My rifle; I had to find it before the gooks got here. I had no sensation from the waist down. I reached over and grabbed the vines beneath me; I pulled myself onto my stomach. I had to get back to the team.

I found my rifle lying next to me. I turned it around and pointed it up toward the top of the hill, then slowly started pulling myself up, hand over hand.

I struggled to reach the top of the hill where I had been sitting before the explosion. I didn't see my team. Smoke filled the spot we had occupied.

Then I saw Linderer's body, lying face down and twisted, in a pool of water next to a crater in the ground. I thought he was dead. I crawled over to him and rolled him over on his side. He was still alive but barely breathing. He had a dazed look. His eyes were dilated. I grabbed his wrist. His pulse was almost gone. I whispered to him.

"Gary! You son of a bitch, come on! Gary!"

I turned and looked back at Sours, who was beneath a tree and appeared to be in shock. He was holding on to a struggling Rucker, who was writhing about uncontrollably. I couldn't see Hillman. I turned back and grabbed Linderer and shook him.

"Gary! Gary! You're okay! Gary! Come out of it, man!"

His eyes opened, and he tried to speak, but I could barely hear him. "Leave me alone, get the fuck away!"

"Hang on, I'll get help."

Now the realization of what had happened struck me. I was scared like I'd never been before.

Sours spotted Hillman and pointed up the trail. Sours and

Hillman seemed in better shape than the rest of us. They were our only effectives—and they were in bad shape.

I laid Gary's head back down in the soft mud. He closed his eyes as if to sleep, then rolled face down in the shallow water. I crawled over to Sours, who was holding his arm and trying to find his weapon.

"Gary's gone, man!"

I was still in shock. We both watched Gary lying there. It was as if he had just given up the will to live.

I was on my hands and knees, but I had no feeling in them. Suddenly, Linderer jerked and started gasping for air.

Sours ran over and turned him on his side again. I crawled back to them and rolled his head toward me.

"You're not dead!" I hissed. Gary blinked his eyes and spit up some of the mud that had filled his mouth. I wiped his face with the tail of my shirt and stayed by his side.

Sours had moved back to Rucker, who was in a lot of pain. The whole scene was terrifying; just to look around and see the smoke and half the jungle blown down was enough to almost drive away all hope. I could smell the pungent odor of cordite and charred vegetation.

Closson ran past me. He must have been tossed down the side of the hill. He had been hit in the face by the blast and looked like someone suffering from a stroke. He couldn't talk. He smacked right into Sours.

I pulled my rifle up next to me and waited for the worst to happen. Finally, Sours got the radio working. He came back over to me and said that help was on the way.

"How's Linderer doing?"

"I don't know," I gasped. "I can't see anything wrong, but he can't move. I think he's paralyzed."

"Gary, help's on the way, man! We'll get you out."

Linderer muttered through the pain, "My legs are gone. I don't care; let me die! I'm not going home like this."

"No, man, your legs are there. You'll be okay!"

I kept talking, and he got pissed at me. He was making no sense. Then out of nowhere, a U.S. Army medevac helicopter filled the open hole above us.

"Medevac!"

I looked up and saw a metal body basket coming down on a cable. The downblast from the rotors blew debris into my eyes. Then something went wrong. The basket got hung up in a twisted treetop and stopped.

Sours ran to the tree and started shaking it, trying to get the basket to fall. Closson ran into the tree with a cross-body block and the basket came loose; I noticed the whole backside of Closson's pants had been blown off, and the bluish-white of his butt stood out like a couple of bald-headed men in a coal bin.

He was trying to help Sours but only managed to knock him down the hill. Sours climbed back up, cursing at the well-intentioned team leader. Sours climbed the tree and guided the basket down to the floor of the jungle. He pulled it over to where Linderer lay and tipped the cage on its side. Then the two of us rolled Gary into the body basket and strapped him down. Sours ran one strap around his legs. I circled his chest with the other. I was having a hard time getting it in the loop, but succeeded, and Gary was ready for the short trip up to the hovering medevac.

I tried to watch as the basket lifted up, but the downblast was too much. In moments, Gary was in the ship. Then the chopper turned right and disappeared.

Rucker groaned, "Sours, the pilot said he thought he took fire. He is going around for another try. Tell everyone the gunships are going to fire up the ridgeline."

I heard several rockets impacting above us. I covered my head as two more rockets exploded to our left flank. The unmistakable sound of a minigun drowned out everything else.

The adrenaline was really pumping, and I seemed to have gained some feeling back in my legs. I found new strength. A Cobra gunship passed overhead. I waved at him. Sours shouted that the medevac was coming back. Closson and I were going out next. He moved me next to Closson. I hated to look at Closson. The left side of his face looked normal, but his right side was distorted, and it made him look like a chubby gargoyle. I had never seen anyone's face look like that before. It was as if someone had clipped all the nerves on the right side of his face. Closson would sit quietly for a moment, then jump up and run. Sours would have to chase him down and bring him back.

I was wondering why the gooks hadn't followed up and killed us yet. But then the medevac returned.

The crew chief lowered a jungle penetrator down through the twisted trees. Sours caught hold and opened it before it hit the ground. I sat down on the open leaf. He pulled Closson over and sat him facing me on the other leaf. As Sours ran the strap around the both of us, I held tight to Closson.

I didn't look directly at Closson's face, but his breath smelled like burnt dogshit. Mine must've smelled as bad. The penetrator cable tightened. As we rose through the trees, my legs went dead. Closson's weight was cutting off my blood supply. He leaned back as we neared the chopper. I was afraid he would fall and take me with him.

As the helicopter hovered, I could see the medic hanging out the door and guiding the penetrator up through the trees. The two of us held on for dear life. Then Closson leaned back again and almost let me go. I yelled at him to hold on. He was rolling his head around, rubbernecking for a better view of his surroundings.

I looked up again at the medic and tried to reassure him that everything was working. A hand grabbed my arm, and we were at the open door. I reached back and clasped the medic's hand, and he pulled us inside the chopper. As we entered the open bay, I noticed the long basket with Linderer still strapped in and lying motionless against the rear fire wall. I could only see his legs.

The rotor noise was unbelievably loud. There was barely

enough room for the medic to maneuver Closson around. The door gunner started firing, and I looked up. He was yelling into his mouthpiece that we were taking fire from the top of the ridge. I braced myself as the ship pulled up, then slid to the side. We just hung there. Rounds were hitting the tail boom.

As the pilot completed his turn, I watched in horror as Closson sat in the open doorway, about to fall.

The medic was pinned back against the pilot's seat and couldn't move. We could only watch as Closson, who was now unstrapped, slipped on some of the mud that covered the cargo floor. His feet went out from under him, and he landed on his bare butt, just missing Gary—who lay motionless, with the look of sheer terror on his face. The medic reached for Closson. I tried to help him, but Closson was dead weight and difficult to move. Finally, the medic pulled him in and secured him against the bulkhead.

Closson sat there half conscious, not realizing how close he had come to falling out of the helicopter.

I was relieved. We were still alive. But there were three Rangers still on the ground. The medevac moved back into position, lowered the penetrator, and retrieved Hillman, Rucker and Sours.

On the flight back, the medic took a good look at us and shouted, "What happened? You look like you just got back from hell!"

I shrugged my shoulders. "We did!"

I lay my head against the bulkhead and tried to relax.

Some feeling began returning to my side and my right leg. My left leg was still numb.

We arrived at the 22d Surgical Hospital at Phu Bai and were met at the chopper pad by a group of medics with three gurneys. They rolled us into triage. I was just happy to be alive, but I realized I still couldn't move my legs.

Inside, a round-eye nurse stuck a thermometer in my mouth and took my blood pressure. She moved over to Closson and Linderer and did the same to them.

I asked her how the other guys were and then proposi-
tioned her. She told me to just relax. She looked at us like
what she was seeing wasn't making any sense. The hair on
our legs was singed, and our pants were ripped and scorched,
but our flesh was untouched.

I looked up and turned my head to see a blond-haired,
round-eye woman walking toward me. She was dressed in
loose green fatigues and was carrying two kinds of scissors.
She stopped at my feet and laid the scissors alongside my leg.
I had a feeling that there was something terribly wrong here.

She reached down and untied my soggy combat boots, then
let them drop to the floor. They hit with a mushy thud. Then
she cut off what was left of my torn and half-burned pants.
Then she started to cut off my belt.

"Don't cut my belt. It's NVA. How does my leg look, is it
okay?"

"Don't worry, it's okay, and I won't cut your belt."

An orderly wheeled Rucker in on a gurney and parked him
next to me. Rucker, who by now was almost back to normal,
laughed and yelled, "He means don't cut off his dick!"

She gave him a dirty look.

"The doc will be in to see you two in a moment. By the
way, your friend is okay. He's still in shock, but he looks
alright."

I was now naked from the waist down and totally embarrassed as she examined me. She finished and ran into the next
room. I've always had that kind of effect on women.

I lifted my head and looked over at the rest of the guys. I
saw Rucker on the bed next to me. We started to laugh.

"What the fuck happened to us? Did we get hit by an NVA
air strike?"

Rucker was almost euphoric as he told me what he remembered. It wasn't much.

"Man, I don't know what came down, but I remember
keying the handset, and the next thing I knew, we were in a
medevac."

"Hey, Closson, are you OK?"

Closson looked my way and tried to smile. His face was returning back to its normal beauty.

Lieutenant Williams had come over to meet the medevac. He was standing at the foot of our beds, watching us with a look of concern.

"That's a hell of a way to get extracted, just to come out a day early."

"Hey, Lieutenant Williams! Boy, I never thought I would love to see your OCS face!" Rucker hollered.

Lieutenant Williams smiled and told us that our medevac pilot had radioed in that they had taken fire. When he got back to Camp Evans, he had twenty-six bullet holes in his tail section.

"They called in a couple of F-4s after they got you guys out, and they took heavy ground fire from the top of the mountain. What did you guys get into out there?"

Rucker grinned, "Little Hanoi, sir, little Hanoi."

Closson, who had been resting quietly, suddenly spoke up. He sounded like someone who just had six hours of dental work.

"We got hit by litnin'!" he muttered.

"You got hit by what?"

"Litnin'! Yeah, it hit aw antenna. Afta Wucka keyed the handset."

"Hell yes, that had to be what happened. That explains why my handset blew up. It must have jumped from the antenna and blew all our mines at once," said Rucker. "The backblast almost killed us."

"Linderer's concussion grenade must have exploded inside his ruck. That's why we didn't find any of his gear or his weapon. He was sitting on it at the time. He must have flown twenty feet straight up in the air," Rucker said.

"Jethus!" Closson added.

"Did you see me, Closson?" I asked.

"Yeah, you dithapeared into thin air, man, you just vanithed."

"God! I did?"

"What did you think happened?" Rucker asked.

I told him I really didn't know. I'd thought the NVA wiped us off the face of the earth. But I did know that Sours saved our butts. He did everything right. Where was he? I tried to raise up to look around.

Just then Sours walked in.

"I bet those dinks up above us were wondering what the hell was going on," he said. "That had to be the loudest explosion they ever heard!"

Rucker wondered if maybe God was trying to tell us something.

"No, man, Buddha was. 'Go home GI, and don't play with dynamite!' " We all laughed.

"Hey, Lieutenant Williams," I said. "When I climbed back up to the spot I had been sitting on, I found my clacker, and it was melted, man. The wire was gone, and there was a half-inch hole burned through the middle. I remember thinking how strange it looked."

Rucker interrupted. "I thought our LAWs blew up."

"Hey," I said, "my pack is still out there with a perfectly good spaghetti LRP and my autographed picture of Jane Fonda as Barbarella in it. Lieutenant Williams, you gotta send in a reaction force to get my pack!"

Lieutenant Williams only grinned and told us he was going to check on Linderer.

"I got most of your weapons. I'll take them back to the company and get someone to put them in the arms conex."

"You got my Swedish K?" Rucker asked.

"Yes."

"See ya, Lieutenant. And hey—thanks for coming by."

Closson sat up and was looking between his legs. "Hey," he said, "I found a leech."

A second nurse came in. She looked shocked at the sight of us. Naked from the waist down, tiger fatigues shredded, hair burned off our legs, camouflage paint and cuts all over our faces—and there was Closson, holding a leech. She looked at us like we were from another planet.

The next day Rucker was released, and they moved Linderer into our ward. After we talked about the whole mission, I asked him about something that was bothering me.

"Gary, did something strange happen to you?"

He looked at me kind of funny.

"What do you mean?"

"I mean the second after we got hit, did you notice something strange?"

I paused to wait for his answer.

"Gary, I saw something I can't explain."

Gary was now propped up on his bunk, listening intently.

"After the explosion, it felt like I was in a dream. I felt like my body was torn apart from the blast, but suddenly a brilliant light was everywhere. I moved into the center of the light and hung there, suspended and safe. It was like something supernatural happened! I felt guarded and safe, as if everything was going to be alright. Then, when I realized what was happening, the light disappeared. Do you think I'm crazy, Gary? It seemed so real to me."

Gary looked around to make sure no one was listening then whispered, "No, I don't think you are crazy, because I saw the same thing."

It was at that point, we decided that it wouldn't be wise to talk about "the light" with anyone.

11 X-ray Team

After a short recovery period, Rucker, Closson, Hillman, and I returned to duty. Gary Linderer left for the States. I pulled one more mission with Closson and Rucker—a BDA (Bomb Damage Assessment) mission into the A Shau, following a massive arclight (B-52) strike. The B-52s were dropping five-hundred-pound bombs. I had pulled a BDA earlier in May. It was strange, like someone had come in and built a line of unfinished swimming pools.

We went into our AO after it had rained, and the bomb craters had almost filled up. They were thirty feet wide, and the vegetation was completely gone. Our teams made contact almost immediately.

The Old Man called in the 2d of the 17th Cav. After three days of fighting, they brought in the 3d Battalion, 187th, who pulled a combat assault near where the Ranger team had made contact.

That next day they found a good-sized cache: 28 mortar tubes, 178 rockets, more than 2,500 mortar rounds, and nearly 50,000 pounds of polished rice.

Because the weather was so bad, they were forced to destroy most of the NVA supplies in place. Luckily for them, the North Vietnamese avoided contact as the days passed. But headquarters back at Eagle decided to establish a new firebase because of all the commotion. And guess where they put it—right in the middle of all the gook supply trails.

Of course, the idea was to slow the enemy down and impede their movement. But all it really did was piss 'em off.

I was asked to take a relay team out to the edge of the A Shau Valley. Our job was to relay all radio communications between our Ranger teams in the field and the TOC back at Camp Eagle.

The clouds had pulled back, and so had the gooks. The firebase was called Airborne and had less than one hundred men on it. About two platoons of infantrymen from the 2d Battalion of the 501st and a handful of artillerymen opened it. We were to set up a radio relay on the new base and relay Ranger teams that would be going into the A Shau.

The night before we were to set up, the NVA tried to take the base. Beginning at 0330 hours, two NVA battalions launched a primary attack from the north of this isolated, little piss-hole of a firebase.

A secondary attack came from the east, and a diversionary attack was launched from the south. Violent fighting lasted over three hours before the gooks broke contact. The 2/501st was in no mood for us to arrive that next afternoon. They had over twenty-six men dead and sixty-two wounded. The whole place was a mess, but the war was not over, and our job was to set up a position for a six-day mission.

After our briefing and hearing that Firebase Airborne had almost been overrun, my adrenaline began to flow. It was still churning as our chopper approached the tiny camp in the northern part of the A Shau Valley.

Saenz was sitting next to me on the chopper, looking out the left side. Larry was a stocky, rough-looking trooper. He was pointing down to the sight below, and I had a hard time believing what I saw—littered around the tiny outpost were dozens of NVA bodies. Some were still in the wire, but most were on the eastern side of the steep hillside. Saenz shook his head, and I did the same.

As we started to come down, the pilot got a call from our commanding officer. He had diverted us to Firebase Eagle

Nest, just five miles northeast of Airborne, on the eastern side of Elephant Valley.

As we pulled up, we both stared at all of the dead bodies lying all over that hillside. I looked at Saenz.

"Saved again, Saenzman."

"I dig it, man."

In a few moments, we were hopping off the chopper onto a steep slope. Next to the chopper pad a small handwritten sign read WELCOME TO THE EAGLE'S NEST. It looked as if they had just blown every square inch of topsoil off the mountain. I checked into the command bunker and was told by a young-looking infantry captain that we could have our own bunker, complete with a chair, and even a panoramic view of the valley below.

Saenz, who we affectionately called Saenzman, found our bunker, and he and Jim Walker, an eighteen-year-old farm boy from Tennessee, went about the task of setting up shop. We were to be there for the next few weeks.

Walker rigged up a field-expedient antenna, and Saenz tried to figure out where he should sleep. Larry had served a year before he volunteered for the Rangers and had pulled his share of missions, so he was used to living on the side of a mud hill like any good boonie rat. He had his priorities straight.

By the time I got back from the evening briefing, they both had the whole show on the road. Our bunker was a place of beauty. The side walls and roof were PSP (perforated steel plates) sandwiched between two rows of sandbags. A small opening that led out to a fighting position faced the eastern edge of the perimeter; a row of barbed wire snaked down the ridgeline. Home sweet home.

Saenz had his shirt off and was already making friends with some of the grunts who were to pull security to our right. He came back to the bunker with a case of C rations, which the grunts had traded him for six spaghetti LRP rations.

I was outside looking off in the direction of Dong Ap Bia.

You could tell we had hit the shit out of it. But still, looking down that steep sidehill that led to the jungle and ultimately the valley floor, it was a bit unnerving. You could hide the entire North Vietnamese Army down there, and never find it.

Whaboom!

"Jesus!" Both Saenz and I bailed into the bunker and hit the ground.

Whaboom!

"155s! We are on the gun-target line, man!"

Whaboom!

"Man, Saenz, no wonder we got this bunker so cheap!"

The rounds were going right over our heads, and each blast left us with a ringing in our ears.

"Man, no way! No one can stay on this end of the perimeter!"

Boy, did I feel like a dumb shit.

"Well, we've been screwed again."

We were like a necessary evil, a Ranger radio-relay team on some infantry commander's firebase. Now I knew we weren't welcome.

"Saenzman, I got to go see the arty commander and see if we can get moved. I'll be right back."

"Every time they get a fire mission into the valley, they'll swing those fucking guns over our heads."

Whaboom! It happened again.

I looked at our antenna shaking and wondered how I could stand two weeks of this.

"You know this is God getting even, Saenz," Walker said.

Saenz nodded. "We should have gone to church last week."

"I know, but I don't know what day Sunday is anymore, do you, Saenz?"

"No, man."

We ate and had a few more rounds blast over our heads, then I walked back to the command bunker and was given a choice. I was told in a very direct manner that I was lucky to have a place to sleep anywhere inside the perimeter, and if I didn't like it, I could sleep outside the perimeter.

I thanked the good captain and returned to tell my team how I had slapped that leg, airmobile officer around but gave in when he begged me to stay. Darkness closed the valley down to the outside world, and we were on our own. The war was about to begin.

"What time do the teams go in?" Walker asked.

"At 0530 hours. No watch tonight; try to get some sleep."

Later that night, Saenz's newfound friends told us they had heard the LPs (listening posts) had beaucoup movement. No one could sleep after that bit of good news; we just sat around and stared at each other.

Pop! A flare lit up the perimeter. I stepped outside to get some air. The flare burned under the small parachute, then it floated out into no-man's land, illuminating the hillside for a couple of hundred feet.

Shadows danced off the trees as the flare settled down to the valley floor below. I walked back inside and tried to find my way around.

I lay back down on my sleeping bag and thought about the world. It seemed so crazy. The TV I had seen on my leave showed protesters in the streets, carrying signs and shouting antiwar slogans. I still believed what we were fighting for was right. It was just the way we were going about it that made no sense. We would take a hill, lose a hundred men, then leave. That made no sense. It was almost like our job was not to win a war, just stall it.

My thoughts were broken when it started to rain. Water soaked our bags. We all got up and wrapped the radios to keep them dry. The way the rain was hitting the metal roof of our bunker we could barely hear the radio transmissions.

The next day, the radios were full of activity as Six inserted two Ranger teams into the A Shau Valley. Five helicopters were used, so the airways were buzzing.

The Black Widows were flying cover, and Kingsmen flew the lead and chase ships. The 160th Aviation Group was both proficient and professional. Everyone appreciated the job they did. I think all of us respected the bravery of these pilots.

After five hours, the teams were laying dog and getting some rest. I heard a shit-hook coming in. I walked outside and watched the big bird unass a quad-fifty.

"Saenzman, you got to see this, man. Look at that puppy. Let's go check it out."

We waited until the 1300 sitrep, then left Walker on the radios and walked over to the nasty-looking gun.

This thing was great. She had four .50-caliber machine guns, mounted one above the other, with two on each side. The shells were as big as my thumb, and each gun had a full box of fifteen hundred rounds attached to its side. The gunner climbed inside, and of course, I couldn't resist getting in. It had a motor drive to elevate and lower the guns and rotate the whole setup.

As we walked back to the bunker, I told Saenz I hoped we got hit just to see what that puppy could do. He agreed it might be worth seeing.

Back in the damp bunker, night came quickly. It reminded me of a cartoon I saw as a child, where an enormous giant closed the cover on his huge toy box and left his toy soldiers in various positions until he returned the next morning to open the lid. We were putting on extra clothes.

"It's going to be wet and cold tonight," Walker said as he sat in the chair for the first of three watches.

Radio-relay, or X-ray teams as they were known, were the most important assets a Ranger team had. We were their only connection to the outside world.

Our teams were out so far now that we were having a hard time hearing them over the radio. And Eagle, some twenty miles to the east, could barely hear us. We would acknowledge the sitreps, and report them back to the company. Every hour the teams were to report in. At the predesignated times, they would just break squelch twice for a negative sitrep.

I crawled into my shelf space but could still see the flickering candlelight casting the shadow of Walker on the wall. He was just sitting there next to the two PRC-25s.

"Shee-it, man, this weather sucks," he lamented.

Saenz changed frequencies on the artillery radio and tried to find out what times they would be firing. The whole firebase was on edge after Airborne got hit.

Their company commander told us that we needed our helmets on at night. The gooks hit Eagle the night before with fifty RPG rounds. And just to the south, sappers attacked Firebase Berchtesgaden. They were hit with everything from small arms, RPGs, satchel charges, to 122 mm rockets. We figured we were next.

That night, we joined in on the mad minutes, every hour on the hour. It was cool watching that quad-fifty light up. Between mad minutes, Saenz kept fiddling with the frequency setting. "I think it's 73/94."

"Saenzman, do you know what their call sign is?"

"Whiskey Two."

I rolled back over on my side and almost fell asleep.

Suddenly, I felt something run over the top of me. I jumped up and hit my head on the shallow roof, less than two feet above me.

"Shit!"

I looked over at Saenz, still playing with the radio.

"Did you see that?"

"What, man?" he said.

"I felt this dog run over me. It was huge, man! It felt like a small dog jumped on me."

I couldn't go back to sleep, so I stayed awake until my shift and then moved out from under that crawl space. I wrapped myself in my bag and slipped into the chair to just wait and listen.

"I roger your transmission. Over. Negative sitreps two six. Over."

I had thoughts of going home more and more now. I was

wondering what my old friends were doing and how much I had changed.

The next morning's first light broke upon the A Shau as a solid, gray cloud filled the valley. There would be no choppers today.

I pulled my poncho liner tighter over my head and peeked out. Large drops of water dripped from inside the bunker ceiling. Saenz stirred in his sleep. He opened one eye and looked at me.

"Hey, Saenz, it's your watch."

Saenz, still in his cammies and jungle boots, slowly rolled out from under his poncho liner.

"You have last watch?"

"Yeah." I said. "Keep an eye on Lawhorn's team. He had some movement last night. But nothing for the last two hours."

"Yeah, okay."

I crawled back up in my space, and once I pulled that poncho liner over my head, I was gone.

I drifted into dreams of childhood fears of monsters and witches. I used to have a dream that an old wrinkled witch was chasing me. She would get close to me, and I would be running as fast as I could, but as I got close to my house, I couldn't make my legs move. She would be gaining, and just as I would climb into my window to safety, she would catch me and pull me back out. It always woke me up. I pulled the liner back over my head.

The rain drizzled all the next day, and I stayed occupied by fieldstripping my rifle and cleaning it. The gray of the day penetrated the bunker, and my only consolation was not being out in the field.

That night, Walker was to pull first watch. During his watch, he had his knife out and was scratching his name on the side of an ammo crate. I felt that thing run across my legs again. But this time Walker saw it and tried to stick it with his K-Bar.

I jumped out of my bag and saw a big rat in a Mexican standoff with Walker. They were less than a foot apart. The rat was at the edge of the PSP shearing as Walker tried to stab it with his knife again. He missed, and the rat suddenly turned and dove for a shocked Walker.

It hit him in the face grabbing the flap of skin just under his nose with his teeth. Jimmy lifted up and hit his head on the roof. The rat wouldn't shake loose.

Both Saenz and I watched in shock as this rat took on Walker and looked as if he was getting the best of him. It finally let loose and scurried away. We tried to calm Walker down, but that rat really shook him. And he was bleeding all over the place.

That next morning Walker was medevaced off the firebase. We heard he had to get a whole series of thirteen painful rabies shots. Saenz and I spent the next two weeks trying to trap that rat, but he outsmarted us. We couldn't kill him, so we decided to make him our Ranger mascot.

That morning I got a call from Sergeant First Class Lockett. He wanted me to fly bellyman. So I grabbed my gear, said good-bye to Saenz, and headed for Camp Evans.

12 Bellyman

One week later

Through the half-open door, I could see the silhouette of a man as he walked down toward the helicopters.

I looked at my watch. It was 0400 hours. I couldn't go back to sleep. I felt homesick for my friends back at the company. I was sick of the endless flying. I was beginning to think that everyone had forgotten about me. I wasn't supposed to be here. I had volunteered to fly bellyman for a day or two. But that was over a week ago! And we'd been flying nonstop the entire time.

I rolled over onto my back and looked up at the ceiling. I decided that I might as well go down to the chopper pad. I got dressed, grabbed my rifle and bandolier and walked quickly to the chopper pad. Smitty, a tall, skinny Kingsman crew chief, who spoke with a slow southern drawl, was already there.

I walked up to the chopper. The dark skin of the Huey reflected the distant hangar lights.

"How'd you sleep?" he asked.

"Man, like a babe in his mother's arms," I lied.

"Yeah, I don't sleep much either, especially when we get into a lot of shit like yesterday."

"I don't know how you guys do this every day. I think I would rather be out in the bush."

"No fucking way, man! You can have that LRP shit!" he smiled.

I laid my gear on the floor of the Huey, then climbed into the dark cargo bay. I looked to the rear of the cabin and remembered unloading a KIA the day before. I could still see the motionless green bag lying against the bulkhead. I knew then that I didn't like this job. Handling dead Americans had always been someone else's job. I'd handled a lot of KIAs, but they had always been the enemy's. My job had been to grease them, search them, and move on. I had never had to deal with the care of our own dead. I had tried not to look at the bag or to think about what was inside. When Smitty and I unloaded the body bag, we each grabbed one end and started to lift. The soldier's body inside slid toward me and made a sloshing sound. I never wanted to hear that again, not if I could help it.

We placed the body on the acid pad as one of the pilots walked up. He told us coldly that the dead man was some cherry, fresh from SERTS, with less than three weeks in country. He had forgotten to check which side of his claymore faced out. He had placed the mine less than fifteen feet from his position. He never realized that he had pulled the biggest screwup of his life. Some local VC probed the cherry's side of the perimeter. He freaked and blew his claymore. One click of the detonator, and he was history. The blast blew his body all over the company perimeter and wounded three other grunts.

Having heard enough, I reached down, picked up my rifle, and secured it with a bungee cord to the structural support post. There was still some blood on the floor of the chopper. I wiped it up with a rag.

My ruck was still lying on the floor under the foldout seats where I'd left it during the extraction the day before. It must have been shoved there in the confusion.

Smitty brought over a wooden box full of smoke grenades and slid them across the metal floor to me. He shook his head and smirked.

"Replacements!" he said.

I took out six of the canisters and fastened them, one by one, to the posts on the side of the cargo bay; two red, two yellow, and two purple smoke grenades.

I turned my head and watched Smitty. He pulled out a fifteen-foot section of belted 7.62 ammo and checked it for kinks. He had jury-rigged his M-60 to avoid jamming by attaching a C-ration can so that the ammo would feed over the can and into the gun without snagging. After meticulously checking the ammo, he reseated the belt. He looked as tired as I felt. It was only 0430, but sweat was already running down his face.

Smitty had been Wild Bill Meacham's crew chief. While with Wild Bill, Meacham had let him ride shotgun up front and taught him how to fly the Huey. It was against regulations, but Meacham thought that if both pilots were put out of commission, it would be nice to know that Smitty could fly the bird back to base.

As dawn approached, the compound came to life. Smitty and I lifted a rectangular can containing fifteen hundred rounds of M-60 ammo onto the cargo deck.

Several other choppers were warming up their engines farther down the flight line. Our Kingsmen pilots, Ken Roach and Chuck Rolle, walked out from the shadows and over to the motionless helicopter. Roach visually inspected the chopper as Rolle stowed their flight bags behind their seats.

Roach circled the ship, inspecting the rotor blade. Rolle trailed behind him and unstrapped the line that secured it to the pad.

As he released the anchor tether, the blade flexed up and down like a teeter-totter.

The two pilots climbed into the chopper and strapped themselves in.

I watched as Roach went through the preflight procedures. I was amazed. There were so many things to remember.

I plugged in my headset so I could hear what was going on up front.

"Coming hot!"

There was a low moaning sound, then a rapid clicking as the ignition switch was thrown. The main rotor blades began slowly turning from right to left, faster and faster as they picked up speed.

The low whine turned into a growing roar as the main rotor increased torque. I thought about the Ranger teams we had inserted six days before and wondered how they were doing. How many days had I been here? More than I could recall.

This one-day job had turned into a one-week tour. I hated flying, but felt that just one day of it would help me overcome my fear. Now, each time the chopper engines wound up, so did my nerves. I was nearly frantic by takeoff. Maybe Captain Cardona, my company commander, had traded me to the aviation battalion for a pallet of beer. Maybe all the contact of the past few weeks had caused him to forget that I existed.

"Clear," Roach said into the intercom.

I braced myself for the liftoff and prayed that we wouldn't get shot at today.

The past week had been the longest week of the war for me. I would prefer hand-to-hand combat than risk getting shot out of the air.

I sat directly behind Roach. A skeleton was painted on the back of his helmet. Below that was a piece of one-inch tape with his name written on it. I could see that he was still busy checking his instruments. Then he eased the cyclic control forward.

The helicopter lifted, rocked back and forth, startling me out of a daydream. I could feel the ship lighten as we continued to lift. I grabbed the mounting post to steady myself.

The Huey moved slowly out to the center of the flight line, then turned to the south and began to climb. I felt the hair stand up on the back of my neck as the chopper lunged forward.

"Morning, guys, just wanted to see if you were awake," Roach cracked over the intercom.

In the distance I could see the sun's first light breaking over the horizon.

The pilots were busy on the radio, getting ground clearance, giving their headings, and checking altimeter readings.

I stood, trying to see where we were headed. I looked through the Plexiglas over Roach's right shoulder, then turned and sat back down. I stared out the open doorway and watched the bunkers and hooches pass by.

We gained airspeed. The camp seemed to extend forever down below. Then we crossed over the perimeter, and in moments Camp Evans was miles behind us. Even with the sun coming up, the sky looked gloomy and flat.

We climbed steadily until we reached fifteen hundred feet. Below us I saw a river.

It must be the Song Bo, I thought. I had pulled several missions down there, so I knew what it was like on the ground; lots of elephant grass, bamboo stands, vines, leeches, and Texas-size mosquitoes. And, oh yeah, a lifetime supply of enemy soldiers.

As we followed the river, I looked down. Kenn Lafferty, Art Monday, Lester Scott, John Sontag, William Calhoun, and Frank Anderson were down there. They had just spent six miserable days in that steamy jungle. Their only sighting had been a sampan at first light on the second day.

"Kingsman Two Four. This is Sparky Peepers Six!"

"Good morning, Six."

It was good to hear a familiar voice. We turned west and flew toward Eagle's Nest and the six waiting Rangers, who had spent the night with the 17th Cav reaction force, while gooks probed their perimeter. I knew they'd be glad to see us.

I wanted someone who knew me to see the new sergeant's bars that S.Sgt. Jeff Ignacio had pinned on me, just three days before. It was not a formal ceremony, just me and Jeff in the back of the slick. He met me on a refueling stop at Evans and pinned the small black chevrons on me. Ignacio, a Hawaiian, loved ceremony. He took a few minutes to bestow my new status on me by standing at attention, saluting, and then shaking my hand. It worked for me. I felt important.

It should have been the benchmark of my tour of Nam. I made sergeant while being in the army less than eighteen months, and I was damn proud of it. No ranks of soldiers standing at attention, no speeches, just a sincere congratulation, and a handshake from a friend.

13

Six more bellyman missions passed uneventfully. Typhoon Tess came and went, with her fifty-mile-an-hour winds and torrential rains. It didn't seem fair that most of my old buddies had long since gone home—and I hadn't had the chance to say good-bye to any of them. I was like a time bomb ticking, and this war had become a waste of my life.

I felt alone. I had proven to myself that I could fight, and I was proud of the job I had done and proud of the job my company had done. But the whole 101st Airborne Division was going through a major transformation in operations concepts and techniques, and it was filtering down to our Ranger company.

In the last two months, our area of operation, which had been centered around the city of Hue, had tripled in size. The AO grew from an area 30 kilometers in length that ran along the coast and 40 kilometers inland toward the mountains to an area which now extended 108 kilometers in length along the coast and 70 kilometers deep to the Laotian border.

We were under a lot of pressure, as we pulled more and more missions, sometimes inserting and extracting twice in the same day. I'd been having a recurring nightmare. It was the same lightning mission, but in my dream, I didn't get up. I lay there. I heard Vietnamese voices—female Vietnamese voices. I heard them coming down the hill, looking for me. I'm paralyzed. I try to get up. I look up. One of the Vietcong women is standing over me. Looking into my eyes, she pulls out a long knife and reaches down to cut my throat. I always wake up shaking and covered in sweat. Meszaros said the Native Americans used to turn captives over to the women and let them cut the poor bastards up. I wouldn't put the same thing past the NVA.

We were spread thin, and I was getting jumpy. On my last mission out, I thought I'd seen gooks, but they turned out to be shadows.

A new first sergeant had come into the company while I was in Australia on R & R. I met him at chow, the first morning my bellyman duties took me back to the company. I didn't even know our old Top was gone.

The new guy was tall, thin, and tough looking.

"I'm 1st Sergeant Gilbert," he introduced himself.

I was impressed. I heard he was on his fourth tour, but more importantly, he seemed interested in everything and everybody. He told me he wanted to talk to me later in the day. I was surprised. I never had any lifer want to talk to me about anything other than burning shit. I wondered why he wanted to talk to me. I went down to the acid pad after chow and jumped aboard the awaiting chopper.

I was just going through the motions. This morning we were going out with a new platoon leader from our company, taking him on an overflight. I felt like I was surrounded by strangers. Even if he was from our company, I didn't know him, and he didn't impress me. I put on my helmet, plugged in my mike, and sat back.

The young lieutenant didn't introduce himself as he climbed into the slick. He hopped in, adjusted his flight bag, and just stared at his maps. On the flight out, he didn't speak much. We flew right down Route 547, past Firebase Blaze, turned to the south, and headed toward Dong Ap Bai Mountain, made infamous by the ten-day battle between the men of the U.S. 3/187, 1/506, 2/506, and the 1st ARVN Division, and the 29th NVA Regiment. It was now known as Hamburger Hill.

It was also where Gary Linderer, Mother Rucker, Larry Closson, Marvin Hillman, John Sours, and I got hit by lightning.

I was nervous about this new lieutenant—maybe because I was getting short; with less than forty days and a wake-up, I didn't need a new second lieutenant in my life.

My mind drifted back to Australia, where I had just spent the past six unforgettable days. I'd gone snow skiing in the Australian Alps, the Snowy Mountains, after a two-hour plane ride from Sydney in the Eastern Highlands. I drank hot wine and sang songs with a group of college kids, who were on holiday. I had forgotten what normal people were like, but this helped me remember.

As I listened to the new lieutenant on the radio, he seemed a little too gung ho. I was also wondering what the new top sergeant wanted from me and why was I out here with this asshole. I'd been busting butt for almost a year now. I needed to do some serious ghosting, but it didn't look like it was going to happen, at least not in my lifetime.

Twenty minutes later, as we approached the A Shau Valley, everyone became tense. The gung-ho second lieutenant told me to start looking for a DZ.

"A what, sir?" I asked. I didn't care if he'd been to jump school and Ranger School, he was still a cherry, and his ink hadn't even dried on his transfer papers.

"DZ, a drop zone," he answered.

Still not sure what he was looking for, but trying to be polite, I pressed my mike switch, and said, "What you mean, sir, is an LZ."

"No, Sergeant," he snapped back. "I know what an LZ is. We are looking for a drop zone."

I couldn't help thinking how easy it would be to throw this asshole out the open door of the chopper, let him run home, and figure out for himself that a new butter bar wasn't going to keep his wise ass alive with that attitude.

"Yeah sure, but what does that have to do with this over-flight, sir?"

I still wasn't getting the whole picture. This guy couldn't be serious about a parachute operation into the A Shau.

"I'm looking for a spot big enough for a combat blast. Intelligence tells us there is a regimental-size base camp near the Rao Lao River on the Laotian border. I'd like to plan a jump in behind the little slope-heads, kick some ass, and show division what a Ranger company can do!"

"Oh," I said.

I slid back in my seat and pretended to be interested. I thought this was the final straw. We were already going out on missions every week, and now this? Who wants to risk a parachute jump into the A Shau Valley? No thank you! If we are going to pull a combat jump, let's jump into Hanoi and cut the bullshit. It'd be safer than the A Shau.

Please God, help us. I sat there thinking the worst all the way back to Eagle. I felt like I was one of the only guys with any sense left.

My worst fears were being realized, and now all I could do was pray we would not pull some crazy Airborne unnecessary jump for some medal and rank none of us would ever live to wear. The cost would be too high for that kind of maneuver.

After we landed, I made a beeline for the tactical operations center to keep my appointment with the new first shirt. I was apprehensive as I walked down the short ramp and into the TOC. I now knew what the new Top wanted to talk to me about. The jump, that must be it. He's going to fill me in on how many body bags to take along.

I stopped for a moment and looked up at all of the captured weapons we'd brought back from earlier missions, which were still hanging on the wall.

Just then the door flew open to the radio room. It was 1st Sergeant Gilbert.

"First Sergeant, you wanted to see me?"

"Yes, Sergeant Chambers, come in and sit down. I have an important mission for you."

As I walked into the radio room and sat down, my stomach churned. I thought, *great, this is about the jump the new LT was talking about.* I sat there, my face expressionless.

"This place is something else," he said.

I nodded.

He was looking down at the file cabinet with its top drawer half-open.

"I have been going through records and brief-back reports. I'm still trying to figure out this Ranger Company. I read in one of these reports jammed in a drawer that one of you guys ate a poison toad and died! What the hell have you guys been doing up here for the last few years? You're all a bunch of wild men."

He took a drink of his coffee and set the cup on the edge of the table.

"Your name keeps coming up. Hit by lightning! My God. Recondo School? Good. How many missions have you been on?"

I looked up. "I'm not sure, they all seem to run together."

"Well, here's what I'm looking for."

I felt my stomach tighten, waiting for the bad news.

"I'm looking for someone I can trust to get me some good volunteers to fill out this company. I need somebody who could represent this Ranger Company in Bien Hoa. You guys have been running understrength for almost two years now. I want to change that. You will work directly for me, not any of the REMFs down there."

I sat back in disbelief.

"You want me to recruit volunteers to join the company?"

"That's right. Your name keeps popping up, and besides, you're getting short. I want a Recondo School graduate who looks the part, not some Stateside commando without combat experience. You'll leave in the next few days. And I want to see some qualified men up here within the month. I don't care if they haven't been in Ranger School. I don't even care if you send up an occasional leg who isn't even Airborne qualified. I just don't want any dick-steppers. Don't send anyone you wouldn't want to break in on your team."

I couldn't believe what I was hearing. I didn't answer. I had nothing holding me here. Most of my friends had gone home months ago.

"Well, go get some chow, Sergeant. I'll fill you in before you head down south."

I stood up, pushed the chair back, and saluted.

"Thank you, 1st Sergeant."

"One last thing."

"Yes."

"Stay out of those Saigon cathouses, and don't start any trouble down south. I'm afraid that one more stunt and we'll all be out of a job."

I walked out into the bright sunlight and took a deep breath. I felt like I was ending a prison sentence. I walked back to my hooch and started to pack.

I'd packed everything that I could cram into my duffel bag and stood looking at the remainder of my belongings, wondering how I'd got it all in the bag the first time.

I was interrupted when Staff Sergeant Meiners hit the wooden door and threw it open. He was breathing like he'd just run his fastest mile. Trying to catch his breath, he yelled to me.

"Miller's got beaucoup gooks on both flanks and is moving to an LZ now. Come on, you're the chase ship!" He turned and hit the door, running. "The gooks haven't hit him yet, but this will have to be a ladder extraction, and they'll hit him if we're not quick."

I grabbed my rifle, a bandolier, and chased him down to the acid pad.

Meiners headed for the extraction ship and began to rig the ladder and McGuire rigs. I ran past his ship to the trail ship and secured my rifle as both Hueys started up. Meiners ran back and checked out my rigging.

"Ya sure you don't want to fly trail, Jim?" I asked.

"Next time," he said and ran back to the lift ship.

I didn't care, I was on my way to the rear in a few days. And besides they hadn't hit Miller yet. Miller was lucky, and they probably wouldn't hit him. Meiners was a good bellyman, and he'd get the team out quick.

Extractions and insertions were done with five helicopters; two slicks, two cobras, and a Loach or slick—the command-and-control ship. Each helicopter used in the extraction had to be specifically outfitted. Normally we had to arrive early to rig the ships, but this was an emergency.

The radio crackled with a call from Team 2-5. I heard Captain Cardona tell him we were on the way.

14 Roung Roung Valley Rescue

Twenty minutes later, Meiners's helicopter circled Miller's position. On the ground, Specialist Fourth Class Glasser threw out a yellow smoke canister to the center of the LZ, a visual signal to the pilot that it was safe to come in.

The chase ship that I was in stayed high and back with the two Cobra gunships. The extraction pilot had just complained to his copilot how badly the ship was running at these higher altitudes in the mountainous terrain. He told Meiners they wouldn't be able to land and they would have to use the ladders.

The helicopter hovered over Miller's position. Meiners rolled the ladder out the door and past the skids. The chopper moved in close.

As Lawhorn started up the ladder, Glasser, the slack man, thought he heard gunfire. It was hard to hear because of the noise from the chopper. The rotor blast was whipping the vegetation around. This was the most vulnerable moment for an LRP team and a helicopter crew. They were sitting ducks. The men tried to climb faster.

With five men hanging on the ladder and one still on the ground, the chopper flipped over.

"We're going down! God! We're hit!" came over the radio.

Buszzz . . . "Kingsman One, this is Red . . ."

The helicopter hit the side of the mountain, bounced once, then flipped up and over onto its back. The five Rangers on the rope fell, rolling down the steep embankment and barely missing the still spinning rotor blades.

I was told later that Dearing, who was on the bottom of the ladder, had fallen down the ridge and landed flat on his back. After the helicopter hit the mountain and flipped over, he watched it come directly down on top of him. He froze as the ship's skids touched down on either side of him and then sprang up and bounced on down the hill. The chopper came to rest, upside down and broken, on the sheer incline.

"We're down . . . We're . . . oh God! We need help . . . *Buszz . . . Buszzz . . .*"

After seeing the lead helicopter shot down, pilot Roach immediately guided his aircraft into position. Within minutes, we were hovering over the downed slick. I looked out the right side and could see a body below.

I could also see Miller's team and the crew of the downed ship, all over the side of the hill. I thought, *God! Please don't let it explode.*

"We just took small arms fire at three o'clock, sir," the door gunner reported. We lifted up and circled to the north. I watched as he swung his M-60 to the front, pulled back the gun-charging handle, then opened fire, less than twenty meters from Miller's team and the downed crew. Two gooks with automatic weapons fired back up at the chopper. I hit the floor and was holding my breath. *Ping . . . ping . . .* Two rounds hit the chopper. *Ping! Shit!* Miller watched as the rounds hit the bottom of the aircraft.

Enemy fire began spraying my chopper, and I closed my eyes and prayed. I looked out the open door and watched a steady stream of green tracers headed for us.

A solid line of green tracers looked as if they were going to hit the ship directly, then seemed to bend away at the last minute. *Thank you, God!*

Both door gunners opened up again.

I looked back following our tracers in.

The two Cobra gunships made a pass with their 40 mm cannons blazing at the enemy position. After that everything got very quiet.

We stayed back and out of the way until the Old Man figured

out what to do. They decided to bring in a medevac. It seemed like it took forever. Someone was dead, one of the team members. All Miller reported was the man's number code, and I didn't know who it was. The medevac took fire but never wavered. Medevac crews had balls the size of Jupiter's moons.

The downed helicopter was on its back and in the thick jungle below. The jungle ran up the steep mountainside, making it nearly impossible for our pilot to keep his blades from hitting trees as he got low enough to get to the team.

It was our turn to try for a pickup.

The pilot spoke through his helmet transmitter to me and his crew chief. He couldn't look forward and down, and fly his aircraft at the same time. The crew chief and door gunner normally help the pilots guide it in, but they were busy watching for the gooks. Maybe I could help. I told him I would climb outside, get under him and guide him in with hand signals. He nodded in agreement.

I untied the sling rope securing the ladder and moved it from the center of the cargo floor to the right side. I then refastened the snap links to the last rung. I extended the ladder all the way out the right side. I kicked it out at sixty feet and grabbed the doorjamb to support myself.

My helmet cord pulled loose from the wall as I climbed outside the chopper. The wind from the rotor blast hit me hard. By standing on the skid of the chopper, I could easily climb down on the ladder. Looking through the lower Plexiglas window, the AC could see my hand signals and still observe the steep mountain to his front. It was working.

Sixty feet, fifty feet, forty feet.

I was also in a good position to help the team up.

Ping!

The metal ladder kicked as a single AK round hit the metal rung below my foot.

"What the . . ." I looked down and to the right. I could see a lone enemy soldier, less than a hundred feet from the team in a small clearing. He was shooting at me! Well, that's what I thought. I'm sure he was shooting at the helicopter, but I took it personal.

I had no gun and no contact with the door gunner, who was looking straight ahead. The enemy soldier pulled his weapon back up to aim. I knew it was all over so I did the only thing I could think of—I gave him the finger.

Just then, one of the Cobra gunships spotted the lone enemy and dusted him. He just disappeared!

Miller's team watching from below started cheering.

Then the pilot pulled in tight over the downed chopper. Before I had climbed outside, the copilot told me the chopper was not running right at this high altitude, and he didn't want more than three people on the ladder at a time.

We got the first three, then flew all the way back to Camp Evans, and dropped them off. Then we returned for the remaining door gunner, Meiners, and the remaining team members Miller sent out.

On the second time in, I had to stop the third man, Glasser, from climbing up. I signaled him to wait. He looked puzzled as we pulled away.

After two more extractions we had only Miller and his senior radio man, McCann, to go back for. It was hard to watch them as we left, but first we had to refuel.

"Kingsman Leader, this is Two Five. Over." It was Miller.

"Hold on Two Five, we'll be right back. Need a little petrol. Over."

"Roger that." The radio in the bird cracked as the slick pilot answered. I could tell Miller was about at the end of his rope. It seemed to take forever to get to Firebase Evans, but that was the closest base with fuel. We were under orders to waste time. A general somewhere had to authorize destruction and abandonment of any downed aircraft, and as long as Miller and McCann were there, the aircraft wasn't abandoned and didn't need to be destroyed. They were sure taking their time.

The skids gently rocked back and forth as the chopper

touched down at Evans. We hurried and gassed up. Miller and McCann were still out there—alone.

As we finished refueling, the fog was starting to get thick. It rolled in like a big gray carpet. I watched it fill the valley floor and start creeping up the sides of the mountain. We knew it could stay socked in for weeks. If we couldn't get back in the next thirty minutes, they would be trapped in the jungle. Miller and McCann would be history.

After thirty minutes, we approached the Roung Roung Valley. By the time we got there, the cloud cover was so heavy that the pilot couldn't see the downed chopper until we were almost on top of it.

The pilot found his mark, and we repeated the process. Once again, my hands started to shake, it was time to climb down the ladder.

I held my breath, the pilot locked the ship in a hover, and I started back down for the last time. At the bottom of the ladder I reached down and grabbed McCann and helped him get started up. As I turned back for Miller the chopper started to drift out away from his reach. It was now or never.

"Jump, you pussy!" I yelled.

He jumped and grabbed hold of the bottom rung. The helicopter pulled away as he started up one hand over the next. Still on the ladder just above him, I reached down and grabbed the back of his web gear and lifted as we started to climb.

As he reached the top rung, and with the help of all the adrenaline rushing through my body, I gave him a real Airborne pull. Up he went, disappeared into the cabin of the chopper and straight out the other side.

I looked under the chopper and saw his dangling legs. *Shit, Miller!* I pulled myself up onto the skid. He was looking across the open-bay door at me.

Miller was hanging on for dear life—his legs pumping wildly in the air. McCann scrambled to pull him back inside.

We had just made four separate extractions, and even with the chopper violently rocking and pitching in the ensuing thunderstorm, I felt safe back inside the Kingsman ship and on our way home. But *something* was wrong. We were still hovering in the dark cloud cover.

Back then, the G-model helicopters didn't have much instrumentation, so if they got too deep in a storm, the pilots could get vertigo and turn the helicopter upside down and never know it. Good pilots had done worse.

"I don't know if I should kiss you or kill you," Miller said. He tried to get up.

"I'd rather have you kill me!" I said, glancing back at the still dangling ladder. The bottom rung was lost.

The chopper bounced and rocked as if no one was at the controls. I was shaking as badly as Miller. The pilots were searching for a hole in the storm.

I plugged my headset back in and listened to the pilot tell his copilot, "We're in trouble! I can't see shit, and she's getting hard to fly." I could see the gauges gyrating wildly.

Then he saw a small opening in the clouds above us, and we headed for it. I tried to steady myself while we climbed higher, trying to fly out of the storm.

I tried to look reassuring as I glanced at Miller and listened to the pilots over my headset. Miller wiped some blood off his hands and started crying, then he got mad. "Shit, man! I should have never let him go. It's my fault!"

I took a breath of reassurance. "It's okay!" I told Miller.

After a few more bumps we lifted above the storm, then the pilot lowered the nose as the whine of the turbine dropped into a steady drone.

I had figured out who was dead. It was Hammond, from commo platoon. Miller had been breaking him in on a team.

I put my hand on his shoulder and tried to comfort him.

"I know how you feel, man, I know how you feel . . ."

We were sort of flying slightly sideways coming back, and gusts of wind blew in the open cargo door, but this time it felt like a cleansing rinse.

The next day, two teams were sitting around on the tarmac

waiting for the choppers to arrive. Ron Reynolds, one of the team leaders, grabbed my sleeve as I passed him and said, "I won't be comin' back," with as serious a tone as I'd ever heard from him.

His arms were limp at his sides, and he had a disconnected stare in his eyes. He didn't seem scared, just that he knew something the rest of us didn't.

I didn't know what to say, so I joked, "Then I'd better take one last picture." I snapped the shot as the helicopters landed, then hurried off to prepare the ship for insertion.

Two days after we inserted his team, he was dead. I heard their sitrep while flying over Thua Thien province. "We've made contact. The TL is KIA." Sitting propped against the back of the pilot's seat, I felt this terrible pain as my eyes burned with held-back tears, recalling our last exchange. But there was no time to grieve. We raced to Camp Evans to pick up the reaction force, and then shuttled them out to help out what remained of Ron's team.

My job as belly man was to stay with the helicopter. But as the seven men from the reaction force stepped off the skids, I wanted desperately to go with them. But I couldn't abandon my post. I knew Ron's body was somewhere close and I felt like I had to see him. As we lifted off the ground, I sat there feeling like a coward for not jumping out with the team.

It was almost a week later before I got a chance to speak to Doc Glasser. Doc had been with Ron in his last moments. "He had been walking point and got shot right in the center of his chest. He just fell over backward in the middle of this waist-deep elephant grass. I held him in my arms, waiting for the medevac. The last thing Ron said was, 'I'm thirsty.' Then he closed his eyes. There was nothing anyone could do."

Twelve days later, we lost another team leader: Sergeant Bill Marcy, killed like Ron by a lone enemy. He was another great guy, an admiral's son, so he was obviously there by his own choice, and he was highly respected by the other men because of that.

Epilogue

There were close to two hundred of us waiting. I watched heat vapors rising off the tarmac, but this time I wasn't listening for the sound of helicopters. A single 707 plane landed and taxied right up to us; the engine revved up, then shut down. A huge cheer went up from everyone going home. The plane's main door opened and fresh troops started down the ramp, their crisp look immediately beginning to wilt. An American stewardess stood in the door frame, and she shot us a friendly smile and waved. This was my last memory of Vietnam.

It was a funny feeling, leaving. I wondered what had happened to that North Vietnamese prisoner from Recondo school—if someday he'd make it home, too. I wore his NVA buckle. The overwhelming emotion that rose up with this thought quickly disappeared when some guy at the back of the crowd began yelling at the patchless new uniforms filing by, "Hey cherries, see you in a year . . . if you live that long," with an exaggerated laugh.

I caught a glimpse over my shoulder at the Spec-4 doing the catcalling. He wasn't wearing jungle fatigues like us, and he didn't have the grunts' look. His khakis looked brand new, like he'd never spent a day outside of Saigon. I could hear him bragging to some other guy about how many Vietnamese civilians he ran over with his bus. I hated guys that profiled.

I instantly forgot the loudmouth when I heard my name being called off the manifest. It was the happiest moment of my life up to that point. I headed up the ramp steps of this beautiful plane. We called them "freedom birds" because it was our ticket back to the States and freedom from the "green machine"—the Army.

My seat was about halfway back in the enlisted men's section; I outranked anyone seated behind me. I had just settled down when I heard the same loudmouth start up again. This time he was yelling at the stewardess, "My seat won't go back. This is a piece of shit."

My jaw set, my back stiffened, and my hands tightened into fists. At that moment, he became the enemy. I tried to ignore him, but he didn't let up. The stewardess attempted to reason with him, "That's because you're in front of the bulkhead."

"I want a different seat!"

"Sir, the plane is completely full."

"Get some private to move," he shouted in her face.

That was when I stepped into the aisle and locked onto his voice like a target. I walked back past several rows. Then, standing over him, I politely said, "Shut the fuck up."

At first, the guy just looked up at me like I was a nuisance. "Go fuck yourself," he muttered, still fighting to make his seat recline.

All was quiet as I stuck my thumbs into his throat. "Shut your mouth. Do you understand me?" I wanted to squeeze the life out of him. He grabbed my hands and gasped for air. I pushed him back in his seat. "Just sit there and be quiet." I apologized to the frightened stewardess and headed back to my seat. Everybody started clapping. I was kind of embarrassed and still shaking as I slid back into my row.

As we flew over the ocean, the stewardess came by and thanked me, then handed me a slip of paper with her name and number on it. I held onto it like an autograph from a movie star. I never heard another word from the jerk in the back of the plane.

Eighteen hours later, we landed stateside. It was four in the morning in Oakland, California, and a small group of protestors held up signs and shouted obscenities as we filed past. I was too tired to flip them the peace sign.

We spent the next three hours inside the repo-depo signing out of the Army. After filling out military release forms and having an exit medical examination, I opened my duffel bag and quickly changed into street clothes. Everyone wearing jungle fatigues tossed them into a huge pile in the middle of the floor. The only thing I wanted to keep was my belt buckle. Then I walked out the back door and was on the street.

That was it—no families or friends—just a few taxis and public buses. It was like nothing had ever happened—like maybe we'd been away at football camp and now we were home. I stood there on the street a moment trying to figure out my next move; I didn't have one. I decided not to go home just yet. I bought a bus ticket for San Francisco. After a couple of days wandering around the Golden Gate Bridge, eating about a hundred hamburgers and drinking dozens of thick milk shakes, I headed home.

I've heard that smell is the most powerful sense and I believe it, because it wasn't until I got a whiff of fresh-cut alfalfa lying in the fields that I actually felt like I was home. Deep down, I wanted there to be some kind of ceremony, or at least a banner saying "Welcome home" over the church or something. I called a few old friends and one of them, Dave Kranig, invited me to a college party.

At first I was excited to be there. Dave was introducing me to some of his friends; there were even a couple of the guys I'd gone to school with. Then reality came crashing down. My crew cut and civilian clothes were way out of date; most of these people were wearing multi-colored shirts and orange or purple pants and boots. No one was wearing black, low-cut Converse tennis shoes but me. And there were round-eyed women. The last time I was around any girls, you could buy them. I wasn't sure how to act or what to say.

It didn't matter because no one seemed to have any interest in where I'd been or what I'd been doing. I really wanted someone to ask. I wanted to tell someone about what it was like trying to survive in torrential rain and mud and thick steamy jungle, and the danger I'd faced. I wanted to recount details about the combat I was in, complete with the numbers of kills and a listing of awards.

Some jock was holding court in the kitchen with a story about how he'd broken his wrist in football practice and everyone was *ooh*ing and *aah*ing. "I sprained my wrist in a helicopter crash in May," I interrupted. "But I was lucky; one of my friends was decapitated when the main rotor sliced through his head." Everyone looked at each other in shock and began to move out of the room—not exactly the reaction I'd wanted.

I walked back into the living room where a blond-haired girl was standing alone and tried to strike up a conversation, but somehow I found myself saying how our lives depend on people we trust. I totally lost her when I began talking about how I believed Vietnam was a pressure relief valve for a much bigger war that could never be fought. She looked at me like I was speaking a foreign language.

It didn't take me long to figure out that nobody wanted to hear about war. About an hour into this party, I was smoking a cigarette with my back against the wall, feeling kind of paranoid, wondering why I had come back in the first place. I pushed my hand into my pocket and felt the piece of paper with the stewardess's phone number on it.

A few days later, Kranig let my borrow his new GTO for my date with Sue Hochstrasser, and I pointed it in the direction of San Francisco. I was so excited to be driving that I was going about 100 mph along this straight stretch of desolate road north of Sacramento. I had just slipped my new tennis shoes under the seat so I could feel my bare feet on the pedals when a California Highway Patrol cruiser zoomed up behind me, lights flashing.

I slowed and pulled to the side of the road. The patrolman's high-beam sidelight filled my car as I leaned over, fumbling around trying to put on my shoes. When I looked up, he was poised at my open side window, pointing his revolver at my head. "Show me your hands . . . Get out of the car and on the ground—now!"

I raised my hands, slowly pulled the door handle, swung it open, and sort of rolled out onto the pavement. "Don't shoot; I'm on your side."

He had me keep my face in the dirt as he searched for my ID and looked under the car seat. "Why were you reaching under the seat?"

I told him I thought it was against the law to drive without shoes.

"Not in years. You might be this Zodiac killer and I'm not taking any chance."

"This . . . what?"

"Where've you been . . . on the moon?"

"Vietnam."

I'd read that in ancient times, the Roman soldiers returning from battle had to live outside the city for a couple of years and slowly integrate back into the culture. Now I understood why.

Appendix A

NVA Trail Marking
and
"Field Expedient"
Mess Facilities

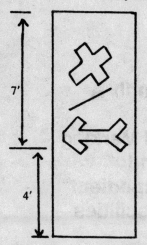

1. These markings were found on
   trees VIC YD421152. These
   markings were approximately 4
   feet above base of tree.

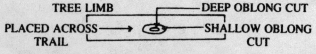

TREE LIMB   DEEP OBLONG CUT

PLACED ACROSS ——→   SHALLOW OBLONG
   TRAIL   CUT

2. This marking was found on a limb placed across trail VIC
   YD419159. Complete oblong sign was about the size of a tennis ball
   with center about the size of a half dollar.

3. Two stumps were found VIC
   YD27157 possibly used as
   table: There were two of these
   smaller stumps, one pulled out
   of ground approx 2 feet
   parallel from taller
   ones—possibly a bench.

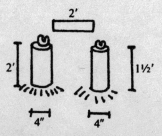

Appendix B

MACV Recondo School
Course Handouts

**MACV RECONDO SCHOOL
5TH SPECIAL FORCES GROUP (AIRBORNE),
1ST SPECIAL FORCES
APO SAN FRANCISCO 96240**

COMMUNICATIONS PROCEDURES
HANDOUT 50452: PASSWORDS AND
THEIR MEANINGS

PASSWORD	*MEANINGS*
THIS IS	This transmission is from this station whose designation immediately follows.
OVER	This is the end of my transmission to you; a response is necessary. Go ahead and transmit.
OUT	This is the end of my transmission to you, and no answer is required or expected.
GROUP	This message contains the number of the group indicated by the number following.
TIME	That which immediately follows is the time or date time group of this message.
BREAK	I hereby indicate the separation of the text from other portions of the message. To be used when there is no clear distinction between the text and other portions of the message.
SAY AGAIN	Say again all of your last transmission.
I SAY AGAIN	I am repeating transmission or portion indicated.
ALL AFTER	The portion of the message of which I have reference is all that which follows . . .
ALL BEFORE	The portion of the message to which I have referenced is all that which proceeds . . .
WORD AFTER	The word of the message which I have reference, is that which follows . . .

WORD BEFORE	The word of the message which I have reference, is that which precedes . . .
I SPELL	I shall spell the next word phonetically.
WAIT	I must pause for a few seconds.
WAIT OUT	I pause longer than a few seconds.
WILCO	I have received your message, understand it, and will comply.
ROGER	I have received your last message satisfactorily.
CORRECTION	An error has been made in this transmission (or message indicated) the correct version is . . .
WRONG	Your last transmission was incorrect. The correct version is . . .
THAT IS CORRECT	You are correct, or what you have transmitted is correct.
GROUP NO COUNT	The groups in this message have not been counted.
I READ BACK	The following is my response to your instructions to read back.
MESSAGE FOLLOWS	A message which requires recording is about to follow. Transmitted immediately after the call.
NUMBER	Station serial number.
READ BACK	Repeat this entire transmission back to me, exactly as received.
RELAY (TO)	Transmit this message to all addresses or to the address designated immediately following.
SPEAK SLOWER	Your transmission is at too fast a speed, reduce speed of transmission.
UNKNOWN STATION	The identity of the station with whom I am attempting to establish contact is unknown.

MACV RECONDO SCHOOL
5TH SPECIAL FORCES GROUP (AIRBORNE),
1ST SPECIAL FORCES
APO SAN FRANCISCO 96240

PATROL TECHNIQUES AND PATROL TIPS
HANDOUT 704-1

1. Make thorough map study.
2. Use difficult terrain in planning your route.
3. "Offset" method should be employed in route of march.
4. Always select an alternate rallying point.
5. Consider the use of special equipment, depending on your mission, the terrain through which you plan to travel, etc.
6. Test-fire your weapon prior to going on any mission. Once you have test-fired it, DO NOT TEAR IT APART TO CLEAN IT AGAIN.
7. Always carry a cleaning rod with you.
8. Use silent hand signals to the maximum.
9. Practice all hand and arm signals prior to departing on a mission.
10. Tape emergency frequencies and artillery-request format to headset of radio.
11. Each night put up field-expedient antenna.
12. Preset artillery frequency on your radio.
13. Occasionally, change point man and compass man on long patrols.
14. Always carry your weapon pointed in the direction in which you are looking.
15. Insure weapon is taped to prevent all noise.
16. Avoid trails, streams, and roads.
17. Don't forget to check trees as you move through the jungle.
18. Avoid human habitations.
19. Sterilize your trail.

20. If men have difficulty in staying awake, have them kneel rather than sit.
21. Sleep close enough to touch each other.
22. If you snore, put handkerchief around your mouth.
23. Do not remove equipment while sleeping.
24. Dead foliage may be old camouflage.
25. Tied-down or cut-down brush may be a firing lane.
26. Avoid streams and moats in an inhabited area; they may contain punji stakes.
27. Unoccupied houses may contain booby traps.
28. Be cautious of all civilians.
29. Do not set a pattern.
30. Always expect an ambush.
31. If ambushed, pick a single point and attack.
32. Take advantage of inclement weather; however, be careful because you cannot call an air strike or call for extraction.
33. Never return over the same route.
34. In sudden engagement, fire low. A ricochet is better than no hit at all.
35. In selection of LZs, avoid overuse or "likely" LZs.
36. Do not smoke while on patrol.
37. Men who cough need to take medicine for it.
38. Be sure to muffle sneezes, coughs, etc.
39. Make sure you observe noise discipline.
40. On hard ground, walk toe to heel; on soft ground walk flat-footed.
41. At meal times, only one man eat at a time; the rest observe security.
42. Keep one ration prepared at all times.
43. MENTAL ALERTNESS—MENTAL ALERTNESS

**MACV RECONDO SCHOOL
5TH SPECIAL FORCES GROUP (AIRBORNE),
1ST SPECIAL FORCES
APO SAN FRANCISCO 96240**

PATROL TECHNIQUES AND PATROL TIPS
HANDOUT 707-8 DEBRIEFING OVERLAY
THE FOLLOWING INFORMATION SHOULD BE
PLACED ON THE DEBRIEFING MAP OVERLAY:

1. Infiltration/exfiltration LZs.
2. Route of movement.
3. Overnight halts.
4. Enemy contacted by hearing, seeing, and actual firing contacts.
5. Called artillery strikes.
6. Called air strikes.
7. Location of enemy KIA, WIA, or captured.
8. Location of friendly KIA, WIA, or captured.
9. Team number or designation.
10. Team member by name and rank and position.
11. Legend.
12. Map tick marks.

**MACV RECONDO SCHOOL
5TH SPECIAL FORCES GROUP (AIRBORNE),
1ST SPECIAL FORCES
APO SAN FRANCISCO 96240**

PATROL TECHNIQUES AND PATROL TIPS
HANDOUT 704-2 TRACKING AND USE OF HUMAN
SENSES IN OBTAINING COMBAT INTELLIGENCE

I. **HUMAN SENSE:** The use of the human sense in obtaining and developing combat intelligence is very important, especially in a guerrilla-type environment such as exists in Vietnam.

Valuable information can be gained about the enemy, just by smelling, touching, and/or listening.

　A. **SMELL:**

　　(1) Smell is very important in that it can be employed to detect the enemy before he sees you; it is also used to determine what he is doing now, or has been doing in the past.

　　Cigarette smoke can be detected up to one-quarter mile if wind conditions are right. You can also smell fish, garlic, and other foods being cooked for several hundred meters. You may even be able to detect a person who has been eating garlic, or other specific food, from a considerable distance, thus discovering a guerrilla ambush before your patrol walks into it.

　　Here in Vietnam, there are many types of wood used for fuel. Being able to identify the smell of some of these types of wood, you may be able to determine the purpose and the general location of the fire, or guerrilla camp, or patrol base.

　　(2) For the man who seldom or never uses soap, after-shave lotion, or other such toiletry articles, it is easy for

him to detect a person using these items for a considerable distance.

In some areas of the world, the best way to prevent detection is not to use these items.

The British discovered this in Malaya. Once they set an ambush on a known guerrilla trail. The guerrillas avoided and bypassed the ambush. Later, one of those guerrillas was captured, and he told the British that he was in the guerrilla patrol that they were trying to ambush. He said they smelled the bath soap which had been used by the ambushing party.

In other cases, the guerrillas smelled the food that had been previously eaten by the ambushing parties and were alerted. Insect repellent is another item that you can smell for a distance.

If the local indigenous population doesn't use it, your recon team shouldn't either.

(3) Another item emitting a distinctive odor is explosives. You can tell that someone has been working with them just by the smell of the hands or clothes.

B. **TOUCH:**

(1) You may find yourself having to search buildings, tunnels, or enemy dead at night with no means for lighting the area; or lights cannot be used for security reasons. When this happens, you rely principally on touch, hearing, and smell.

(2) To use the sense of touch to identify an object, you consider four factors: shape, moisture, temperature, and texture.

   a. By shape we mean the general outline of the object.

   b. Moisture refers to the moisture content of the object (wet or dry).

   c. Temperature is the heat or lack of heat of an object.

   d. Texture is the smoothness or roughness of the object.

You will be able to basically identify the object. Your

ability to determine what, by considering all of these aspects, an object is by touch may save your life.

A good example of this is the timely detection of trip wires by using the exposed portion of your arm for feeling. Another method of searching for trip wires is the use of a very fine branch. Hold it in front of you, and you can feel it strike anything.

Another method is the use of a piece of wire with a small weight on one end, hold it in front of you as you walk. This method has proven to be quite effective.

During the Korean War, on occasion, the Turks would remove all their clothing prior to departing on patrol. If while in no-man's-land, they came in contact with someone, they merely felt or touched them, if they felt clothing they killed them. This, too, has proven effective.

C. HEARING:

(1) The sound of a safety latch being released on a rifle or machine gun could warn of an ambush or a sniper. The sound of sudden flight of wild birds may indicate enemy movement. The sounds of dogs barking could warn others of your approach to a village.

You must be able to determine whether you have been discovered or whether the dogs are barking for another reason.

Sudden cessation of normal wildlife noises may indicate passage of the enemy, or the animal's or bird's detection of you. Thus, it is important that you become familiar with distress or warning cries of birds and wild animals of the area of operation. The sound of a man talking, running, or crawling are important sounds to recognize.

In reconnaissance work, the team should always move cautiously enough to hear sounds made by the enemy before the enemy hears or sees the recon team.

Another very important sound is the striker of a hand grenade and the sound of the handle flying off. Sound can also assist you in determining range to an explosion or blast.

If you can see the flash of the explosion and can determine the number of seconds from the flash to the time you hear the sound, you can determine the approximate range.

To use this method you must be able to see the flash of the explosion. Sound travels at approximately 1100 feet per second; for all practical purposes we can say sound travels at 400 meters per second.

With a little practice, you can learn to determine range of enemy weapons using flash/bang method of range determination. It is also important that you be able to identify the type and caliber of various types of weapons by the sound of the report of the weapons.

Whenever you hear a noise, if you will rotate the upper body, with your hands cupped over your ears, until the noise is the loudest, the direction you are facing will usually be the source of the noise. When there is no wind, air currents generally flow downhill at night, and uphill in daylight.

These elements can also be a disadvantage; for example, if following a trail that leads into a guerrilla village, and the wind is to your back, dogs may bark warning of your approach. A good tracker constantly considers all of these factors.

II. TRACKING

Tracking, combined with the use of the basic human senses is another important source of combat intelligence, as evidenced by the following examples:

As the recon team moved through the jungle, it came upon a crest, which had recently been evacuated by the enemy. The crest was pocketed with rifle pits. In the spoil around the pits were blurred footprints. The holes were deep but not as wide as American GIs dig them. It was concluded from these signs that the hill had recently been held by the Vietnamese.

Several men prowled the jungle below and found numerous piles of elephant dung; enough to suggest that upwards of twenty of the animals had been picketed there. The dung was still fairly fresh, about two days they figured.

In one area there was a small frame house, carefully camouflaged and well bunkered, that looked like a command post. There were a dozen or so split gourds strewn about the room. Bits of cooked rice—perhaps 15 or 20 grains in all—still clung to the sides. They were still soft to the touch. Adding these things together, it was speculated that an enemy force of approximately battalion strength had held the same ground not more than 48 hours before.

A. **Displacement:** The disturbance of soil, vegetation or wildlife from its natural state.

(1) Footprints: Footprints can indicate several things: the number of personnel in a party, direction of movement, sex, and in some cases the type of load being borne by the person in the group.

By studying a set of prints for worn or unworn heels, cuts in the heels, tread pattern of the soles, one may be able to recognize them again. Also note the angle of the impression from the direction of movement.

Prints normally spaced, with exceptionally deep toe prints indicates that the person leaving the prints was probably carrying a heavy load. If you follow the tracks you may find where the load was placed on the ground during a rest break. Then, by studying those prints and the surrounding area, you may get some idea of what the load consisted of.

(2) Vegetation: When vegetation is stepped on, dragged out of place, or when branches are broken, the lighter colored undersides will show unnaturally. This will be easier to see by looking into the sun at the trail.

a. Vines will be broken and dragged parallel to or toward the direction of movement.

b. Grass, when stepped on will usually be bent towards the direction of movement. When the bark on a log or root is scuffed, the lighter inner wood will show, leaving an easily detected sign.

3) Shreds of clothing: The jungle environment is very hard on clothing. It is not uncommon to find threads or bits of cloth clinging to the underbrush, particularly if movement was hurried.

(4) Birds and animals: Another type of displacement may occur when wild birds and animals are suddenly flushed from their hiding places.

a. Birds, in particular, usually emit cries of alarm when disturbed. Animals will also run away from man. You should definitely be familiar with the distress signals of the wild animals and birds of your area of operation.

B. **Staining:** The deposition of liquids or soil not natural to a specific location.

(1) Bloodstains: Look for bloodstains on the ground, on leaves, and underbrush to the average height of a man. Examine stains for color and consistency.

(2) Soil: Observe logs, grass, and stones for signs of soil displacement from footgear. The color and composition of the soil may indicate a previous location or route over which a party has been moving.

The muddying of clear water is a sign of very recent movement which can be picked out by the most untrained eye. If the water in footprints is clear, this may indicate the trail is an hour or more old.

C. **Littering:** Littering is a direct result of ignorance, poor discipline, or both. If the enemy should litter the trail, take full advantage of his carelessness. Some examples of littering are cigarette butts, scraps of paper and cloth, match sticks, ration cans, and abandoned equipment.

Observe along the trail and to the flanks for these items. Uncovered human feces is another example of littering.

D. **Weathering:** The effect of rain, wind, and sun on the appearance of trail signs.

(1) Rain.

a. On footprints: A light rain will "round out" footprints and give the appearance that they are old. A heavy rain will completely obliterate footprints in a very short time.

b. On litter: Rain will flatten paper scraps and other litter such as ammunition bandoliers and cloth scraps. By close examination you can determine whether the litter was discarded before or after the last rain. It is very important that you always remember the day of the last significant rainfall.

(2) Sunlight.

a. On footprints: Footprints, when first made, will have a ridge of moist dirt pushed up around the sides. Sunlight and air will dry this ridge of dirt, causing a slow crumbling effect.

If actual crumbling is observed by the tracker, this is an indication that the prints were made very recently, and increased stealth should be employed.

b. On litter: Sunlight bleaches and discolors light colored paper and cloth. Such litter will first go through a yellowing stage and then, eventually, turn completely white. Of most interest to us is the yellowing stage.

After one night, yellow spots will begin to form; it takes about three days for such litter to become completely yellow. On dark colored paper or cloth, you must determine how much the paper has faded. The only guideline for this is experience.

3) Wind.

a. On footprints: Wind may blow grass, leaves, sand and other light litter into the prints. Examine the litter to determine whether it had been crushed. If not, it will be important to remember when the wind was last blowing.

b. Litter: Litter may be blown away from the trail; therefore, it may be necessary to search back and forth along the trail to locate it.

(4) Combination of all the above. All of the elements of the weather will cause metal to rust. Check recently exposed portions of metal. For example, closely examine the rim of ration cans where the opener stripped the paint. Rust will form in these places within 12 hours or less.

(5) Effects of wind and air currents while tracking. Be aware that wind and air currents carry sound and odor. This knowledge can be used to your advantage when attempting to locate the enemy.

**MACV RECONDO SCHOOL
5TH SPECIAL FORCES GROUP (AIRBORNE),
1ST SPECIAL FORCES
APO SAN FRANCISCO 96240**

PATROL PREPARATION
HANDOUT 707-2 BACKWARD PLANNING

Make a time schedule based on time available. Use the "Backward Planning Technique." Start your schedule time you infiltrate back to the time you received the order.

Example:

1945–	Infiltrate
1930–1945	Move to Helicopter
1845–1915	Final Inspection
1800–1845	Rehearsal
1745–1800	Inspection
1700–1745	Supper Meal
1630–1700	Briefback
1600–1630	Issue Patrol Order
1500–1600	Complete detailed plans
1400–1500	Make Recon
1330–1400	Issue Warning Order
1130–1330	Preliminary Planning
1130–	Operations Order Issued

**MACV RECONDO SCHOOL
5TH SPECIAL FORCES GROUP (AIRBORNE),
1ST SPECIAL FORCES
APO SAN FRANCISCO 96240**

PATROL TECHNIQUES AND PATROL TIPS
HANDOUT 707-1 PATROL PLANNING STEPS

1. PLAN USE OF TIME
2. STUDY SITUATION
3. MAKE MAP STUDY
4. COORDINATE (CONTINUOUS THROUGHOUT)
5. SELECT MEN, WEAPONS, AND EQUIPMENT
6. ISSUE WARNING ORDER
7. MAKE RECONNAISSANCE
8. COMPLETE DETAIL PLANS
9. ISSUE PATROL ORDER
10. INSPECT AND REHEARSE
11. BRIEFBACK

MACV RECONDO SCHOOL
5TH SPECIAL FORCES GROUP (AIRBORNE), 1ST SPECIAL FORCES
APO SAN FRANCISCO 96240

FIELD EXPEDIENT ANTENNAS
HANDOUT 502-1 JUNGLE ANTENNA

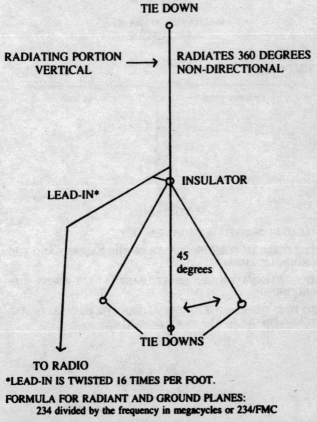

TIE DOWN

RADIATING PORTION VERTICAL → RADIATES 360 DEGREES NON-DIRECTIONAL

INSULATOR

LEAD-IN*

45 degrees

TIE DOWNS

TO RADIO

*LEAD-IN IS TWISTED 16 TIMES PER FOOT.

FORMULA FOR RADIANT AND GROUND PLANES:
234 divided by the frequency in megacycles or 234/FMC

THE RADIANT SHOULD BE AT LEAST 15 FEET ABOVE THE GROUND, HOWEVER THE HIGHER THE BETTER.

**MACV RECONDO SCHOOL
5TH SPECIAL FORCES GROUP (AIRBORNE),
1ST SPECIAL FORCES
APO SAN FRANCISCO 96240**

**FIELD EXPEDIENT ANTENNAS
HANDOUT 502-2 HORIZONTAL DOUBLET
ANTENNA**

**RADIATES 90 DEGREES
BROADSIDE**

INSULATOR

TIE DOWN   TIE DOWN

¼ wave length   ¼ wave length

LEAD-IN*

TO RADIO

*LEAD-IN TWISTED 16 TIMES PER FOOT.

THE FORMULA FOR THE LENGTH OF THE RADIANT AND THE GROUND IS 234/FMC.

THE ANTENNA SHOULD BE AT LEAST 15 FEET ABOVE THE GROUND.

TO FIND THE LENGTH OF THE RADIANT OR GROUND OF ANTENNA FREQUENCY OF 46.80 MEGACYLCES . . .

$$234/46.80 = 5'$$

$$\begin{array}{r} 5.0 \text{ feet} \\ 46.80\overline{)234.00} \\ \underline{234.00} \\ 0 \end{array}$$

MACV RECONDO SCHOOL
5TH SPECIAL FORCES GROUP (AIRBORNE),
1ST SPECIAL FORCES
APO SAN FRANCISCO 96240

FIELD EXPEDIENT ANTENNAS
HANDOUT 502-3 VERTICAL DOUBLET ANTENNA

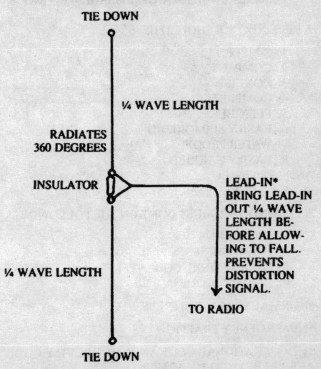

TIE DOWN

¼ WAVE LENGTH

RADIATES
360 DEGREES

INSULATOR

LEAD-IN*
BRING LEAD-IN
OUT ¼ WAVE
LENGTH BE-
FORE ALLOW-
ING TO FALL.
PREVENTS
DISTORTION
SIGNAL.

TO RADIO

¼ WAVE LENGTH

TIE DOWN

LEAD-IN TWISTED 16 TIMES PER FOOT.

FORMULA SAME AS HORIZONTAL DOUBLET.

ADD SIX INCHES TO RADIANT AND GROUND PORTION, FOR TIE
DOWN.

**MACV RECONDO SCHOOL
5TH SPECIAL FORCES GROUP (AIRBORNE),
1ST SPECIAL FORCES
APO SAN FRANCISCO 96240**

SOI AND MESSAGE WRITING
HANDOUT 504-1 SOI AND MESSAGE WRITING

A RECONDO SOI SHOULD BE:

1. SIMPLE
2. COMPACT
3. CONCISE
4. COMPLETE
5. FLEXIBLE
6. EASILY MEMORIZED
7. WATER PROOF
8. EASILY CARRIED

AND ABOVE ALL

9. SECURE!!!!

A RECONDO SOI MUST CONTAIN THE FOLLOWING:

1. CALL SIGNS
2. FREQUENCIES
3. OPERATIONAL CODE*
4. BREVITY CODE**

*NORMAL TRAFFIC, SITREPS, ETC.

**EMERGENCY TRAFFIC

THE OPERATIONAL CODE AND THE BREVITY CODE
ARE *NEVER* USED TOGETHER.

A RECONDO SOI SHOULD ALSO CONTAIN:

1. MESSAGE FORMATS
2. CODED MESSAGE INDICATORS
3. GROUND TO AIR PANEL MARKINGS

MACV RECONDO SCHOOL
5TH SPECIAL FORCES GROUP (AIRBORNE),
1ST SPECIAL FORCES
APO SAN FRANCISCO 96240

PATROL PREPARATION
HANDOUT 707-4 BRIEFBACK OVERLAY

Team Leader	SANDUL	MSG
Asst Tm Ldr	ALLEE	SFC
Point Man	MORRIS	SFC
Tm Member 3	ZUMBRUN	SSG
Tm Member 4	LIGHTNER	SSG
Tm Member 5	MRSICH	SSG

MAP INFORMATION

Map Name: **NHA TRANG**
Map Scale: 1:50,000
Map Sheet: 6833 III

LEGEND

Primary/Alternate Infil LZ's

Primary/Alternate Exfil LZ's

Initial Rally Points RP

Proposed Route of March →→→→

Proposed Overnight Halts With Nights Numbered 1 2 3

Special Points of Interest ×—×—

Escape and Evasion Route With Azimuth E&E 180

MACV RECONDO SCHOOL
5TH SPECIAL FORCES GROUP (AIRBORNE), 1ST SPECIAL FORCES
APO SAN FRANCISCO 96240

HANDOUT 707-7 DEBRIEFING MAP OVERLAY EXAMPLE

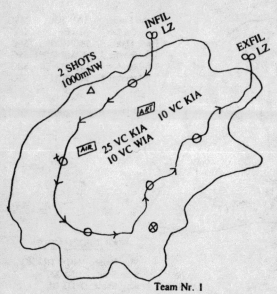

Team Nr. 1

Team Leader	ROGERS	SFC
Asst Tm Ldr	JONES	SSG
Tm Members	TELFAIR	PFC
	NICOLS	PFC
	RETTER	PFC
	HAMILTON	PFC

<u>LEGEND</u>

Infiltration/Exfiltration LZ's ⫝

Route of march →→→→→

Overnight halts ●—●—●—●
            1   2 3   4

Arty called 10 VC KIA [ART]

Air Strike called 25 VC KIA 10 VC WIA [AIR]

2 shots heard 1000 M NW of team △

2 VC with weapons moving south on trail ⊗

2 VC KIA in ambush ①

MACV RECONDO SCHOOL
5TH SPECIAL FORCES GROUP (AIRBORNE),
1ST SPECIAL FORCES
APO SAN FRANCISCO 96240

FO PROCEDURES AND ARTILLERY ADJUSTMENT
HANDOUT 803-4 BINOCULAR RETICLE

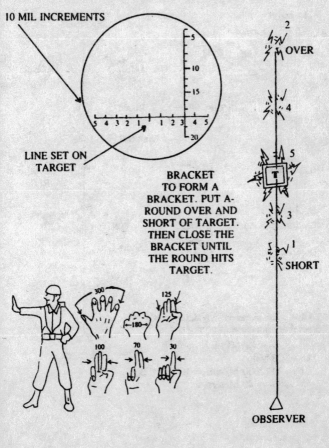

10 MIL INCREMENTS

LINE SET ON TARGET

BRACKET
TO FORM A
BRACKET. PUT A-
ROUND OVER AND
SHORT OF TARGET.
THEN CLOSE THE
BRACKET UNTIL
THE ROUND HITS
TARGET.

OVER

SHORT

OBSERVER

MACV RECONDO SCHOOL
5TH SPECIAL FORCES GROUP (AIRBORNE),
1ST SPECIAL FORCES
APO SAN FRANCISCO 96240

FO PROCEDURES AND ARTILLERY ADJUSTMENT
HANDOUT 803-5 MIL RELATION

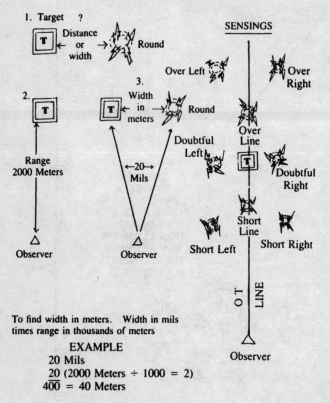

To find width in meters.   Width in mils
times range in thousands of meters

EXAMPLE
20 Mils
20 (2000 Meters ÷ 1000 = 2)
$\overline{400}$ = 40 Meters

MACV RECONDO SCHOOL
5TH SPECIAL FORCES GROUP (AIRBORNE),
1ST SPECIAL FORCES
APO SAN FRANCISCO 96240

SPECIAL PATROL EQUIPMENT
ANNEX A—STUDENT UNIFORM AND EQUIPMENT

Camouflage fatigue uniform	1 each
Floppy brimmed hat	1 each
Jungle boots	1 pair
Insect repellent	1 bottle
Panel, signaling	1 each
Pen flare gun	1 each
Flares, pen gun	10 each
Mirror, signaling	1 each
Compass, lensatic	1 each
Triangular bandages	2 each
Ammunition pouches	2 each
Compress bandages	3 each
Magazines	11 each
Ammunition	200 rounds
Grenade, smoke	2 each (1 red, 1 yellow)
Grenade, fragmentation	3 each
Canteen, plastic	4 each
Cover, canteen	2 each
Water purification tablets	4 bottles
Pistol belt	1 each
Harness, pistol belt	1 each
Snap link	2 each
Bayonet with scabbard	1 each
Pouch, first aid	1 each
Rucksack, indigenous	1 each
Nylon rope, 12 feet	1 each
Gloves, rappelling	1 pair
Poncho, lightweight	1 each
Individual weapon	1 each

Glossary

(A)

AC—Aircraft commander, pilot.

acid pad—Flat, hard-surfaced area designed to accommodate helicopter landings and takeoffs.

air bursts—An explosive device, such as a grenade, a bomb, an artillery round, or a mine, rigged to detonate above the ground to inflict maximum damage by expanding the range of shrapnel.

air strike—Surface attack by fixed-wing, fighter-bomber aircraft.

AIT—Advanced Individual Training following Basic Combat Training.

AK47—Communist made 7.62 caliber automatic assault rifle. It was the primary individual weapon used by the NVA/VC forces.

AO—Area of Operations. A defined geographical area where military operations are conducted for a specific period of time.

ao dai—traditional Vietnamese female dress, split up the sides and worn over pants.

ARA—Air Rocket Artillery. Military description of Huey gunships.

arclight—B-52 bombing mission.

Article 15—Punishment under the Uniform Code of Military Justice. Less severe than general court-martial.

artillery fan—Area within range of supporting artillery.

ARVN (Arvin)—Army of the Republic of Vietnam.

ATL—Assistant Team Leader. Second in command on an LRP or Ranger team.

AWOL—Absent Without Leave.

(B)

BCT—Basic Combat Training. Initial course of training upon entry into the United States Army.

BDA—Bomb Damage Assessment. A special operations mission for the purpose of verifying results of an aerial bombing attack.

beaucoup—Derived from the French word for very many.

berm—High, earthen levee surrounding most large, permanent U.S. military installations as part of the perimeter defense system.

black box—Sensor devices planted along trails, roads, rivers, and at intersections and junctions to detect body heat, perspiration, or sound given off by passing enemy troops.

blasting cap—The detonator inserted into claymore mines, grenades, satchel charges, and other explosive devices, which initiates the actual detonation.

blood trail—Blood signs left by the passage or removal of enemy wounded and dead.

blue line—Designation on maps of streams, rivers, and other natural waterways.

body bag—Rubberized canvas or plastic bags used to remove dead U.S. casualties from the field to Graves Registration locations.

body basket—A wire litter lowered by cable from a medevac helicopter to aid in the evacuation of critically wounded personnel, where landing is impossible because of terrain conditions.

boonies—Informal term for unsecured areas outside U.S. military control.

boozers—Slang term for military personnel who frequently indulge in heavy alcoholic consumption.

bush—Informal term for the jungle, also called boonies.

butter bar—Second lieutenant.

(C)

CA—Combat Assault.

CAR-15—Commando version of the M-16 assault rifle.

C-4—Plastic explosives.

Cs or **C rats**—Canned individual rations.

C & C—Command and Control.

CIB—Combat Infantry Badge.

CID—Criminal Investigation Division.

CO—Commanding officer.

COSVN—Commanding Officer, South Vietnam.

CS—Riot-control gas.

cammies—Camouflaged jungle fatigues-blouses, pants.

cammo-stick—Dual-colored camouflage greasepaint in a metal tube.

canister round—M-79 round containing numerous double-O BB shot.

Cav-Short for Cavalry.

chieu hoi—An enemy soldier who has rallied to the South Vietnamese government.

cherry—New, inexperienced soldier recently arrived in a combat zone.

Chicom—Designation for Chinese Communist or an item of Chinese Communist manufacture or origin.

chopper—Informal term for any helicopter.

chopper pad—designated landing or takeoff platform for one or more helicopters.

Chuck—Informal term describing the enemy, also Charlie, Mr. Charles, Victor Charles, or VC.

clacker—Term describing the electric firing device for a claymore mine.

claymore mine—Command-detonated, antipersonnel mine, designed to saturate an area six to eight feet above the ground and over an area of sixty degrees across its front, with 750 steel ball bearings.

cockadau—Vietnamese slang derivative meaning kill.

cold—Term describing an area of operations or a landing zone that is devoid of any enemy sign or activity.

commo—Communication.

commo check—Radio operator's request to verify the reception of his transmissions.

compromise-Enemy discovery of the presence of an LRP/Ranger in its vicinity, thereby resulting in the termination of the mission and the extraction of the team.

concertina—Coiled barbed wire, strung for perimeter defense.

contact—Firing on or being fired on by the enemy.

contour flying—Low-level, high-speed, daring helicopter flight, adjusting altitude only for terrain features.

crapper—Slang term describing single-hole or multi-hole latrines.

(D)

daisy chain—More than one claymore mine wired together with det cord to effect simultaneous detonation.

DEROS—Date of Estimated Return From Overseas.

det cord—Detonator cord, demolition cord: used with plastic explosives or to daisy chain claymores together.

dex tabs—Dexedrine tablets: an aid to prevent sleep; could cause hallucinations if taken to excess.

di di or *di di mau*—Vietnamese phrase meaning "get out" or "go."

diddly bopping or **diddy boppin'**—Slang term meaning to move about foolishly and without taking security measures.

dopers—Slang term for soldiers who use drugs.

double canopy—Phrase used to describe primary jungle with a lower layer of undergrowth.

dragging ass—Slang term to describe a condition of physical exhaustion.

deuce-and-a-half—Two-and-one-half-ton military transport truck.

dust off—Helicopter conducting a medical evacuation.

(E)

early out-Termination of military service prior to normal ETS.

E & E—Escape and Evasion.

EM—Enlisted man.

ETS-Estimated Termination of Service.

exfiltration—The procedure of departing a recon zone after completion of a mission.

extending—Prolonging one's tour of combat duty beyond the normal DEROS date.

extraction—The removal of troops from the field, usually by helicopter.

(F)

F-4 (Phantom)—McDonnell-Douglas fighter-bombers that saw heavy use in Vietnam.

FAC—Forward Air Controller.

FNG—F—ing New Guy, slang term meaning an inexperienced soldier, newly arrived in a combat zone.

FO—Forward Observer.

FOB—Forward Operating Base.

fast mover—U.S. fighter-bomber.

firebase or **fire support base**—Forward artillery base.

firefight—Small arms battle.

fire mission—Directed artillery barrage.

flak jackets—Vests worn by U.S. soldiers to lessen the impact of shrapnel.

foo gas or **phoo gas**-A mixture of JP-4 aviation fuel and naptha, which performed like napalm when detonated. It was placed in fifty-five-gallon drums and buried outside military perimeters as part of the frontline defense. Very effective against massed troops.

frag—Fragmentation grenade.

Freedom Bird—Name given to any military or commercial aircraft that took troops out of Vietnam.

free-fire zone—An area declared off-limits to all personnel. Anyone encountered within its confines was assumed to be hostile and could be fired on without verification or authorization.

(G)

G-2—Division Intelligence section.

G-3—Division Operations section.

goofy grape—Slang for purple.

gook—Derogatory slang term for any Oriental person, especially Vietcong or NVA. Also dink, slope, slant, or zipperhead.

go to cover—Move into heavy concealment.

Graves Registration—Section of the military service charged with reception, identification, and disposition of U.S. military dead.

grunt—U.S. infantryman.

gunship—Heavily armed helicopter used to support infantry troops or to independently attack enemy units or positions.

(H)

HE—High explosive.

H & I—Harassment and Interdiction, preplotted artillery fire designed to keep the enemy on edge and possibly catch him off-balance.

HQ—Headquarters.

halazone tabs—Halazone tablets, used to purify water before consumption.

heads—Slang term for soldiers who smoke marijuana.

heat tabs—Heating tablets, small, blue chemical disks that burned slowly and gave off an intense, smokeless heat when ignited. Used for heating rations and boiling water.

heavy team—A LRP or Ranger team of ten or more personnel.

helipad-Acid pad or chopper pad.

Ho Chi Minh Trail—A vast network of roads and trails running from North Vietnam, down through Laos, Cambodia, and South Vietnam and terminating just to the northwest of Saigon. It made up the transportation system that enabled the North Vietnamese Army to replace its losses of manpower, arms, and equipment.

Ho Chi Minhs—Slang name for the sandals worn by the Vietnamese, made from discarded automobile tires and inner tubes.

hooch—Slang term for any small civilian family or military shelters in Vietnam.

horn—Term used to describe radio communication.

hot—Term describing an area of operations or a landing zone where contact has been made with enemy troops.

Huey-UH-1 helicopter, the primary helicopter troop transport in Vietnam.

hump—The midpoint in a soldier's overseas combat tour, usually the 183d day.

hump (to)—To walk on patrol, usually heavily laden and heavily armed: to perform any difficult task.

(I)

I Corps-Northernmost military district in South Vietnam.

II Corps—Central military district in South Vietnam.

III Corps—Southernmost military district in South Vietnam.

IG—Inspector General.

in country—Term used to refer to American troops serving in Vietnam.

Indian country—The jungle, also known as the bush, boonies, boondocks, the field.

infiltration—The procedure of entering a recon zone without detection by the enemy.

insertion—The placement of combat or recon forces in the field, usually by helicopter.

instant NCO or **Shake 'n Bake**—Derogatory informal terms used to describe soldiers who received their rank as noncommissioned officers not by time in service and time in grade but by graduation from the NCO school in Fort Benning, Georgia.

(J)

Jody—Universal name for the guy back home who tries to steal the GI's girl while he is overseas.

jungle penetrator—Metal cylinder with fold-out legs, attached by steel cable to a helicopter-mounted hoist, used to medically evacuate wounded soldiers from thick, jungle terrain.

(K)

K-bar—Type of military combat knife, used primarily by the Marines, LRPs, and Rangers.

KIA—Killed In Action.

killer team—LRP or Ranger team with the primary mission of inflicting casualties upon the enemy through the use of ambush or raid.

kill zone—The target area of an ambush.

Kit Carson scout—Former VC/NVA soldier, repatriated to serve as a scout for U.S. combat forces.

klick—One thousand meters, a kilometer.

(L)

LAW—Light Antitank Weapon: a single-shot, disposable rocket launcher.

LBE—Load Bearing Equipment.

LOH or **Loach**—Light Observation Helicopter.

LP—Listening post.

LRP—Long Range Patrol.

LRRP—Long Range Reconnaissance Patrol: also a dehydrated ration used by special operations units.

LZ—Landing Zone.

land line or **lima-lima**—Ground telephone communications between two points.

lay dog—Going to cover after insertion, to wait and listen for any sign of enemy movement or presence in the area.

lifer—Career soldier.

Lima Charlie—The phonetic military designation for the letters L and C, which is used as a reply to the radio commo request, "How do you read me?" It means loud and clear!

Lister bag—Waterproof canvas bag, suspended from a beam or tripod, providing potable drinking water to troops in bivouac.

lock 'n' load—To chamber a round in one's weapon.

(M)

M-16—Lightweight, automatic assault rifle used by U.S. forces in Vietnam: 5.56 caliber.

M-60—Light, 7.62 caliber, belt-fed machine gun used by U.S. forces in Vietnam.

M-79—Single-shot, 40 mm grenade launcher: also called a blooper or a thumper.

MACV—Military Assistance Command, Vietnam.

MIA—Missing In Action.

PC—Military Payment Certificate: funny money or scrip issued to U.S. military personnel in Vietnam.

mag—Ammunition magazine.

McGuire rig—Nylon sling or seat attached to a 120-foot rope, used to extract special operations personnel from dense jungle under extreme conditions.

meal-on-wheels—Mobile snack trucks found at major U.S. military bases.

medevac—Helicopter conducting a medical evacuation.

Mike—Phonetic military designation for the letter M: usually means minutes or meters.

monsoon—The rainy season in the Orient.

(N)

NCO—Noncommissioned Officer: ranks E-5 through E-9.

NCOIC—Noncommissioned Officer in Charge.

NDP—Night Defense Position.

NVA—North Vietnamese Army.

Nam, or **the Nam**—Short for Vietnam.

nouc mam—Rotten-smelling fish sauce used by the Vietnamese.

number one—Slang, means the very best.

number ten—Slang, means the very worst.

(O)

OCS—Officer Candidate School.

OP—Observation post.

one-oh-five—105 mm howitzer.

one-five-five—155 mm artillery.

one-seven-five—175 mm artillery.

op order—Operations order, a notice of an impending operation.

Overflight—Pre-mission aerial scout of a recon zone for the purpose of selecting primary and secondary landing zones and extraction points, determining route of march, and locating possible trails and enemy supply depots, structures and emplacements; usually conducted by the team leader and his assistant team leader. The inserting helicopter crew flies the overflight.

(P)

PAVN-People's Army of Vietnam.

PF-Popular Forces: South Vietnamese irregular forces.

Pfc.—Private First Class.

PLF-Parachute Landing Fall.

POW—Prisoner of War.

PRC-25 or **Prick-25**—Portable radio used by American combat troops in the field.

PSP-Perforated steel plating, used for airstrips, helicopter pads, bunker construction, and bridge matting.

PT—Physical Training.

PX—Post Exchange.

PZ—Pickup Zone.

peter pilot—Copilot of a helicopter.

piasters, or **Ps**—Vietnamese currency.

pig—Affectionate slang nickname for the M-60 machine gun.

pink team—Airborne, hunter-killer team, consisting of one or more LOH scout helicopters, a Huey C & C helicopter, and two or more Cobra gunships.

piss tube—A twelve-inch pipe or the shipping case for an eight-inch artillery round, with one end buried at a sixty degree angle and the other end projecting thirty inches above ground and covered with screen wire mesh. It served as a semipermanent urinal for U.S. troops in bivouac.

point—Unit's advance man in line of march, or the scout in a combat patrol.

Psy Ops—Psychological Operations unit.

pull pitch—Term used by helicopter pilots that means they are taking off.

punji stakes—Sharpened bamboo stakes, hidden in grass, vegetation, in covered pits, or underwater, to penetrate the feet and lower legs of unwary troops. They were often dipped in feces to cause infection to the wound.

(R)

REMF—Rear Echelon Mother F——er; slang derogatory term of endearment that combat troops called noncombat administrative and support troops.

RPD—Communist-made, drum-fed, light machine gun used by the VC/NVA forces in Vietnam.

RPG—Communist-made rocket launcher, firing a B-40 rocket: used by both the VC and the NVA, it was effective against U.S. armor, fixed emplacements, helicopters, patrol boats, and infantry.

R & R—Rest and Recreation: five- to six-day, out-of-country furloughs given to U.S. military personnel serving in a combat zone.

RTO—Radio Telephone Operator.

RZ—Recon or Reconnaissance Zone.

radio relay or **X ray**—A communications unit, usually set up on a firebase, with the mission of relaying transmissions from units in the field to their rear commands.

rappel—The controlled descent, by means of a rope, from a tall structure or a hovering helicopter.

reaction force—A military unit established to respond quickly and determinedly to another unit's request for rescue or reinforcement; also called "blues."

rear seat—The gunner in a Cobra gunship and in certain dual-seat fighter-bombers.

Recondo School—An exclusive training program, conducted by 5th Special Forces personnel in Nha Trang, which taught small-unit, special-operations techniques to members of U.S., South Vietnamese, Korean, Thai, and Australian special operations units.

redlegs—Informal name given to artillerymen.

revetment—Sandbagged or earthen blast wall erected to protect aircraft and helicopters from shrapnel and blast caused by hostile mortars, artillery, rockets, thrown satchel charges, or demolitions.

rock 'n' roll—A slang term used to describe the firing of a weapon on full automatic, as opposed to semiautomatic.

ruck or **rucksack**—infantryman's backpack.

(S)

SAR—Search & Rescue.

SERTS—Screaming Eagle Replacement Training School; orientation course given to all new replacements in the 101st Airborne Division upon their arrival in Vietnam.

Sfc.—Sergeant First Class: E-7.

SKS—Communist-made, 7.62 mm, semiautomatic assault rifle used by the VC and the NVA in Vietnam.

SOG (MACV)—Studies & Observation Group, also known as Special Operations Group; specialized in deep-penetration patrols across the borders into South Vietnam's neighboring countries.

SOI—Signal Operating Instructions; the booklet that contained the call signs and radio frequencies of all units in Vietnam.

SOP—Standard Operating Procedure.

sapper—Specially trained enemy soldier, with the mission to penetrate the perimeters of U.S. and Allied military installations by stealth, and then to cause as much damage as possible to aircraft, vehicles, supply depots, communication centers, command centers, and hard defense positions. He would utilize satchel charges, grenades, demolition charges, and RPGs to accomplish his mission; sapper attacks often preceded mass infantry assaults and took place under heavy shelling by their own mortar and rocket crews.

selector switch—A three-position device on the M-16 and CAR-15 assault rifles, enabling the operator to choose safe, semiautomatic, or automatic fire merely by thumbing it in ninety degree increments.

shit-burning detail—The most detested extra duty in Vietnam; it involved the disposal of raw human waste by burning it in half fifty-five-gallon drums; diesel fuel was poured into the barrels and ignited; the mixture was allowed to burn until a layer of ash accumulated on the surface, then it was stirred back into the raw sewage by means of large paddles and reignited; this procedure continued until only dry ash remained.

short or **short timer**—A term to describe a soldier whose time remaining in country is less than sixty days.

single canopy—Phrase used to describe low, dense jungle or forest growth, with no overhead cover from mature trees.

sitrep—Situation report; regularly scheduled communication check between a unit in the field and its rear command element, to inform it of their present status.

Six—Radio call sign for a unit's commander.

slack—The second position in a line of march or in patrol formation; also means "go easy on."

slack jump—A rappel involving a short free-fall before commencing a standard rappel.

slick—Informal name for a Huey troop-transport helicopter.

smoke—Informal name for a smoke grenade; they came in a variety of colors and were used to signal others, to mark positions, to determine wind direction, and to provide concealment.

Snake—Informal name for the Cobra gunship.

snatch—To capture a prisoner.

spider hole—A one-man, camouflaged, enemy fighting position, often connected to other positions by means of a tunnel.

spotter round—Artillery or mortar shell producing a dense cloud of white smoke; they were used to mark targets or to assist units in establishing their correct locations.

stand down—An infantry unit's return from the field to a firebase or base camp for rest and resupply.

starlight scope—A night-vision device, utilizing any ambient light source, such as stars, the moon, electric lights, distant flares, etc.

Stars and Stripes—U.S. military newspaper.

strack—A term used to describe or designate the ideal in military dress, demeanor, and bearing.

(T)

TAOR—Tactical Area of Responsibility.

TDY—Temporary Duty.

TL—Team Leader.

TOC—Tactical Operations Center.

Tac Air—Fighter-bomber capability of the air force, navy, and Marine air wings; as opposed to the strategic bombing capacity of the air force's B-52s.

tanglefoot—Fields of barbed wire stretched tightly over a grid of metal stakes, approximately twelve inches above the ground; it was part of perimeter's static defense and was designed to discourage rapid and uninterrupted penetration.

tarmac—A term describing the hard-surface coating used to construct permanent airstrips, helicopter pads, and roads; the word comes from tar and macadam.

ten-forty-nine, or **1049**—The U.S. military slang term for requesting a transfer to another unit.

toe popper—A small, plastic U.S.-made antipersonnel mine, designed to cripple rather than kill.

tracer—Ammunition containing a chemical compound to mark the flight of projectiles by a trail of smoke or fire.

triple canopy—Phrase used to describe mature jungle or forest with a third layer of ancient trees, often reaching heights of two hundred feet or more and blocking out the sun.

typhoon—An Asian hurricane.

(U)

Uncle Ho—Familiar title for Ho Chi Minh, the leader of North Vietnam.

(V)

VC, Vietcong, Victor Charles—Slang names describing members of the People's Army of Vietnam.

(W)

WIA—Wounded In Action.

WP, willie peter, willie pete, or **willie papa**—White phosphorus grenades, mortar rounds, or artillery rounds that exploded into a spray of chemical fire, which ignited on contact with air and could only be doused by removal of the source of oxygen.

wait-a-minute vines—Strong, barbed ground creepers that caught at the boots and clothing of American soldiers and retarded their forward movement.

warning order—A directive that gives final approval for an upcoming mission.

white mice—A derogatory slang term for the military police of the South Vietnamese government.

World—The States, USA, home.

(X)

XO—Executive Officer.

x-ray team—See radio relay team.

(Z)

zapped—Killed, slain in combat.

zipperhead—Derogatory name for the Vietnamese, or any Oriental.

On the ground with the Special Forces in Afghanistan.

THE HUNT FOR BIN LADEN

Task Force Dagger

by ROBIN MOORE

In this acclaimed, groundbreaking bestseller about America's war against al-Qaida in Afghanistan, Robin Moore—with exclusive access and his trademark expertise—takes you on a top-secret tour of the most covert conflict since the CIA's war in Laos. This is a blistering, behind-the-scenes account of America's first strike in its war against terrorism. From the international outrage of 9/11 to its immediate aftermath—the unprecedented Special Ops assault on Osama Bin Laden's bases—all aspects of this astonishing story are revealed for the first time. Here is how a few hundred Green Berets toppled the Taliban and how Bin Laden may have made his escape.

Published by Presidio Press
Available wherever books are sold